John Weeks

ASSAULT
from the SKY
A History of Airborne Warfare

G. P. Putnam's Sons New York

Publisher's note on the photographs
In cases where the actuality and interest of a picture
are unique it has been reproduced in spite of the
blemishes that inevitably result from photography in
battle, in preference to sacrificing authenticity for
artistry.

Published in 1978 in the United States by
G. P. Putnam's Sons
200 Madison Avenue
New York
N.Y. 10016

Library of Congress Catalog Card Number: 78-53430

SBN: 399-12222-2

Printed in Great Britain

CONTENTS

Introduction

Airborne warfare has caught the popular imagination since the first German parachute troops carried out their daring and alarming invasions in early 1940. The airborne assault is fast, spectacular, dynamic and unpredictable. It dominated the thinking of the Allies in the difficult and dangerous days at the beginning of World War II when a German invasion from the air was foreseen at any moment in Britain and the wholesale advances of the Wehrmacht in Scandinavia and the Low Countries were almost daily expected to be repeated in Britain. The swift and shattering fall of Crete seemed to 'confirm the infallibility of the airborne method of making war, and it accelerated the Allied efforts to raise similar forces. From then on the tide turned against the Germans and resulted in the massive and overwhelming might of the First Allied Airborne Army which spearheaded the Normandy invasion and the advance into Germany. Parachute troops became a fixture in Western forces, though they have now been equalled, if not overtaken in numbers and variety by those of the USSR.

This book sets out to give as comprehensive a picture of the background to airborne forces as is possible within the limitations imposed by the space available. Technicalities have been eschewed and the intention is to give a full and rounded picture of what is a modern and innovative method of warfare. The greatest centre of interest is of course World War II, and it is no accident that the greater part of the book is devoted to the rise of airborne forces during that war. We shall never see again the thousands of aircraft of all types which filled the skies for the D-Day invasion, or Arnhem, or the Rhine Crossing. The last military glider flew over a quarter of a century ago, and none will ever fly again. The entire scope and size of airborne warfare has changed to something quite different today; the helicopter carries men right to their objective and lands them on it without the necessity of having to drop by parachute or fly in a glider. Guns and vehicles are nowadays lifted underneath a helicopter with no more preparation than hitching them on a sling. However, 30 years ago a similar load could only be carried in a glider which made a one-way journey at great cost.

There are enough publications and films which deal with the glamorous battles and the large campaigns. These battles and campaigns have their place in the whole story and all of them will be found within these pages, but each is treated as a part of the overall development of airborne warfare, and so the reader will find that the ground fighting which followed each operation is not closely examined unless it was affected by the air plan. Where this happened, and Arnhem is an outstanding example, then it is chronicled. Many small raids have been omitted, not because they were unimportant in themselves, but either because they added little to the actual method of airborne warfare, or for reasons of space. To have recorded every single use of airborne troops would have meant several volumes and much boring repetition of similar actions.

Probably the most interesting feature of airborne warfare is the difficulty which some generals had in understanding how they could and should use their airborne troops. In Germany, General Student had from the very start a clear and precise vision of the way in which his highly mobile forces should be employed, though he tended to overstretch himself at first. His superiors, however, either could not or would not fully support him; and when he showed how successful his ideas could be he became the object of jealousy and intrigue. The Allies took their lead from the Germans and tried to use the same surprise techniques against the men who had invented them; they found it more difficult than they had planned. The answer was found to lie in using overwhelming numbers and the campaigns from D-Day onwards are really exercises in the use of an airborne sledgehammer. Subtlety reappeared with the French in Indo-China where the virtues of economy and surprise were once again shown to be more valuable than overwhelming numbers. The Suez operation was an humiliating example of the lack of progress in Britain since 1945, though again the French were able to show that they had learned the essentials of the airborne method and had had the wit and daring to use that knowledge.

After the French came the American army in Vietnam and the use of the helicopter. The story of the war in Vietnam can conveniently be looked upon as the story of the helicopter in modern warfare and it is due to that unpopular and expensive campaign that helicopters and their tactical use have reached their present stage of development. There is still more to come, but it will come more slowly now.

Finally there is the future, for all that has happened is only the prologue. The Soviet army has a vast airborne army, how large we cannot say with any accuracy, but large enough to be able to carry out a small war on its own without involving any other forces. In the NATO countries we have ridiculously small airborne forces and even smaller reserves. Continuous peace-time military budgets and steady reductions in the size of defence forces have brought about a position where the NATO armies can only muster a fraction of the numbers that oppose them. We are steadily putting ourselves into the same position that we were in in 1940, and the same shock may occur all over again.

Parachute jumping instructors of No 1 Parachute Training School, RAF Abingdon, taking part in a spectacular simultaneous drop by sixty parachutists (*Ministry of Defence, Crown copyright*)

1 Early Developments

It seems a sad reflection on Man's inability to live at peace that within 20 years of the first balloon flight being made someone was already thinking of using them to carry soldiers and invade a neighbour. When Napoleon was massing his invasion barges at Boulogne it was quite seriously suggested that he could use balloons to carry his assault troops, or at least part of them, across the Channel. One idea was for 2,500 balloons each carrying four men to be launched before the sea invasion, and to land in England a few hours in advance of the main body and cause confusion, if not complete surrender. Another and more fanciful notion was for the construction of an airborne fort, but the exponent of that idea had not done his sums, whereas the four-man balloon idea was certainly just feasible even if, as we now know, it could not have failed to be anything other than a disaster for all concerned.

After this episode the idea of airborne troop carrying passed out of fashion until 1918 when the aeroplane had reached the stage of development where it could carry reasonable loads in safety and with acceptable standards of reliability. General Billy Mitchell, the maverick of the American army, drew up a plan for lifting part of the American 1 Division over the German lines and parachuting them several miles behind the Metz sector. For this operation he intended to use the only large aeroplane available to the Allies, the Handley-Page bomber, and he would have required just about the entire bomber force. Planning reached an advanced stage for the campaign of 1919, but General John Pershing vetoed the idea even before the Armistice ruled it out. Pershing was probably right; air operations were too little understood for there to have been any better than a very slim hope of success; for one thing it is apparent that Mitchell had no idea of the training needed for parachute troops, nor indeed could he have had, for it had never been done before and with the primitive radios of that time co-operation between air and ground forces would have been slight. But like Napoleon,

Mitchell had the right idea. He wanted to take his troops over the enemy defences in order to attack an objective that could not be reached in any other way. The object of airborne forces remains the same today. They are forces which can take advantage of a particular line of approach to put themselves in an advantageous position from which they can influence the battle or strike a blow at a vital part of the enemy defences.

There were others who shared Mitchell's enthusiasm and vision, though none made such an impact. However, the theories of Giulio Douhet in Italy bore some fruit when, in 1927, Italy became the first country to try practical military parachuting using an improved form of the escape parachute supplied to balloon observers and aircrew. This was in many ways a significant technical step forward, since most of the military parachutes that followed used the same general methods. The Italian 'Salavatore' was carried in a pack on the man's back and operated by a line hooked to the aircraft. The line pulled out the canopy, which inflated with a jerk but flew steadily and slowly to earth. In November 1927 the first formation drop was made; by 1930 there were complete battalions trained in parachuting. These later became the Folgore and Nembo Divisions of World War II, but they never made an operational drop.

The US army carried out some small-scale experiments in 1928 using the Irvin ripcord parachutes, but these were not as practical for dropping troops as the Salavatore since they needed far more training for the men and a greater dropping height for the aircraft. However, the few trials showed that there was some potential for sabotage groups and small parties of demolition experts. The idea was then abandoned. Russia was the country which took the airborne theory the furthest, and the Soviet government encouraged parachuting and gliding as national sports from 1922 onwards. Experiments with parachute troops were started in about 1928, and by 1930 a small group of para-

chutists 'captured' a corps commander on an exercise. In 1936 a force of 1,500 men was dropped by parachute before an invited audience of military observers and caused no small stir in the Western capitals, though it soon died down thanks to indifference, apathy and other more urgent matters. Most European countries were rearming to fight Germany and had no resources to spend on untried ideas; for the majority of them it was to be a substantial effort to raise a modern army at all, much less a force of transport aircraft and specially trained airborne troops.

In Germany the atmosphere was different, though the difference was largely fortuitous and not the result of any particular national policy. As in Russia, there had been a government-sponsored movement to popularize all kinds of aviation and to some extent the German interest kept pace with that of Russia; it was all helped by the secret military agreements which Germany had made with Russia in 1922. Germany was well aware of the Russian experiments with airborne troops and had been following them closely; the 1936 manoeuvres came as no surprise in Berlin,

for the groundwork had already been laid. Since 1928 the German airline Lufthansa had been buying aircraft which could be utilized as transports in time of war, or which were virtually prototypes of bombers. When, therefore, the military restrictions of the Versailles treaty were torn up by Hitler in 1935 almost 250 useful military transport machines were already serving in civilian markings and the type was in mass production. It was a substantial start and it ensured the success of the German airborne arm, though there was hardly any particular enthusiasm for it at that time.

The idea of airborne warfare suited the German military philosophy of that time. Surrounded by potential or imagined enemies, determined to strike the first blow, and fully realizing, above all else, the value of the element of surprise in destroying morale, airborne forces appeared to be tailor-made for the blitzkreig. Germany's frontiers were blocked on several fronts by old-fashioned linear defence works such as the Maginot Line and there were good bases and airfields all over Germany from which any number of airborne assaults

Jumping from a Russian TB-3. Men are climbing out from a hatch in the top of the rear fuselage, and going over the port side. At the same time another stick is climbing out of a hatch on the starboard side just above the wing and these jumpers are sliding or rolling down the wing walk-way and dropping off. The figure nearest to the machine has just done this and he is hunched up into a ball. All are using ripcord parachutes. The plane must be flying very slowly, notice the pilot in an open cockpit and the man standing in the extreme nose holding a small flag. He is thought to be controlling the two sticks. This picture could have been taken at any time between 1934 and 1940 (*Imperial War Museum, London*)

Soviet soldiers boarding a TB-3. The size of their main parachute pack indicates that the canopy is made of a bulky material, perhaps cotton, silk or a mixture of the two. Presumably they are going to jump with their weapons still slung from the shoulder as there is no indication of any sort of container (*IWM, London*)

could be launched without warning. It seemed that all that remained was to train the troops and equip them. In fact it turned out to be a little more difficult than that.

In 1936 Major Immanns was sent to a training camp in Stendal, Bavaria, and ordered to set up a small experimental and training school for parachutists. He had 15 officers and 70 NCOs and men, and within a few months he had decided firmly on the static line parachute, similar to the Italian Salavatore. At the same time he tested and developed equipment and training methods and within the space of a year Stendal was a parachute school, ready for its first pupil. It was the first such school in the West. The Russians had had a military school for some years, and the Poles were to open a small parachute centre based on Russian teaching within a few months of Stendal starting. Having laid the foundations, Immanns was superseded by General-Major Oswalt Bassenge, more staff appeared, and serious training began.

The interesting thing is that at this point nobody in Germany had any clear idea of what the parachutists would be used for, nor how they would be organized, nor – and this was to be crucial – under whose auspices they were to come.

The army had vague ideas of forming a parachute battalion, trained and equipped for ordinary military ground operations, but there was no notion of how they would be employed except perhaps as a rapid reinforcement to advancing units. The Luftwaffe approached the idea quite differently. They had foreseen the time when there might be targets that had to be bombed, but which were too heavily defended for the bombers to get through to them. In these cases the Luftwaffe proposed to parachute in demolition parties some miles from the target, which they would then approach carefully and sabotage using equipment and explosives carried on them. They would then withdraw to open country and either prepare a landing strip, or select a piece of road for use as a landing strip, and be picked up by aeroplanes. It was an interesting idea, to use what we now call Special Forces as an extension of the bomber. Finally there was the SS who were not going to be left behind whatever was happening, no matter for what reason, so they sent a platoon for training. Fortunately there was no shortage of support or equipment and the school could call on up to 100 Junkers 52s whenever it needed them. There was widespread jealousy between the army and

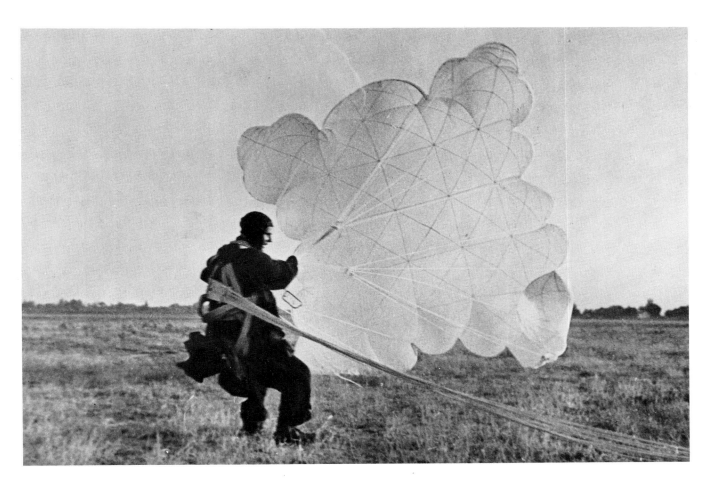

Pre-war Russian parachutist immediately after landing. His main canopy is out of the picture and he is controlling his inflated second or reserve parachute. It was a common Russian habit up to 1941 to jump with both canopies inflated. The square shape is a distinction of Russian pre-war parachutes and was originally intended for simplicity of manufacture; it also gave a stable and directional flight (*IWM, London*)

the Luftwaffe over the ownership of the parachute arm, and nobody in Berlin would make a decision, but the school kept going just the same.

Bassenge was no fool and he pushed his troops into taking part in the 1937 manoeuvres in West Prussia. The Luftwaffe demolition parties did well and were judged to have disrupted the enemy rear areas, but none of them could be picked up as they had no suitable radios and this vital part of the demolition theory could not be practised. Indeed it never was and it is highly unlikely that it would ever have worked except under the most favourable circumstances with a totally disorganized enemy, and in those cases anything goes. Next day a complete parachute infantry company was dropped, more as a demonstration for Hitler than for any good tactical reason, but it served its purpose of showing the possibilities to all the top-ranking generals at once, even though it was still to be some time before they made up their minds.

Meanwhile other experiments were going on at Stendal and at the end of 1937 trials were being made with the first cargo gliders for carrying the support weapons and their ammunition. The actual glider used was what later became the DFS 230.

It was too small and light for anything except minor loads, but was an invaluable machine for teaching the tactics of glider operations both in the air and on the ground. Germany had already realized that the parachute force would always be widely spread on landing, and that a glider or aircraft-landed group arrived in one compact unit, ready to fight the moment it cleared the aircraft. Despite the drama of the Russian drop in 1936 Major-General (later Field-Marshal) Archibald Wavell who was the British observer, noted that one and a half hours after the first troops had landed small numbers of parachutists were still being collected together, and there is no reason to suppose that the Germans in 1937 were any better. Parachuting is only half the story, and at Stendal it was quickly being realized that there was much more to the business of flying to the battle than had been imagined, but still no decision came on who would control the airborne force, nor how they would be employed.

Meanwhile political events were speeding up. In 1936 the Rhineland was reoccupied by Germany, and the Spanish Civil War started; in March 1938 Germany occupied Austria and immediately planned to take over Czechoslovakia by the autumn of that year. For this latter operation it was decided to give the infant airborne arm their opportunity and Bassenge was called to Berlin. There he was told to select volunteers from an SA (*Sturmabteilung*) regiment, the Felderrnhalle Regiment, and have them trained as a parachute battalion and an air-landed battalion by the following autumn, i.e. within four months. In addition he was to ensure that all the existing trained airborne units were ready for operations behind the Czech lines at the same time. For Bassenge this was almost the last straw. He still had no idea who was to command the airborne operation, nor which department would direct it; he had trained one army battalion, one Luftwaffe battalion, some SS and was now being told to train extra men from a purely political organization – the SA – still without any proper direction as to how they would be employed. Furthermore it was quite obvious that he, Bassenge, would be expected to command this mixture of troops in whatever operations it pleased the political branch of the Reichschancellery to devise. He jibbed, particularly at the prospect of the SA being used as infantry. He advised the Chancellery that it was impracticable for one man to train and command at the same time, and advised the appointment of a separate ground force commander. This was accepted, and Major-General Kurt Student, who was commanding a division of the Luftwaffe, was summoned by Göring on 4 July and told to form an airborne division by 1 September, ready to invade Czechoslovakia.

He did it, though his division was never put to the test as the Sudetenland was annexed without a fight; but Student managed to have the 16 Infantry Regiment air-landed into open fields near their objectives in Moravia as an exercise. This took place in one day, on 1 October 1938, and was entirely successful. No men were hurt and all but 12 aircraft which were damaged were flown out again. The division was now called the 7 Flieger Division, and consisted of no less than nine battalions. There were the two parachute battalions and seven air-landed ones, the latter coming from the Luftwaffe Hermann Göring Regiment, the SA Felderrnhalle and the 16 Infantry Regiment. There were also elements of the necessary supporting troops and an artillery troop of four Skoda guns. In support were transport and fighter squadrons of the Luftwaffe and a dozen gliders. In all, the division was 9,000 strong, not counting the air-

crews – an astonishing advance for 1938, though it must be remembered that most of the men had only had three months training or less, there had been no major exercises, very few minor ones and there was no proper idea of how to employ all these expensively trained troops.

The winter of 1938 was not an auspicious one for the new airborne force. The army recalled the 16 Regiment and the SA took back the Felderrnhalle men and it looked bleak for Student. However, he was a man of action and he persuaded the Luftwaffe to take command of all parachute units, the army to take all air-landed troops, and pressed for the establishment of an inspector of parachute and airborne forces. Student had himself made inspector, and put all policy on airborne forces under the Luftwaffe. He then set about rebuilding 7 Flieger Division and got the army to agree that 22 Infantry Division would become an airborne (air-landed) division. By September 1939, 1 Parachute Regiment had been re-formed from the pieces left after the return from Czechoslovakia, two battalions of 2 Parachute Regiment were forming and there were some independent anti-tank companies and an anti-aircraft troop. There were continual airborne exercises during 1939 and in July both the divisions took part in an exercise at the same time. In this exercise a complete battalion of 1,000 men jumped in one lift on to one drop zone. Arrangements for rallying and collecting the men were being explored, if not actually perfected, during this time. Both divisions were given tasks in the Polish campaign, but were not needed and in October 1939 Hitler personally ordered Student to prepare for airborne operations in Western Europe in the following spring. Airborne warfare was once again recognized in Germany and Student was determined to see that it played a major part in whatever actions were to come in the war.

While all this activity was going on in Germany it is almost incredible to have to report that practically nothing was being done in any other European country. In Britain there was an indifference amounting almost to hostility, and in France much the same feeling prevailed. As the Continent drew ever nearer to war, only in Germany, and to a lesser extent in Russia, was there any real attempt to use the theories and practice of the airborne assault. A stiff price was going to be extracted for this blindness.

November 28, 1941. Men of 3 Battalion, 9 US Infantry Division unloading a 37mm gun from a DC-3. This was a very early exercise in the use of airportable troops, and it was an assault landing on Maxton Airport N.C. (*US Army*)

US experiments in the mid 1920s. A Curtiss JN-4 taking off with five parachutists, four clinging to the wings and one in the rear cockpit (*US Army*)

Russian parachutist soon after the jump. His reserve parachute has not yet inflated (*IWM, London*)

2 Europe 1940

During the winter of 1939 the German general staff considered several different plans for the invasion of the West. Hitler demanded an immediate follow-up to the Polish offensive, but the idea was never fully supported by the military and a combination of a severe winter season and an unfortunate security breach convinced the staff that it was better to wait until the spring. The security breach was the loss of the Stendal parachute school commander who force-landed in Belgium while flying to a conference in Berlin in bad weather. As he was carrying copies of the plans for an attack on the French and Belgian armies, and as he was captured by the Belgians with all his papers intact, his loss caused no small stir in Germany, and in the West too, since none could decide if his crash was a deliberate plant or not. But the Germans had pushed ahead with their training despite the uncertainty of the planners, and it is typical of their methods that they practised for winter jumping by jumping in sub-zero temperatures on to snow-covered drop zones.

Hitler began thinking of invading Scandinavia around Christmas 1939, and he returned to the idea in early 1940. His motives were fear of the British forestalling him and seizing his supplies of iron ore, and a wish to push the British naval blockade as far away from the German coast as possible. The Norwegian traitor Quisling seems to have played on these fears in the hope of gaining power for himself, and Hitler appears to have believed his tales. At any event, planning went forward with a rush from February onwards, when the British seizure of the German ship *Altmark* in Norwegian waters set Berlin in a frenzy. Invasion was now certain.

Denmark and Norway

The success of the invasion plan depended heavily on surprise. Both Denmark and Norway were to be invaded on the same day. For the troops to have the best chance of landing along the extended coasts it was essential that no warning be given and also – a significant point – that air superiority

was retained throughout the operation. For the first time in war parachute troops and air-landed troops were to be used together, the parachutists to seize the airfields, and the air-landed units to consolidate and spread out from these bases. The date was fixed by the clearance of the spring ice packs, and was late, it was early April before the waters were clear of hazards, though it was still very cold.

Moonrise fixed 9 April as the ideal date, and all was prepared for then. It was vital to the plan to have the airfields in Denmark and Norway captured at the very outset so that the troops could have air cover for their landings, for the range was too great for the fighters to operate from Germany. For this important task only the 1 Parachute Battalion could be spared. It seems incredible now that a full-scale invasion of two separate countries could even be contemplated with the support of only one battalion, but, at that time, there was no understanding of the capabilities of parachute troops, and the greater part of the German army was already deployed awaiting the far more important invasion

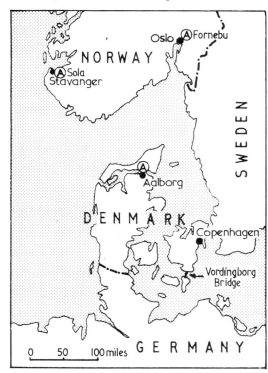

Reinforcements landing during the Narvik operation, June 1940 (*Bundesarchiv*)

of Belgium and France which was due to start straight afterwards. There were neither troops nor aircraft to spare; one battalion had to do.

The commanding officer was given four tasks to fulfil, two in Denmark and two in Norway, all to be carried out at about the same time. In Denmark he had to capture a long and vulnerable road bridge in front of the invading ground forces, and do it before it was blown by its Danish defenders. He also had to capture two airfields at Ålborg, luckily they were close together. He allotted one company to this part of the day's work. In Norway the battalion had to capture Sola airfield at Stavanger, and for this he allotted one more company. Battalion headquarters and the two remaining companies were to capture the main Oslo airfield at Fornebu and hold it as a bridgehead while air-landed troops built up a large enough force to occupy the city.

April 9 dawned stormy with winds up to gale force and no sign of an improvement before 0800 hours when the parachutists were due to jump. The 500 transport aircraft warmed up their engines and the operation began. At Ålborg a 30-man

platoon dropped without any trouble in clear sky and within half an hour the two airfields were completely under German control. Within two hours the Luftwaffe was operating from the runways and establishing a forward fighter base.

The capture of the road bridge to Copenhagen was more dramatic. There were two platoons for the task and the company commander dropped one at each end simultaneously. He used surprise as his only real weapon, relying on the early-morning torpor and slow reactions of the Danish conscripts for his success. The parachutists wasted no time on landing but without collecting any weapons they rushed straight at the defence positions at each end of the bridge firing their pistols into the air and shouting at the Danes to surrender. Bewildered, unaware of any war being declared, and terrified of these tough, determined paratroopers, the Danes did not fire a shot. The bridge was captured within ten minutes by just 60 men.

The story at Sola airfield near Stavanger was a little different. Although there were no actual anti-aircraft defences there were some machine gun installations and a couple of pill boxes. The murk and cloud

Opposite: (*Above*) The heroes of Fort Eben-Emael in a posed photograph with the Führer after being presented with their Iron Crosses. All are wearing the early pattern overall with long legs, and all have side laced boots and black leather gloves. There appears to be some variety in the arrangements for the overall pockets as well as in belts, and at least two men have pistol holsters (*Bundesarchiv*)

(*Below*) German parachute troops leaving a plane, Holland, 10 May 1940 (*IWM, London*)

were so bad for the fly-in that the Junkers were down to 30 feet and most of the escort fighters turned back, but six got through and strafed the defences sufficiently to both quieten them and alert their crews as to what to expect next. Within minutes the Junkers arrived, co-inciding with a clear patch of sky, and out jumped number 3 Company, straight into a hail of fire from the defenders. It took them 35 minutes to collect weapons and rush the defending positions, helped by two more Messerschmitts which arrived in the nick of time, but the casualties were heavy. Two anxious hours later the first air-landed troops arrived and secured the surrounding area and harbour.

So far, so good, but things were not encouraging at the prime objective at Oslo. The Norwegian government bravely refused the German call to surrender and decided to fight, full mobilization was ordered and the king and government moved out of the capital to conduct the war from the mountains. The German air attaché went to Fornebu and radioed to Germany to tell them to sieze the airfield immediately. The 1 Battalion was alerted and despatched immediately, but the

weather was even worse than on the way to Sola and after two aircraft had collided the force was recalled. The commanding officer of the air-landed troops got the call just as Fornebu came in sight, once again in a providential clear patch, and he decided that the recall was a hoax. Messerschmitts were strafing the defences, and he went straight in to land. His aeroplane was shot to bits as it approached, and his pilot just managed to pull up and circle again. Meanwhile the Messerschmitts had run out of fuel, and their flight commander decided on a typically brave and daring move. He landed his force and used them as machine gun support for the shattered Junkers to come in again. The Norwegians, who could have destroyed the lot, gave up and moved back to Oslo.

Five days after the successful invasion of Norway, there was a small but significant follow-up operation when an attempt was made to prevent the Norwegian army retreating from Oslo by seizing a narrow pass in the hills near Dombås. It failed miserably, probably because the fly-in was too low – many men were killed by hitting the ground before their parachutes opened, and all the rest were rounded up.

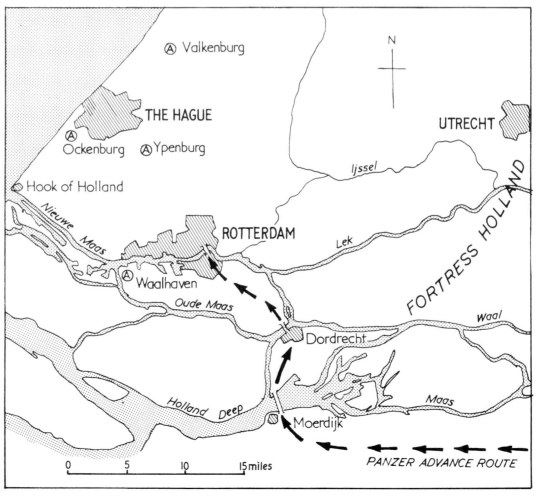

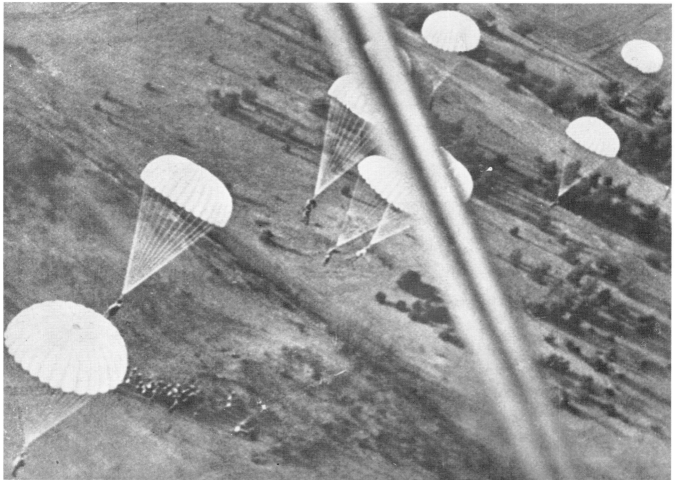

The lesson was not ignored, though all reports about it were suppressed.

There was no doubt that Scandinavia had been won by an enormous airborne bluff, and a great deal of luck, and it was unlikely to succeed a second time on the same scale. There were many lessons in it for both Germans and Allies. For the Germans there was the realization of the vital importance of reliable radio communications between the various elements of the entire force, and also the follow-up troops. For the Allies there was the fact that airborne warfare existed at all, and the tales of the assaults on Norway and Denmark grew mightily in the telling, doing little for morale among those who waited to see who would be next. A few clear-headed thinkers tried to find the chinks in the airborne armour, but the general atmosphere was one of grave alarm and a feeling of being menaced by an implacable foe whom nothing could stop. For the first time in history no part of a defender's country was safe from attack.

Holland

But despite the histrionics and success of the Scandinavian campaign nobody could pretend that it had been real war. The airborne arm still had to prove itself and show that it was something more than just another way of carrying ordinary soldiers to the battlefield. Such a demonstration was almost ready, for Hitler's plans for the invasion of the West were now about to be put to the test. After much changing and rethinking, the German army was to sweep through Belgium and the Low Countries. On the way Holland was to be swiftly engulfed, thereby securing the right flank and providing the Luftwaffe with air bases close to the North Sea and the British east coast. The main armoured threat, the blitzkreig, would strike through the Ardennes and on into France. Speed was essential, and as Holland was allotted primarily to the Luftwaffe, 7 Flieger and 22 Infantry Divisions became part of the invading force; only a small airborne element was to be used elsewhere though they played a vital and glamorous part.

Student was given virtually a free hand in deciding the uses of his airborne troops in the Dutch campaign, and because he had to allow time for the planners to put his ideas into effect, the tactical plan was fixed well before the Scandinavian adventure. In retrospect we can see that this was a mistake since he used the same general principles and though they worked well

enough in Denmark and Norway, it was to be different in Holland. There were three main features to the plan: firstly the airfields were to be seized by small parachute forces followed by air-landed units. Secondly, there was to be no warning of the attacks; and thirdly, the ground troops must catch up quickly. There was one other element which Student could have been expected to have appreciated and done something about. He actually commanded both the divisions, though only in his capacity as overall commander of the airborne forces; he was never officially a corps commander, nor did he have any tactical headquarters. His enthusiasm was such that he jumped with the leading unit, and so once the first wave had gone in there was no effective control of the remainder of the operation. Nobody could make decisions as to which sector to reinforce, or to withdraw, or to re-supply, or any other necessary feature of war. Once the commander had flown off the plan had to be followed exactly and each separate battalion had to fight it out as best it could. In the end it worked, but this time the price was high and the margin of success small.

The plan was as near a stroke of genius as makes no matter, whatever may be the criticisms of its application. One division, the 22 Infantry, was to be dropped right into the heart of the enemy country, almost on top of the capital itself, and about as far from the follow-up troops as possible without actually landing in the North Sea. Its objective was the capture of The Hague, including the Dutch government and, if possible, the royal family. For this the division had one parachute battalion and two infantry regiments, the 47th and the 65th. The 7 Flieger Division was to carry out an operation which later became known as 'laying an airborne carpet' in that they were to capture the bridges and communication centres between their drop zone and the 22 Infantry Division's position, so allowing the follow-up units to move quickly across the country to give support. The geography of the Netherlands is such that the main obstacle is the river Maas, which runs just south of Rotterdam on a west-east course almost to the German frontier, where it turns south and follows the line of the boundary. If the Germans could 'bounce' a crossing of the Maas at the frontier they would have a good run along the south bank of the river until they were opposite Rotterdam, but to get into the

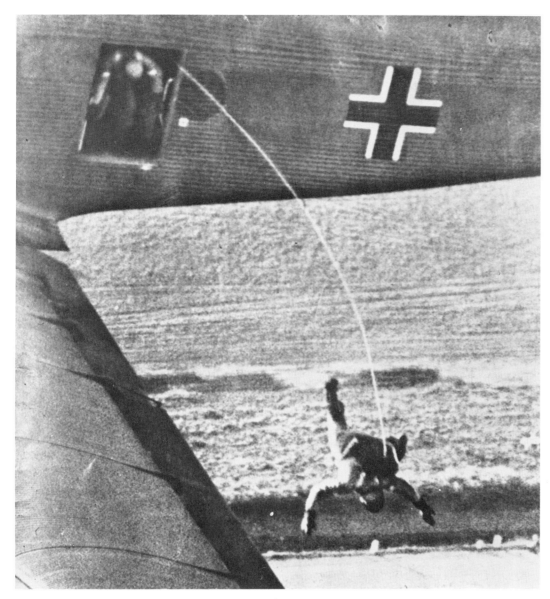

A stick jumping into
Holland, 10 May 1940.
No 1 leaving the door of
a JU-52, No 2 just pulling
himself clear of the
door-sill. Early morning,
height about 500ft (*IWM,
London*)

Parachutists and infantry
at Waalhaven, 10 or 11
May 1940. The infantry
are probably from 22
Luftlande Division who
were flown in after the
parachutists captured the
airfield (*IWM, London*)

city they would have to cross no less than three rivers, for at that point the Maas spreads out into a near-delta. It was these crossings which 7 Flieger was sent to hold while the main part of General Georg von Kuechler's army pushed the ill-prepared and ill-equipped Dutch army out of its way and stormed through southern Holland towards the prizes on the west coast. It was the classical use of airborne forces in an assault.

Unfortunately, although the strategy was correct, the tactics were weak. The Dutch were forewarned of what to expect by the Scandinavian campaign, and altered their deployment to suit. Instead of sending their reserves well forward, they held them back around the airfields, realizing that the airborne attack depended for its success on landing infantry in aircraft which had to make repeat trips. Had there been no advance warning it is just possible that Student's plan would have worked, but with the example of Norway to study, it was in jeopardy from the start.

On 10 May the invasion began, and at 0530 hours wave after wave of fighters, bombers and Junkers transports droned over the Netherlands en route to their targets. The air raids helped to confuse the Dutch while 22 Division tried to seize the airfields at The Hague. At each airfield, however, the defenders were ready and the parachutists were either rounded up or

chased off the airfield itself. As the air-landed units came in to land they were shot up in dozens, and by the end of the day the survivors were scattered over the countryside, holding out in houses and farms and firmly pinned down by the Dutch. There were smoking wrecks of Junkers all over the Hague area and the Dutch were triumphant, but also bewildered and nervous. Alarmist reports of parachutists in disguise spread throughout the nation, and it is from this day that the stories of German parachutists dropping in nun's dress, or Dutch uniform date. They were all quite untrue and the figments of excited imaginations, but they gained sufficient credence to be believed by some today. At the time they caused continual false alarms which exhausted the Dutch defence.

South of Rotterdam 7 Flieger Division fared better, perhaps because it had three parachute battalions to the 22nd's one, and so was a little less dependent on the landing of aircraft to get troops on the ground. To capture a bridge on the Rotterdam waterfront 12 seaplanes landed on the river and taxied up to the bridge, discharging 120 men who swarmed over the structure, removed the demolition charges, and held on. Elsewhere the story was similar. The parachute drops were largely successful, though most of the men had to fight as they landed and the defence was fierce at all points. The position of the division was not secure until the afternoon, when two battalions of 16 Infantry Regiment were landed on to Waalhaven airfield. The aircraft, however, came under artillery fire from the Dutch whose observers had the runways under complete observation. With these extra troops the bridges could be held, and despite some anxious moments they were held until 12 May, when 9 Panzer Division caught up. Holland surrendered on the evening of the 14th.

While the invasion of Holland was being launched, another but smaller operation was taking place on the Belgian frontier. At the point where Belgium is nearest to Germany there is a finger-like projection of Dutch territory pointing south from Holland, called the Maastricht Appendix, from the name of the town which almost fills the area. To the west of the Appendix is the Albert Canal, a formidable obstacle with road bridges over it into Belgium. It was obvious that any attempt to cross the Appendix with troops would warn the Belgian defenders who would blow the

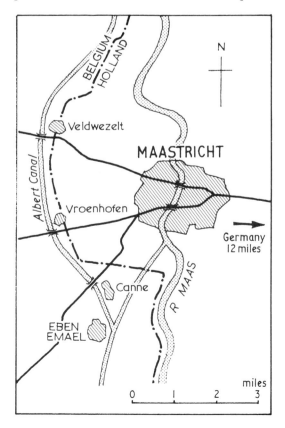

bridges long before the Germans could reach them. The requirement was to seize the bridges first of all, without warning.

There are three bridges that lead west out of Maastricht and over the canal and all were defended by a Belgian company with concrete pill boxes and an anti-tank gun. Each bridge was mined and wired for demolition. In addition there was a huge fort dominating the area, Fort Eben-Emael. The fort was entirely underground, with only concrete cupolas above the surface and thick barbed wire entanglements around it. The banks of the canal were cut almost vertical, and were faced with concrete in places. The positions seemed impregnable from land attack, but there were neither anti-aircraft defences nor any aerial look-out points. These were fatal omissions.

The German approach to this problem was to use gliders to put troops on top of each objective and to back them up with parachutists in the second wave. It was a plan of enormous daring and considerable complexity, calling for great courage and steadiness on the part of the troops, and precise timing, but it was so novel that there was no reason why it should not succeed. And so it turned out. Two of the three bridges were captured intact but the highlight of the day was the reduction of Fort Eben-Emael by a force of only 78 men.

All the gliders were released at 8,000 feet while still inside Germany, and glided in total silence over the Maastricht Appendix to land on their Belgian targets just as dawn was breaking. The surprise was complete, for the use of gliders meant that there was none of the usual warning from aircraft engines. Each glider carried ten men in a formed group, fully equipped, ready to fight, to within a hundred or so yards of their objective. The defenders stood little chance. On the fort the casemates were smashed with explosive charges, the doors blown in, and the upper works occupied. The defenders were cooped up in their subterranean tunnels quite unable to strike back. They surrendered next day. The attack had cost six German lives.

After the surrender of Holland the divisions were withdrawn to Germany to reform and retrain while the next stage in the war was prepared. Student was wounded in Rotterdam and took some weeks to recover; meanwhile his command was enlarged. The Dutch invasion was to be the last airborne operation in 1940, but the new arm had proved itself fully and convinced the German military leaders that this was a worthwhile way to wage war. The 7 Flieger Division was expanded so that all its members were parachutists, and an assault engineer regiment was added to it. But the Germans made another gain, one that was more subtle but none the less valuable. Their successes caused extreme alarm everywhere.

In Britain the entire population was mesmerized by the conviction that they were in mortal danger of being invaded at any moment by hordes of German parachutists wearing disguises of all kinds, who would descend on any point in the islands from an apparently unstoppable air fleet accompanied by continuous bombing attacks. It was a terrifying prospect, and it took several months for it to subside. Meanwhile the failures of 22 Division around The Hague were quietly obscured.

In fact there were plans to use airborne troops in the invasion of Britain and they were allotted the task of seizing a bridgehead on the south-east coast; however, General Putzier who was commanding in Student's absence, vetoed the idea on the rather flimsy grounds that there were too many anti-airborne obstacles on and around the landing areas. Student would have reacted differently. So, as the year faded out in an autumn of anti-climax after the successes of the spring, the airborne arm could look back with pride and confidence.

3 Crete 1941

The winter of 1940/41 was usefully spent in consolidating the German airborne army; it was formed into a proper corps, with a central command structure and communications. This became XI Flieger Corps, consisting of 7 Flieger Division, 22 Infantry Division, the XI Air Command, comprising all the transport aircraft and gliders, and finally the Corps Troops in which were the signals battalion, the medical and supply battalions, a reconnaissance aircraft squadron and the Parachute Assault Regiment – an airborne engineer unit descended directly from those which had attacked Fort Eben-Emael. For air operations the XI Flieger Corps would be put under the command of an air fleet, thereby remaining under the control of the Luftwaffe, but also ensuring that the aircraft, airfields and support aircraft were available and properly integrated into one force. However, there was one weakness: despite the high standard of individual training and the undoubted capability of the junior commanders, this large and formidable force had never had a chance to train as one command. Of necessity it had had to be spread over Germany during the winter and there had been little chance to carry out more than battalion-sized exercises, nor had the command structure been tried out, as most of the time had been spent in training the reinforcements and in experimenting with new dropping techniques.

As Hitler prepared for the Russian invasion in early 1941 it became clear to him that first of all he would have to extract his ally Mussolini from the mess he had got himself into in Albania and Greece, thereby securing his southern flank. To leave Greece still fighting the Italians was to invite the Allies to invade and push up into Rumania while the Wehrmacht was tied down in the north. Hitler therefore decided, reluctantly, on a quick campaign to clean up the Balkans. In the event it took longer than expected, owing to a stubborn revolt in Yugoslavia, but early in April Greece was invaded and the Greeks and their British allies were pushed steadily southwards. The 7 Flieger Division was moved to Rumania with the intention that it should seize the island of Lemnos, but this mission was cancelled and instead it was given the job of blocking the British retreat across the Corinth Canal. Most of the British troops were crossing this canal by a single road bridge into the Peloponnese to the south, and being picked up by the Royal Navy from the many little ports along the coast. If the canal could be secured, then the main escape route would be cut. The 2 Parachute Regiment was allotted to the bridge, together with a platoon of engineers from the Parachute Assault Regiment.

The attack was mounted from the airfield at Larissa in central Greece, which had only dirt strips and few hangars or fuel stores. There were sufficient Junkers for two battalions to be carried in one lift, and for towing the gliders of the assault platoon. The plan was an exact copy of the one used on the Belgian bridges the year before. Assault engineers in the

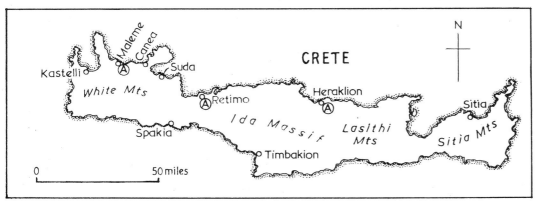

The parachute drop on the Corinth Canal. A close formation of Junkers over the drop zone (*Bundesarchiv*)

gliders would arrive first, right on the objective, and dismantle the explosive charges. The parachutists would drop very shortly after and overwhelm the defenders, landing more or less directly on their defensive positions. It was to be a dawn attack, quick and concentrated. But the bridge was heavily defended by infantry and anti-aircraft guns.

The attackers were lucky, the glider engineers got between the defenders and the bridge and secured the explosives while the parachutists confused the defence by dropping all round them, but the southern end was strongly held and bitter fighting broke out. In the fighting a stray shell hit the bridge and blew up the demolition charges, so cutting the road and blocking the canal but in spite of this the operation was a success. The German casualties were only 240 and loss of the bridge resulted in the capture of 2,000 British and Commonwealth troops and 8,000 Greek and Yugoslavian. But those who escaped had learned something of the strengths and weaknesses of airborne assaults, and would be putting it to the test in the following month.

With Greece secured Hitler wanted to get on with the Russian invasion, but the Luftwaffe was anxious to take Crete also in order to ensure that there was no base

26 April 1941. Air landing troops loading a Junkers 52 for the assault on the Corinth Canal bridges (*Bundesarchiv*)

left from which the Allies could attack the German flank, either by bombing the Rumanian oilfields, or by direct landings. Student flew to Berlin and persuaded Göring, who probably needed little urging in any case, that Crete could be taken by airborne invasion alone. Hitler was less sure, and offered objections that were later justified by events; but eventually he gave way and the Luftwaffe was allowed to make the attempt to take Crete. There was little time to spare; on 21 April Hitler agreed to the attack and fixed 15 May as the date for it. The Luftwaffe squadrons were to be released to Russia immediately after that, so Crete had to be taken in one non-stop assault.

Student returned to Greece to start the planning, and ran into difficulties at once. In order to get guns ashore on Crete he would have to use shipping as he had no means of delivery by air. There was almost no shipping in Greece that could land on open coasts, nor was there any sizeable naval force to escort them. The Royal Navy controlled the sea by night using its new radar detection equipment, so the assault would be short of support fire for the initial attacks apart from the Luftwaffe fighters and dive-bombers. The 7 Flieger Division was split between Germany and Greece and the 22 Infantry Division was

bogged down holding the Rumanian oil-fields. Roads and railways were sketchy all across the area and it was a nightmare to move anything at all. The 7 Division containers were all packed ready for the invasion of England, and were stored in France; they finally reached Athens via Austria, Rumania, the Black Sea and Piraeus. Other stores took less dramatic but equally tedious routes and it was only by extraordinary feats that a more-or-less complete corps was assembled at Athens on 14 May. The 22 Division had to be left on the oilfields and in its place Student took 5 Mountain Division which had done well in Greece, and was on the spot.

The four weeks had passed in furious activity. The 5 Mountain Division had been trained in air-landing techniques, mounting bases had been set up, the local airfields had been stocked, and amazingly all 500 Junkers of XI Corps had been flown back to bases in Germany, Austria and Czechoslovakia, overhauled, and returned to Greece. But it was not quite enough and 15 May had to be abandoned as the date of the invasion. On the 17th most of the petrol for the Junkers was still on board a tanker jammed in the Corinth Canal by the wreckage of the blown bridge. Divers were flown from Kiel to clear it, and the fuel reached the airfields

Crete, 20 May 1941. The first parachutists coming down at Canea (*Bundesarchiv*)

on the 18th. The attack was then fixed for 20 May.

Crete lies about 150 miles south of Athens, but less than 100 miles from the southern coast of the Peloponnese. A one-way flight from Athens took less than an hour for the slowest machine, and for the fighters and dive bombers whose bases were nearer there was adequate 'loiter time' over the target. The island is a long thin strip, running west to east about 160 miles long and 30 or 40 miles wide. The topography is uninviting. The island's main feature is a mountain chain that runs more or less continuously along its entire length, dropping steeply into the sea on the southern side, and sloping down to the north to give a narrow coastal plain. The few rivers run off the mountains to the north, cutting across the plain in deep gulleys and draining small valley pockets in the mountains. The few towns of importance are on the northern coast, and the only lateral road follows the coast joining them. The north coast has some small harbours, which in 1941 were only developed for light coastal shipping, but there is a superb bay at Suda, big enough to take a battle fleet in comfort and safety. The southern coast has only one or two tiny fishing harbours crouched at the bottom of the cliffs. The only airfields were alongside the towns and harbours on the north coast, at Maleme, Retimo and Heraklion. The remainder of the plain was ill-suited to landing aircraft, being deeply indented with gulleys, and containing terraced fields surrounded by stone walls. Significantly, the plain was heavily cultivated with crop-bearing trees such as olives, carobs and citrus. These were to prove invaluable to the defence, and misleading to the air reconnaissance units of the Luftwaffe.

To defend this island the British had a considerable force. There was the original garrison of a reinforced brigade numbering about 5,000 men. These were disposed at Heraklion and Canea and had about 30 obsolete light tanks and the same number of light anti-aircraft guns in support, they knew the island and had prepared defensive positions. In addition, another twenty-odd old tanks had been sent from Egypt with a battery of artillery, a fresh infantry battalion and some marines. But the most significant reinforcement was in the shape of the 6 Australian and 2 New Zealand Divisions who had fought through Greece, been evacuated from the Peloponnese and then landed by the Royal Navy at Suda Bay. They had little more than their rifles

and light machine guns and they had suffered fairly severely at the hands of the Luftwaffe already so that morale was not as high as it could have been, but they were trained men and were in complete units. Indeed, the shortage on Crete was not men, but material and munitions. There were scarcely any mortars, anti-aircraft guns, artillery pieces or tanks, nor were there radios to control the troops. Unit could not speak to unit, neither could they speak to HQ; even the tanks were without radios. It was not a good base on which to build a defence capable of rapid reaction to an airborne attack, but the commander was a redoubtable New Zealand general, Bernard Freyberg VC, and he put the defences in such good order that they quickly represented a major threat to any air landing. He also insisted on the strictest attention to concealment and camouflage so that German intelligence never discovered the presence of the extra two divisions, and thought that the only force they had to deal with was the original brigade.

German intelligence also made another serious error. They convinced themselves that the Cretans would be friendly, though they had no reason to think so, and indeed the Cretans were anything but. Almost 10,000 of them turned out carrying rifles to join with mainland Greek irregular units in defence of their homes. Air reconnaissance from Greece did nothing to alter the German view of the island, and in this the trees on the plain played an important part. Under their shade the defenders waited each day, only moving along the roads at night. The airfields were continually attacked, and the few RAF aircraft that could be spared from Egypt were either shot down or pulled back to Alexandria. The air was easily cleared for the German assault.

The German plan was fairly complicated and once again based on the one used in Holland, where it had only partially worked. Student planned to put down as many parachute assaults as he could, with the intention of seeing which one would succeed and then reinforcing that one quickly. He did not anticipate much resistance, and once again the strength of the attack lay in the air-landed troops who would come in on the airfields captured by the parachutists. Despite the presence of the Air Assault Regiment, who were all engineers, there was no provision for making improvised airstrips away from the airfields proper. Yet it had been shown

(*Above*) After the drop at
Corinth, a short pause in
battle. Time for a smoke,
a drink and a quick look at
the map (*Bundesarchiv*)

(*Left*) The end of a
Junkers 52 as it runs in
across the drop zone
(*Bundesarchiv*)

in Czechoslovakia that the Junkers could operate from open fields with little trouble. Student was, however, fixed on the capture of the airfields, and as was soon apparent, these were heavily defended. There were not enough transport aircraft to carry more than half the parachute force and tow the required gliders, so the assault was divided into two lifts, which would be about eight hours apart. For the first crucial hours only 4,300 parachutists would be fighting on the island, isolated entirely from their base, with only the light weapons that they could carry in their containers, but with the Luftwaffe giving close and continuous fire support. Against them they would have ten times their number, though in the actual battle areas the ratio would be less. Both sides would be fighting with roughly similar weapons, both would be foot-mobile, for the British had few trucks on the island, both would be unaware of the strength and casualties of the other. As Student saw it from his headquarters in the Hotel Grande Bretagne in Athens it was a fair gamble, in fact a good one. The only chance he was taking was in attempting to get through at night with a seaborne flotilla to reinforce his troops, for he knew the narrow straits were continually patrolled by enemy warships as soon as it was dark. On Crete 20 May dawned clear, warm and bright, and with the sun came the first air attacks falling with a ferocity and duration

that alerted the defenders to look for a reason, and the direction in which they looked was north. On the airfields around Athens the Junkers loaded up and took off in clouds of dust, causing the later pilots to lose their formation, and straggle.

The Battle of Crete is well-known and well-documented elsewhere. To describe it here other than in the barest outline would take too long, for we are more concerned with its outcome and effects. Student's plan went wrong from the start. The assault parties in gliders who came in near Maleme airfield were in difficulties even before they landed. The parachutists fared similarly and that battle quickly stalled. Elsewhere the story was similar and none of the first day's objectives were gained. At Retimo, Heraklion and Canea the parachutists were held down and rendered ineffective, suffering heavy casualties. The second lift was late, and the whole schedule went astray. Surprise was never actually achieved. Communications from Crete to Greece were all but non-existent so that Student had no idea what was happening, and pilots brought back contradictory reports. Chaos reigned on the makeshift airstrips as the second lift struggled to refuel the planes, load up their containers, and take off in the order dictated by the flight plan. Few did and the troops arrived on the drop zones in piecemeal batches, to be dealt with promptly by carefully sited defenders dug in around

The Corinth drop zone. A machine gunner and in the distance behind him a group of men who are probably unloading a container (*Bundesarchiv*)

Wrecked Junkers on the side of one of the landing zones. From their appearance these machines were damaged by rough landings (notice the stone walls) rather than by AA fire and the crews and passengers may well have survived (*Bundesarchiv*)

the perimeters. German intelligence reports had predicted glider landing zones where there were actually terraced hills, and gliders crashed hopelessly, killing their passengers and wrecking their loads.

Throughout the first day Student held his nerve and waited for a sign of change. It came that evening when he could see that the only area where he had a toe-hold was at Maleme. He sent liaison officers in aircraft to report on what was happening on the island, and only the one who went to Maleme came back. His report was not encouraging, but it was Student's best chance, and he sent his few remaining parachutists to attack the airfield on the second day, with a feint attack further east. The feint failed, but owing to an unfortunate withdrawal by the defenders during the night, the Germans gained control of the airfield in the late afternoon. It was the beginning of the end, for with an airfield the Junkers could ferry troops, supplies and ammunition to the exhausted parachutists. The first Junkers came in to land with troops of the 5 Mountain Division at 1700 hours. It was greeted by a hail of fire, but survived, as did most of the others which followed it. Those that did not added to the number of burning

wrecks already littering the dirt runways. There were still enough British troops in the area to eject every German on Maleme, but the fatal shortage of radios made it impossible to pass the orders in time, nor did the right information get back to the commanders, and the expected counter-attack started late, moved slowly and lacked purpose. At dawn it was far short of its objective, and the Luftwaffe quickly finished it off.

The landings of 5 Mountain Division continued all day, despite the fearsome losses of aircraft. Maleme was now confirmed as the main point of effort of the invading army, and the Luftwaffe concentrated on the New Zealand positions overlooking the airfield. Within a few hours the guns were silenced and the fire from the trenches slackened. To all intents and purposes the battle was now over. The 5 Mountain Division was steadily reinforced and then moved eastwards, fighting hard, but with the certainty of victory before it. The isolated groups of parachutists in the centre and the east, pinned down since the first day, were relieved one by one as the defence was, in Student's own words, 'Rolled up from the West'. On the 27th the Commonwealth troops began withdrawing to the tiny port of Spakia on the south coast, and during the next day and night they were ferried out to warships of the Royal Navy. At Heraklion a brigade was taken off in one night, but that was the only large evacuation from the north coast for the German advance units swept along the coast road and had captured all the ports by the 28th. For the remaining Commonwealth and British troops the only route out was a painful one over the mountains to Spakia, soon to be attacked throughout daylight hours from the air. The dismal process of crouching in caves all day, and standing on the beaches all night, waiting for a boat, was a miserable and frightening conclusion to a campaign that had bemused most of the troops, and caused doubts in the minds of many as to the quality of the Allied war machine and its leaders. At Retimo and Heraklion the defenders had received their orders to retire with incredulity. They had beaten the parachutists, pinned them down, and were ready to take on more. Retreat was the thing furthest from their minds and it was with disgust and alarm that they finally withdrew.

The Germans were equally subdued. There was no doubt that they had won, but the price had been frightening. Accustomed to quick, cheap victories from the airborne arm, the losses in Crete caused deep thought, but in fact the ratio was still good overall. Out of the attacking force of 22,000 men about 5,000, one in four, were dead, most of them coming from among the junior leaders – the corporals, sergeants and young officers. About 2,500 were wounded and there were other losses in a reinforcement flotilla that the Royal Navy had totally destroyed on the first night. All the gliders and 170 Junkers transports were wrecked completely. About 50 other transports flew back to base but were too damaged to continue.

The British lost far more heavily. The casualties were about the same, over 4,000 killed and 2,500 wounded, but 11,800 were captured. In addition 10,000 Greek and Cretan irregulars and some Cypriot labour troops were left in German hands. Nine warships were sunk, 17 damaged so badly as to need dockyard repair, 46 aircraft were destroyed, and the entire equipment of the British troops on Crete fell into German hands. By any calculation it was a massive win for the Germans and it demonstrated as no other campaign had done the full effectiveness of properly used airborne warfare.

Nevertheless, despite these important gains, the Crete campaign did not really affect the German war plans to any degree. Russia was the main target, and even before the last Allied troops had surrendered on Crete, elements of the air fleet were being taken away to regroup for Operation Barbarossa. The 7 Flieger Division was withdrawn to Germany where the men were treated as heroes, but it was to

Crete. Mopping up after the battle. A German section gingerly advancing up a track *(Bundesarchiv)*

be for the last time for most of them. All too soon they would be frittered away as infantry in Russia, and die in the snow in front of Leningrad. The British, dispirited and bewildered, unaware of the crisis that had befallen the Germans on the first day, settled down to learn as much as they could from the campaign, and to devise their own tactics from what they had seen from the receiving end. Crete marked the beginning of British airborne thinking, it also marked the virtual end of the German. Student was quietly snubbed by his fellow generals for risking too much expensive manpower and equipment, and so, into the mincing machine of the Russian Front went the men, the weapons and the aircraft of the *Fallschirmjaeger*; they were only ever to undertake minor airborne operations in the future.

Special Feature: German Airborne Forces

Despite the Russian and Italian experiments Germany was the first country to appreciate the full potential of airborne forces, and the first to fully explore the use of them. Others may have had the initial idea, and demonstrated that it could be done, but as with so many inventions, it is rarely the inventor who develops and markets the final product, and so it was with airborne warfare. The Germans took the idea and developed it, and whatever were the reasons for the Italians and Russians lagging behind, they are not relevant to the main story.

Training and Organization

The backbone of any military force is always the men, and the Germans took particular care with the selection of their recruits. From the start both officers and men were treated alike in training, and there were no relaxations for anyone, whatever his rank. In the *Fallschirmjaeger* everyone took the same risks, and everyone faced the same tests. It was a useful yardstick which all the other airborne armies copied. All ranks were volunteers, coming from existing units, so that they were trained soldiers when they started. When the first volunteers were trained in 1936 the link with flying was so strong that the first batch of officers were put through the full pilot's course, the normal Luftwaffe practice, before they ever approached the parachute school, but it stopped after that. In fact, the parachutists were looked upon as a sort of airborne marine force and just as marines live and fight alongside the navy, so did the *Fallschirmjaeger* live and fight alongside the Luftwaffe. On the forward airstrips in Greece they helped to refuel the planes, load the containers, hitch up the gliders, and even marshal aircraft around the perimeter, the sort of jobs that marines do without thinking, but which no other air force would have allowed for a moment.

That they were tough goes without saying. It was part of their training, and the Luftwaffe quickly caught on to the fact that by imposing a rigorous training régime and rejecting two-thirds, which

was the usual failure rate, they automatically advertised themselves as an élite. These parachutists were by no means the unthinking heel-clicking automatons that British propaganda tried to convey. They were self-reliant, aggressive, and capable of thinking for themselves at all times. Their training taught them that they were the pick of German youth, and until 1942 they undoubtedly were. The first three months of training were spent in refining their infantry skills and included unarmed combat and the use of enemy weapons. There was a considerable emphasis on physical training, marching and agility. In the latter half of the course the recruit learned aircraft drills and in particular, the unusual head-first dive that was used to leave the Junkers 52. At the same time the man was introduced to parachute packing.

After passing out from that they went for a short 16-day parachute course in which they actually packed their own parachutes and made six jumps. The course was highly compressed, and in retrospect must have needed later revision, for there was too much to absorb in so short a time. After this the student received his parachute badge, a diving eagle surrounded by a wreath which he wore on his formal uniform, and he became a full member of a parachute unit. Curiously, he would not have done a night jump, nor would he have had much practice in such important requirements as rallying on the drop zone or packing containers. This had to come from his unit.

Uniform

The distinctive uniform of the *Fallschirmjaeger* was the combat dress. In barracks and on normal training they were indistinguishable from other Luftwaffe troops, except for the parachutist badge. They wore the same yellow patches on the collar of their jacket, but had a regimental title embroidered on the cuff. The 7 Flieger Division wore a dark green title, the regiments a light green one, and for Crete there was a special cuff title.

The combat dress was entirely different. The first and most striking change was in

Opposite: *(Above)* Joseph Goebbels inspects a 'flying club' in 1933 prior to the repudiation of the Treaty of Versailles *(J G Moore Collection, London)*

(Below) A reinforcement jump in Norway, 1940. This was taken just after the invasion and probably took place on the high plateau to the north of Oslo. Four men are running to help the parachutist, perhaps to collapse his canopy and ensure that he is not dragged over one of the outcrops of rock *(J G Moore Collection, London)*

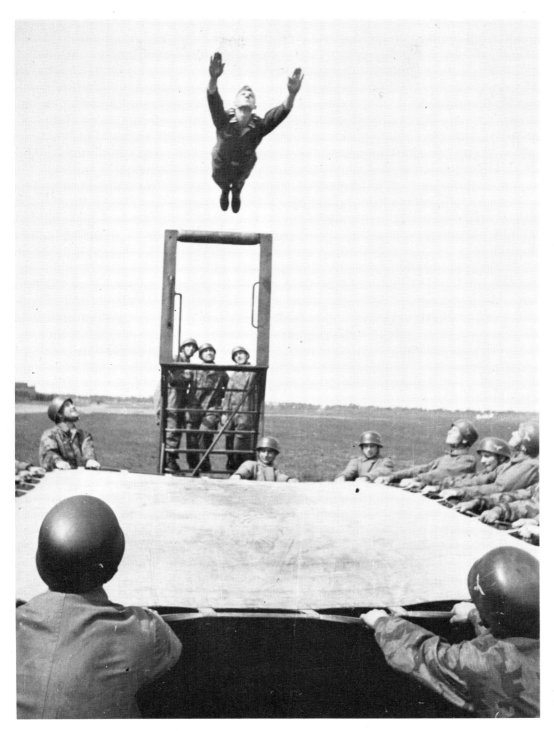

(Opposite) The Messerschmitt Me 323 powered glider, the largest operational aircraft in World War II. Powered by six captured French Le Rhone engines, it could carry a light tank, or an 88mm gun and tractor. Two of the defensive machine guns can be seen in the nose (J G Moore Collection, London)

An instructor demonstrating a perfect exit from a mock door of a Junkers 52. Other pictures in this book show how different was an actual jump. This picture is about 1942 and shows the trainees wearing a late variety of overalls (Bundesarchiv)

the helmet which was a standard German 'coal scuttle' with the rim cut down to prevent the parachute lines catching it. It had a distinctive and practical shape and was immediately recognizable by the chinstrap leading from three points on the rim, either side and the back. Inside it was thickly padded with foam rubber, and on the left side was the Luftwaffe eagle, facing forward.

The remainder of the uniform, apart from its loose cut, would scarcely raise any eyebrows today. The trousers were very full, as was the general fashion at the time, with buttoned pockets on the sides running almost down to the knee. There was an internal pocket below the right knee, with a snap-fastened flap, in which was kept a folding knife. This knife was expressly intended for cutting loose the parachute harness when being dragged by a strong wind, and its blade could be flicked out and locked with only one hand. Dragging was an unpleasant danger with the RZ-16 parachute which had a buckled harness, and recruits were trained to deal with it by being blown across the airfield in the slipstream of anchored aeroplanes.

An early photo of flight training with dummy rigging lines on pulleys. The man is hauled up, set swinging, and then released so that he makes a swinging drop on to the mat in what is a good representation of an actual landing. The uncomfortable harness shows up clearly, with the large belt taking the bulk of the strain, and the two ropes which are clipped to it running to a single suspension point behind the man's head. This picture must be 1940 or 1941 judging from the side-laced boots *(Bundesarchiv)*

In extremis the parachutists were allowed to cut the two suspension ropes which ran to their waist belt.

The trousers tied round the ankle with tapes and tucked into the top of the boots. The boots were interesting in that they were also special. They had thick rubber soles and were designed to come high up the calf to give ankle support; in order to minimize the danger of catching in the parachute they were laced up at the sides. This is a strange idea, which the British slavishly copied, and is based on no accidents known to the author. After Crete, when the equipment underwent an over-

haul, boots were laced at the front; one trouble was that the side-lacing was uncomfortable for marching.

The most distinctive feature of the parachutist's dress was his overall, or smock as the British called it. Until late 1940 this overall was a plain green colour, reaching almost to the knee and snap-fastened at the front. It was very loose in cut and for parachuting it went over all the parachutist's personal equipment. The pre-war and early-war versions had short legs sewn into them, so that in putting it on the wearer had to put a leg through each, before fastening the front. Having landed

the parachutist took off his overall, removed his equipment, put on his overall again, and finally put his equipment on over the top. He was then ready for battle. This must have taken a little time, however well trained the man was, though surviving veterans make light of it today. After 1940 the overall became a little shorter, and the sewn legs disappeared, to be replaced by a button-through tab. There were four large pockets which were intended to be used for ammunition and rations.

Parachutes

The design of the German parachute was such that it held the man in a face-forward position while in the air, and it was mandatory to land with a forward somersault. This was a fruitful source of minor injuries, and to protect himself the jumper usually wore some sort of ankle support and knee pads. The former were either his boots or linen bandages, the latter were strapped on over his trousers. He was also issued with leather gauntlet gloves, all of which went to emphasize the rigours and dangers of parachuting. Finally there was a special ammunition bandolier for carrying rifle ammunition. Instead of being slung over the shoulder, it hung round the neck and ran down the wearer's chest to tuck into the waistband of his trousers. There were 12 compartments, carrying 10 rounds in each, and the idea was that it could be carried under the overall during jumping without risk to the wearer. Most of the parachutist's equipment was designed with the single aim of not producing injuries on landing, since the actual jump itself was fairly hazardous, and always produced a crop of sprains and minor bone breaks even in good weather.

As the war went on there were slight changes to the combat dress just described. The overall became a patterned camouflage colour in 1941, though some troops seem to have worn their plain ones for some time thereafter, perhaps until they wore out. The helmet was fitted with a hessian cover, and scrim bands for attaching camouflage were added. Later helmet covers were made in a patterned material similar to the overall. By 1944 it was less and less easy to distinguish individual parachutists by their uniform and the only reliable indicator was the helmet. In Italy and Africa this was painted sand-yellow and much standard army equipment was worn.

Training in France, 1943. Boarding a Junkers 52 for a jump. All except one man are wearing rubber knee pads and all but two have a hessian cover on their helmets. The RZ parachute shows clearly, as does the suspension rope clipping to the belt. The centre man is having a last drag on a cigarette, and the belt clip can be seen under his raised arm
(*Bundesarchiv*)

The parachute did not allow a man to carry anything more than a pistol, or a sub-machine gun with him on the drop. The canopy opened with a severe jerk, and the harness was very tight and restrictive, so that any solid objects underneath it were highly likely to injure the man. Landing was a minor gymnastic feat, which required as few encumbrances as possible, so every man had to get to a weapons container as soon as he could, in order to get his arms and additional equipment before he left the drop zone. The necessity of finding a container was a severe handicap, and it led to the virtual extinction of two units in Crete when they dropped on to defended positions. It probably also accounts for the fact that the Germans carried out only one parachute assault by night, and appear to have done little night training at all. The one operation which was tried, the dropping of a battalion in the Ardennes in 1944, was a total disaster but there were reasons other than lost containers to account for that.

In an effort to emphasize the special role of parachute troops the Luftwaffe authorized a special parade dress, one of the very few exceptions to the laid down standards. The parade dress was a modified and smartened combat dress, it consisted of the jump overall worn over a shirt with collar and tie, and a parachute harness without the pack containing the parachute. This has given rise to the idea that the parachute could be detached from its harness, but this is not so, and the parade harness was only for decoration. With this uniform the soldier wore the normal German leather boots, which were more suitable for marching than the rubber jumping variety, and any medals and decorations were pinned to the overall. Leather gloves were worn and for a formal review parade when arms were carried, the parachutist's cloth bandolier was slung round his neck and tucked under the harness waist-belt.

Further Training and Recruitment

The 7 Flieger Division was not left in peace for long after the Battle of Crete was over. By late 1941 the entire division was in action as infantry before Leningrad, and it drew heavily on the manpower in the training organization in Germany for its reinforcements. During 1942 a number of large airborne operations were planned, but none was actually carried out. For the first, 7 Flieger Division was withdrawn from Russia for an attack on Malta in conjunction with the Italian Folgore Division.

When this was cancelled the attack was switched to Gibraltar, and when that was abandoned the division went back to Russia where its name was changed to 1 Parachute Division while it was in the line in front of Smolensk. A special brigade was raised under General Bernhard Ramcke for desert operations and sent to the Western Desert in June 1942 where it was intended it should jump into Cairo; however, it too was committed as normal infantry and frittered away. When the Allies invaded North Africa (Operation Torch) all available parachute units were swept together and rushed to Tunis and Bizerta as reinforcements. They suffered severely in the heavy fighting.

During this time the training and development of airborne techniques continued, partly in Germany and partly in France, where most of the individual training was done. A new parachute harness was produced, with a quick-release box to reduce the number of casualties from dragging. Night jumping was practised as was the carrying of weapons on the man, all in imitation of the Allied methods. New methods of using gliders were tried, but, for the most part, only the old DFS 230 models were available; the new Gothas were being used in Russia. In 1943 XI Flieger Corps formed and trained parachute units for Bulgaria and supplied them with equipment, and while this was happening Hitler changed his view on airborne units. Realizing that the Allies were raising and training large airborne armies he gave General Student the task of training all the German army in the West against possible airborne invasion, and authorized the expansion of the German airborne forces.

Student, together with XI Flieger Corps, moved to Brittany and set up a parachute school at Dreux. The 1 Parachute Division was recalled from Russia and retrained and 2 Parachute Division was formed. When the Allies invaded Sicily, 1 Parachute Division was flown in as reinforcements and a few men were actually dropped on to Catania airfield to save time. That division remained in Italy, fighting throughout, until the end of the war. The 2 Division was sent to Rome to bolster the wavering Italians and in the autumn of 1943 was withdrawn to reinforce in Russia. In the spring of 1944 it was rushed back to Normandy to resist the Allied invasion, but left some units on the Eastern Front where they remained until 1945. While in Italy one battalion of

2 Division parachuted on to the island of Elba, unopposed, and captured it. At the same time Mussolini was rescued in a dramatic and daring action by the highly specialized Parachute Lehr Battalion under Otto Skorzeny, using a combination of parachute and glider assault.

Both 1 and 2 Divisions were the real parachute troops, but in late 1943 there was a considerable expansion in which divisions were formed which never fought other than as infantry, and which never flew in aircraft at all. Göring decided to form parachute divisions from the many redundant Luftwaffe men who were available, owing to the decline of German air power. Student was promoted to Commander-in-Chief Parachute High Command and 3, 4, 5, and 6 Divisions quickly formed, together with I and II Parachute Corps to control them. Despite the difficulties of wartime, all men were as far as possible volunteers, and about 30 per cent were trained as parachutists, though none jumped in action, nor were there enough aircraft left to lift more than one or two battalions. Parachute schools were set up at Wittstock and Freiburg in addition to the one at Dreux mentioned previously. Parachute divisions now began

to form everywhere. Early in 1944, 4 Division was quickly put together in Italy and went into action straight away. It remained in that country fighting alongside 1 Division until the end of the war. The 3 and 5 Divisions were formed in France and were complete divisions, but of 6 Division only one regiment was ever made up. To train this large force no less than eight training battalions were set up, together with special training camps, nearly all in France, and all went ahead at full speed. By the time the Allies invaded Normandy the parachute army consisted of 160,000 men.

The Last Year

Student was ordered to counter-attack the Normandy bridgehead using his parachutists, but nothing came of this. The 3, 5 and 6 Divisions covered the retreat of the German army from northern France and by September were reduced to only a few thousand men altogether. The survivors were re-formed into a composite unit under II Parachute Corps until they could be reinforced. In fact they were never full fighting formations again and became reserve divisions. With the retreat from France the Parachute High Command

A training jump, perhaps in France. The static line has just started to pull out the canopy of the lower man, who is holding a good position in the air. The second man has just left the door and appears to be turning towards the tail *(Bundesarchiv)*

39

Close-up of a DFS 230 glider, Italy 1943. The small size and cramped cabin show very well in this photograph. The fuselage side panels and cockpit canopy have been removed to show the interior better and it can be seen that the passengers sit on a central bench, facing forward, a leg on each side. The defensive machine gun is a late addition and is virtually useless *(Bundesarchiv)*

pulled back to the Berlin area and set about forming still more divisions. The 8 Division appeared in Holland in December 1944, fought in the Reichswald Forest area, and withdrew into Germany in 1945. The 9 Parachute Division was put together in early 1945 from Luftwaffe ground personnel and was intended for the defence of Berlin. It surrendered to the Russians in May after a brief battle. The 10 Division was formed in Austria in March 1945 from detachments of 1 and 4 Divisions who were still in Italy. This division never really got into the war at all, and surrendered to the Russians in May 1945. There were several other independent units and formations, of which only the Parachute Lehr Battalion and Otto Skorzeny's specialist unit ever saw action as airborne troops.

The latter history of the German parachute troops, with its confusing number of divisions, rather detracts from the dynamic and impressive early years. The real reason for the virtual disappearance of the airborne arm was the invasion of Russia. Not only were the experienced men lost on the Eastern Front, but so also were the

transport aircraft and their pilots. The parachute divisions were then used as high class light infantry, a well trained all-volunteer force who could be quickly moved to threatened parts of the Front, but who took little heavy equipment or support weapons with them. They were an ideal mobile reserve to plug gaps, but not a force which could sustain prolonged operations. When the High Command broke these rules of use, as at Leningrad and in Normandy, the parachutists suffered appalling losses. After 1943 the divisions were parachute in name only, they could never have repeated the Crete operation, though they fought fiercely enough. It is instructive to see that the few small parachute drops which did occur after 1943 were all carried out by units of 1 and 2 Divisions, the only ones with any pretence to operational experience. But despite the saddening finale, great credit must go to the Germans for having the foresight and courage to form the first effective airborne army in the world, for giving it such high standards, and for using it with such dash and daring right from the beginning. It set an example for others to follow.

Colonel-General Student,
the architect of German
Airborne Forces *(IWM,
London)*

Generaloberst STUDENT

4 North Africa and Sicily 1941-43

British parachute troops in flight in North Africa in 1942. All are strapped in to X-type parachutes with a sleeveless jump-jacket over their equipment and clothing. Hence the odd shape of each man. All except the man nearest the camera have removed their helmets for the flight, and some have kneepads. All are wearing smocks, battle-dress trousers, webbing gaiters and ammunition boots. All are hooked up to the wire which runs along the right-hand side of the picture, and the webbing static-lines of the left-hand row of men can be seen leading across the central gap *(IWM, London)*

Early in 1942 the Allies decided on a policy of 'Germany first' in the general conduct of the war: in other words, Germany was to be knocked out of the war before turning the combined Allied effort on to Japan. With that aim in view the decision was taken to clear the North African coast of Rommel's army as a prelude to invading Europe through Italy. The German main base and supply ports were in Tunisia and the Allies planned to land the First Army to the west along the shores of French North Africa between Casablanca and Algiers and advance eastwards towards the Eighth Army who were pushing in fast from the Western Desert, thus pinching out the Germans. It was known that Tunisia was lightly held and there was confidence that the whole coast-

line could be rolled up fairly quickly.

In the early stages of the planning only one parachute battalion was allocated, the American 2/503 Parachute Infantry, but Major-General Frederick Browning who was the official British adviser on airborne matters to the C-in-C, suggested that there was scope for many more in such far-ranging operations as were foreseen by the planners. Accordingly the War Office added the British 1 Parachute Brigade, consisting of 1, 2 and 3 Parachute Battalions who were scarcely ready and had to be made up to strength by some hurried cross-postings within the division. The Air Ministry was unable to offer any aircraft or crews to drop the parachutists and the US Army Air Force immediately and enthusiastically took on the job of flying

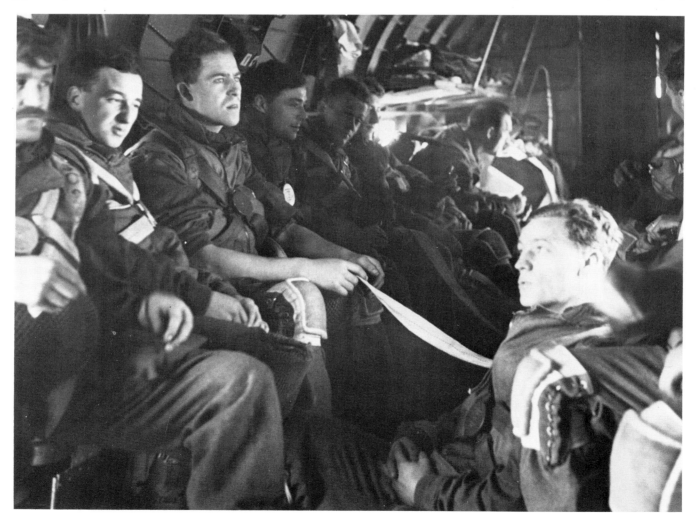

the battalions to war and allocated 60 Group of 51 Wing (Dakotas) to the job. Unfortunately there was not enough time to train either the parachutists or the aircrews, none of whom had ever dropped parachutists before and most of the brigade went to North Africa without having done a jump from a Dakota.

One of the reasons for this was that the British static line used in the Whitley was much shorter than was necessary for the Dakota and in the first practice jump from a Dakota three men had been killed when their canopies hit the tail-plane and ripped. By the time alterations were made to the parachutes it was time to go.

There were sufficient aircraft for two battalions to fly to North Africa, and these were the 2/503 under Lieutenant-Colonel Raff and 3 Battalion from 1 Brigade under Lieutenant-Colonel Geoffrey Pine-Coffin. The 2/503 took off from England on the night of 7/8 November and flew direct to Oran, where it was to seize La Senia airfield which was under the control of the Vichy French. Lieutenant-Colonel Edson Raff was given worrying orders for this, his first, operation. If the French were friendly, then Raff was to land and quietly take over the airfield without ruffling any feathers. If the French had decided to fight, he was to choose a suitable drop zone in a nearby dried lake bed, and take the airfield by force. It was up to Raff to decide from his reception over La Senia which plan to adopt. As they approached the coast in the early light of a cold dawn, Raff's pilot came and told him that nine of the planes were missing from the formation and that all of them were lost. Luckily there was no lack of initiative and when shortly afterwards land appeared below the pilot promptly put down beside a small hut. The incredulous Arab owner was interrogated in bad French and pointed towards Oran, still 100 miles away. Happy that they had hit the right country, the

formation flew on and arrived over La Senia where Raff had no trouble making up his mind about his reception as he was fired on by anti-aircraft batteries. He thereupon landed his force on the lake bed and reconnoitred. He soon met a mobile American column who told him that they could manage La Senia and that the military aerodrome of Tafaraoni was also in US hands, but being counter-attacked by large French forces. Raff immediately sent off three Dakotas to reinforce (none of the others had any fuel left) and marched the remainder of his battalion towards the battle. He chose the wiser course, for French fighters shot down all three aircraft shortly after take-off. It was a grim beginning for the 503rd.

The British 3 Battalion staged at Gibraltar and from there flew without incident to Maison Blanche near Algiers. They were immediately briefed to jump the next morning on to Bone airfield and capture it. As with the 2nd/503rd it was not possible to give a proper briefing since too little was known and Pine-Coffin was told to be guided by his own appreciation of the ground situation. One aircraft came down in the sea, but there was no opposition and the airfield was secured. Since the battalion was flown by the US Army Air Corps this operation ranks as the first ever Allied airborne action, the forerunner of so many to come.

The remainder of 1 Brigade arrived by sea on the 13th. The First Army now started to use their airborne force in a curiously haphazard way; they had no experience to guide them, and the record of the Germans in the two previous years had suggested that parachute troops could undertake enormously ambitious tasks with every chance of success. The First Army therefore copied the German technique of going for the airfields, though without the necessary air-landed troops to consolidate the rather tenuous hold that

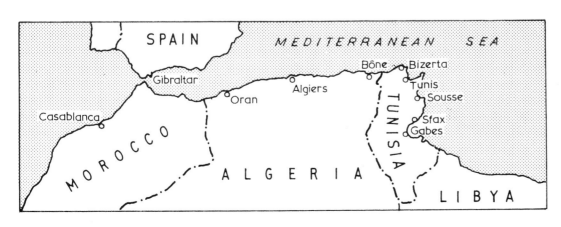

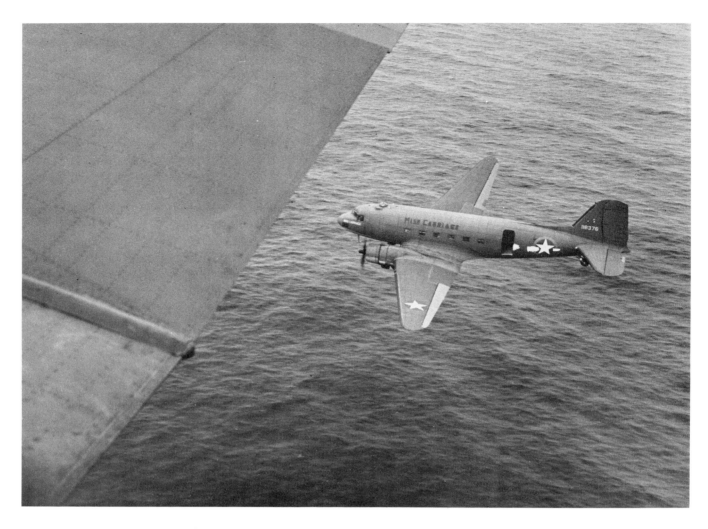

A Douglas C-47 Dakota en route to North Africa with paratroopers on board. Note the open door. All parachute Dakotas flew without a door (*IWM, London*)

parachute troops achieve and without the air support that lightly armed parachutists need if they are to survive counter-attacks. On 14 November both the 2nd/503rd and 1 Battalion were briefed to jump the next day. The 2nd/503rd were to take the airfields at Tebessa and Youk les Bains, south of Bone, and 1 Battalion was to pick a drop zone near Beja, push east until the enemy was found, and remain in contact with him. This was a remarkable battle plan since it had no clear objective and committed the battalion to the most dangerous type of warfare that can face airborne units, namely a lone battle in strange country with no follow-up force and little hope of re-supply. Bad weather frustrated this jump, but it was repeated on the 16th and the CO was told that if the weather was bad again he was to jump as far to the east as he could, and to march the rest of the way!

As it happened the drop succeeded and ground troops linked up quickly. For 1 Battalion, the First Army had several objectives, none of them really practical since they envisaged jumping up to 50 miles ahead of the ground troops and hoping

to be relieved. But the Germans were in Tunisia in force now and the opportunity for quick 'seize and hold' operations was already past, as was soon proved.

The first enemy reinforcements came into Tunis within a day of the Allied landings. Hauptmann Saur was in Athens with a company of Ramcke's Brigade and they were quickly flown out in Junkers 52s to Tunis, landing on 9 November. His troops were in action straight away, using the same tactics as the 2nd/503rd, dropping or landing on airfields and holding them until fast-ranging armoured columns came up, then moving on to another airfield to repeat the process. By this means he secured both El Aouina and La Marsa and troops from Rome were flown in to hold them. Saur also tried to capture Bone airfield, but as his aeroplanes approached the lead pilot saw the Dakotas of Pine-Coffin's 3 Battalion wheeling away after the drop and the Junkers turned back. On 14 and 15 November the German 5 Regiment arrived in Tunis after an exhausting but rapid journey by rail and truck from their base in France, to Naples, and from there by Me 323 transports, across the

(*Above*) Tunis 1942 or 1943. *Fallschirmjaeger* mortar crew loading a Grenatenwerfer 82 short-barelled airborne mortar (*Bundesarchiv*)

(*Left*) Three officers of I Parachute Brigade in North Africa, 1942. (*From left to right*) Captain Stark, Lieutenant Brayley and Major Ashford. Major Ashford has a fighting knife on his left side (*IWM, London*)

(Opposite) Men of the 505 Inf 82 Airborne Division, loading parapacks under a C-47 Dakota, 3 June 1943. This is a posed picture as no man would attempt to lift and struggle with such heavy loads while wearing steel helmet, full equipment and two parachutes. These men might be jump-masters as their main parachutes are rip-cord operated, but it seems unlikely that a jump-master would carry full equipment so it may be that the entire picture is fraudulent. However it shows a parapack very well *(US Army, Washington)*

Mediterranean. The first company arrived as Tunis airfield was being strafed by fighter-bombers, and they were continually in action after that. They largely contributed to the slowing down of the Allied advance and when the first Axis counter-attack went in on 11 December, 5 Regiment was in the lead.

But while the First Army was still moving eastwards, on 29 November, Lieutenant-Colonel John Frost's 2 Battalion was launched on to Depienne airfield with the objective of destroying aircraft on Ouda airfield, 20 miles away and itself only 18 miles from Tunis. After a scattered drop the battalion marched by night to Ouda only to find the field was disused. They extracted themselves from the area with great difficulty in the face of determined German armoured attacks, crossing nearly 50 miles of hostile country on foot and losing half the unit in the process. The action has become a minor classic of deception and withdrawal, but it should never have happened. There was sufficient air reconnaissance effort in North Africa to have determined whether or not the airfield was occupied and used, and sufficient fighter-bombers to deal with any planes that were there. Why it should have been thought necessary to send a valuable battalion to do a job that four or five aircraft could have done equally well, and far more quickly, has not yet been explained.

The last airborne action in Tunisia was carried out by the Germans who air-landed a force on to Gabes to secure their lines of communication to the troops holding off the Eighth Army. This happened on 11 December, and after that both sides used their parachute troops as infantry, and the casualties were heavy.

The Germans emerge from North Africa with some credit in their use of airborne forces, although in the end they all but destroyed them in the ground fighting. The Allies can be offered few congratulations; the degree of optimism with which the First Army launched parachute battalions on to unknown objectives, without reconnaissance, planning or support is amazing. That the losses were not far heavier can only be due to luck and the remarkable skill and ability of the men involved, and perhaps the planners were banking on that too. But it was no way to make war, and the operations of the next year showed that there had been some thinking in the intervening winter.

Sicily

The invasion of Europe was to start in Sicily in July 1943 with Operation Husky and airborne troops were to play a major part in it. By this time there were two divisions in North Africa, the American 82nd and the British 1st. The 82 Division was newly arrived from the United States, commanded by Brigadier-General Matthew Ridgway and consisted of the 504 and 505 Parachute Infantry and 325 Glider Infantry, supported by 12 Troop Carrier Command flying 331 C-47 Dakotas. The

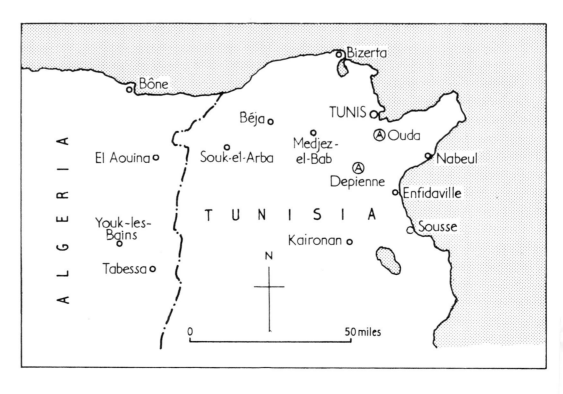

North Africa 1943.
1 Air Landing Brigade
unloading an early model
Waco CG-4 in training.
They are pulling small
handcarts which were
loaded with ammunition or
signal batteries and pulled
off the LZ to the RV,
where they were dumped
until needed

British 1 Division was roughly the same composition and size with 1 and 2 Parachute Brigades and 1 Air-Landing Brigade, however there were no British transport aircraft, and very few gliders. Only 19 of the 29 Horsas towed out from England arrived, after a hair-raising journey going around France and Spain. The 150 American Waco C-G4 Hadrians which were shipped in crates from the United States were erected on dusty airstrips by inexperienced men with minimal instruction. They all flew, which speaks volumes for their designer.

Sicily is shaped roughly like a large triangle with one apex on the south side. The Allied plan, code-named 'Husky', was to make a two-pronged pincer movement on to both sides of this apex, Americans on the west, British on the east. Both landings would take place at last light, allowing a full night in which to get troops and vehicles ashore without interference from enemy air attacks. The combined advance would then go northwards, following the main roads and taking the major towns. When this was completed a crossing into Italy could be made from the north-east tip of the island across the Straits of Messina. Each of the Allied landings was to be supported by a brigade-strength airborne drop inland of the beaches. On the American side the objective for Colonel Jim Gavin's 505 Regiment was to prevent enemy reinforcements reaching the beach-head by seizing and holding a prominent piece of high ground, the Piano Lupo. As secondary tasks he had to isolate the Ponte Olivo airfield by fire, and destroy or hold a river bridge. He could be reinforced if need be on the second night by the 504th.

On the British side the plan was more complex. The first objective was to capture the road north from the beach-head area to Syracuse. This could only be done by taking and holding the Ponte Grande canal bridge which was only a mile south of Syracuse. The next phase was to take Syr-

acuse harbour and, at roughly the same time, a coastal battery which could cover the invasion beaches. All three objectives were to be assaulted at night and secured by daylight. For these tasks the glider-borne air-landing brigade was allotted, the parachute battalions were to come in on the second night further up the coast and take other vital bridges as the advance required. The 2 Parachute Brigade was in reserve with an expected task of the capture of the town and harbour of Augusta. In the event the advance went fast enough not to need this operation, and 2 Brigade stood down, somewhat disappointed.

Unfortunately these apparently straight-forward missions were hampered by an unnecessarily complicated flight plan which involved flying a long and devious route to the targets. There were other difficulties too. The aircrews were largely new to the idea of navigating on their own. Some were still untrained and nearly all were unused to war and straight from

peace-time flying in the United States. Finally there was some friction between the Americans and British over the use of US aircraft. The only transports in the Mediterranean were the Dakotas of XII Troop Carrier Command, and 82 Division felt, understandably, that they should have first call on them. But 1 Division had to use them also because the RAF could only provide 28 Albemarles and 7 Halifaxes to tow gliders, and no parachute aircraft at all. Also, since there were so few British gliders, 1 Air-Landing Brigade took the Wacos too.

On the night of 9 July there was a gale blowing from the south-east. The 1 Air-landing Brigade took off first in the evening light raising clouds of dust from the primitive airstrips. The stream of gliders was battered by winds of up to 45mph, which moderated to about 30mph as they approached Sicily, but even this was enough to blot out the land with an impenetrable wall of dust and to deny the

Training for Sicily, 1943. Gunners of 1 Airborne Division firing the US 75mm pack-howitzer which was the standard gun of allied airborne forces throughout the war

A nicely contrasting photograph of a Junkers-52 and a Messerschmitt Me 323, the latter sitting back on its tail skid *(Bundesarchiv)*

The Rescue of Mussolini
Opposite: *(Above)* The 'Commando' waving an elaborate, and obviously staged, farewell to the great Roman dictator as his plane revs up on the tiny airstrip *(J G Moore Collection, London)*

(Left) Skorzney's paratroopers before setting off to rescue Mussolini. Note the typically German way of draping machine gun belts around the neck *(J G Moore Collection, London)*

(Right) Mussolini, in rather shabby clothes, is helped into a Fieseler Storch after his rescue on the Gran Sasso *(Lorobe)*

navigators a sight of their landmarks. A feeble moon did little to help. The plan called for the gliders to be slipped over the sea and to make a silent approach over the beaches to their targets, a throw-back to the Maas bridges and Fort Eben-Emael, but without the vital close air support from fighters and dive bombers that was such a feature of the German attacks, and without their intensive training and rehearsing.

It was a dangerous idea at best, and in the early hours of 10 July 1943 it turned out to be a tragedy. About 60 per cent of the gliders were slipped too soon and crashed into the sea. Some men survived by clinging to wooden wreckage, a few swam ashore, but 252 drowned. Of the 52 gliders which actually crossed the coast only 12 landed near their targets. At Ponte Grande where it had been intended that six gliders should seize the bridge by a *coup de main*, only two actually arrived and one blew up on landing. The bridge was held by a reinforced platoon until the next afternoon when they were swept away by the Italians, but they had removed the demolition charges and the bridge was recaptured by the beach-head troops before it could be destroyed. The advance northwards was saved by a hairsbreadth.

In that hairsbreadth 1 Air-Landing Brigade lost 490 men out of 2,000 and 88 glider pilots out of a total of 145.

Wherever the gliders landed their passengers and crews took violent action against any enemy they met. The coastal battery was captured by one glider load of 7 officers and 10 men who were part of Brigade Headquarters. They killed 6 Italians, wounded 6 others and took 40 prisoners. Another glider landed 250 yards out to sea under fire from a machine gun. Only 10 men reached the shore. Four were too exhausted to go further, but 6 crawled through 20 yards of barbed wire and marched 10 miles to rejoin their battalion. On the way they captured 2 pill boxes, 21 Italian soldiers, 3 machine guns and an anti-tank gun. Similar actions occurred all along the coast and led the baffled Italian radio to report that 'Five or ten airborne divisions have been landed in Sicily'!

Colonel Jim Gavin and his 505 Parachute Infantry fared little better. The pilots flying the 505th were confused partly by having to fly low in the bumpy atmosphere caused by the gale and partly by lack of navigational aids. The groups began to straggle soon after take-off and the approach to Sicily quickly became a shambles with planes coming in from all

Me 323 'Gigant'
(*Bundesarchiv*)

directions and pilots vainly searching for landmarks. Once again there were dust clouds and many aircrews, tired, lost and in some cases frightened by anti-aircraft fire, dropped their parachutists and turned for home. The regiment was scattered over a distance of 65 miles which was 60 miles more than anyone had planned. Furthermore the men landed on stone ridges, olive groves, barbed wire, beaches – and a few in the sea. Captain Edward Sayre landed close to the objective, collected 95 men together and seized a fortified position on the Gela Ridge itself. From here he and his tiny force fought off two tank attacks and continual infantry assaults until relieved at 11.30 hours the next day. They had managed to block the main reinforcement route to the beach-head. Meanwhile Colonel Gavin himself was 30 miles away, having landed with two officers and three privates. They fought their way towards Gela, collecting other stragglers as they went. On the way Gavin led an assault on the Biazza Ridge which was held by a reinforced battalion of the Hermann Göring Division. The parachutists took the ridge

and held it for 12 hours until relieved; then they went on to Gela, arriving on 12 July. While they had been making their way across Sicily the 504th had been called up to reinforce by jumping in on the Gela airstrip.

It turned out to be another disastrous action. As Colonel Reuben Tucker's two battalions neared the coast, flying in close formation over the anchored invasion fleet, a single machine gun opened up on them, firing from the land. Within seconds every gun in range was firing at the planes and all fire control was lost. The pilots weaved and scattered, most of them diving for the shore where the Allied army shot at them even harder and when the harrased paratroopers jumped some of them were killed too, by men who thought they were being attacked by German *Fallschirmjaeger*. Of the 144 Dakotas, 27 were shot down, 37 were badly damaged and 8 flew back to Tunisia with their parachutists. Of the 2,000 men, 229 were casualties, and the remainder were so scattered that by the middle of the following afternoon no more than 558 of them had been located, yet

(*Opposite*) Loading a jeep into a Waco Hadrian CG-4A glider. This is an early model of the Waco and this picture, although undated, may have been taken in North Africa just before the Sicily landings (*US Army*)

53

Italy, 1943. DFS-230 in flight, towed by Ju-87 Stukas. Stukas were frequently used for training when their operational value as a dive bomber declined (*Bundesarchiv*)

the regiment had neither been in action nor flown over enemy territory.

On the eastern side the rapid advance had caused 2 Brigade's drop to be cancelled, but 1 Brigade was needed to gain another vital bridge, this time the Primosole, on the night of 13 July. The Primosole bridge was seven miles south of the next important town, Catania, and it spanned the river Simento which was not otherwise crossed for some miles inland. The plan was to drop one battalion to the north and two to the south, forming a brigade-sized garrison which would await the arrival of the main force, expected within 24 hours. The operational orders give strong hints that more powerful enemy resistance could be expected at Catania, and this must have been the reason for dropping a full brigade whereas only a few months before a battalion would have been thought sufficient. Nowhere is there any sign that the importance of the ground force linking-up without delay was recognized. The 1 Brigade was only taking 12 anti-tank guns with it

and a determined attack by armoured units would be all but impossible to stop.

Once again the drop was scattered and confused and once again a large number of brave men were quite unnecessarily killed and drowned. The lead aircraft took off at 1900 hours on 13 July in clear weather. As before, navigation went astray and anti-aircraft fire from the Allied fleet and enemy batteries caused further casualties and distraction. Recollections of the 504th's reception three nights before were too recent to expect the pilots to be other than wary, and it must be remembered that these early Dakotas were very much civilian airliners which had been quickly converted, without such luxuries as self-sealing fuel tanks. One hit from an anti-aircraft gun was usually enough to produce a fireball. Of the 1900 men who took off only 295 arrived according to plan; 39 planes dropped men on the planned drop zones, 48 dropped theirs up to 10 miles away, 29 did not find any drop zone and 11 were shot down. Of the gliders, 4 landed successfully on the landing zone,

7 landed successfully in the wrong places, 6 crashed on landing and destroyed themselves and 3 were lost at sea. For the parachutists the success rate was 20 per cent, for the gliders 25 per cent, and this was on a clear night.

The 295 men on the bridge had only three anti-tank guns; ranged against them were most of an Italian division and 3 Parachute Regiment of the German 1 Parachute Division. These men had been flown in from France and the 1 *Fallschirmjaeger* Battalion had actually parachuted on to a drop zone south of the Primosole Bridge shortly before 1 Brigade arrived. There is a tale, treasured still by the Parachute Regiment, that a young *gefreiter*, dazed in his landing, wandered into the rendezvous for 2 Battalion, asked where his Schmeisser was, and found nothing strange in what was going on around him.

This German drop was another good example of the use of airborne troops as rapid reinforcements in a fast-moving battle, and they immediately set about attacking the few men of 1 Brigade on the bridge. Primosole Bridge was captured, recaptured and captured again before the main advance could continue. It took two days for the Allied ground forces to arrive at the Simento River, and there were few survivors from 1 Brigade by that time. Despite the seizing of the bridge, the advance was bogged down by stubborn Axis resistance, though the operation had not been in vain.

Primosole Bridge was the last use of airborne troops in Sicily and they were not left in the line as they had been in North Africa, but were quickly withdrawn to reform and reinforce. In later years the Germans were to pay extravagant compliments to the stubborn little bands of airborne men who so delayed the movement of Axis reinforcements and at the time the Allied airborne leaders were anxious to say the same things as they were only too aware of the cost of the operations, and the small gains that had resulted from them. In the United States there was strong opinion against using airborne forces at all, and their value was reassessed in Britain. Eisenhower decided the issue by roundly declaring that with proper training and larger troop formations there was no need for failure. The British thought much the same, and plumped for the use of pathfinders to ensure that the right drop zone was found as well as advocating more centralized control over the whole operation. It was apparent that the days of the individual battalion drop were over, except for very special reasons; from now on airborne warfare was to be a highly organized joint affair with large numbers of aircraft, large bodies of troops and, with luck, proper air support. Few objected, certainly nobody who had landed in Sicily.

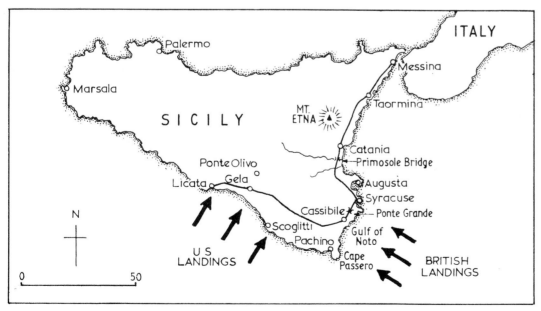

Special Feature: US Airborne Forces

Although General Billy Mitchell had first advocated using parachutists in 1918, virtually nothing was done to try out his idea until the late 1920s when, in common with several other countries, the US army experimented with a small party of parachutists operating from airfields in Texas. After a few months of inconclusive trials the idea was dropped and did not reappear until 1939 when the chief of infantry suggested the creation of an airborne force. There was more support for his idea than seemed possible, but those who supported it wanted to control it. The engineers considered that parachutists would only be saboteurs, hence they should be engineers. The Army Air Corps thought that they should be under their control, as the Germans were under the control of the Luftwaffe, and like the Germans they looked to the parachutists to be a sort of air 'marine' force. The chief of infantry, not unnaturally, had quite different ideas and in the end he got his way. However, it was not until the spring of 1941 when the success of the German invasion of Crete became known that there was any real drive to form airborne units in the United States.

Formation and Training

Late in June 1940, Major William Lee was ordered by the War Department to form a parachute test platoon and experiment with ways of delivering men to the battlefield from aircraft. Major Lee was a remarkable character and exactly the man for the job. He collected 48 volunteers from the 29 Infantry Regiment at Fort Benning, Georgia, and took them up to New York to the site of the 1939 World's Fair. One of the features of the Fair had been a parachute tower, installed by the Safe Parachute Company, which offered a controlled descent by means of a parachute which ran down on wire guides. As a fairground stunt for the public it had had great success. Lee and his men used this and other towers built by the company for training aircrews in parachuting. They then returned to Benning and built a replica of one of these towers, and started more serious experimenting.

Tower jumping has been a feature of US airborne training ever since, and at Fort Benning now there are three towers, each a more-or-less exact replica of the original one used in New York in 1939, though the 1940 version built by Lee fell down in a gale a few years ago. Each tower has four arms at the top, sticking well out so that when a parachutist is hanging from an arm, he is clear of the tower. The parachutist is hauled up from the ground in his harness, with the canopy spread out by a large metal hoop. He is pulled up to the top of the arm, where his instructor prepares him for the drop, then he is released from the hoop and floats down on to a soft base around the tower. It is a very easy and informal way of learning to land, and a gentle introduction to real parachuting.

The test platoon quickly mastered tower jumping and made its first drop from an aeroplane, a Douglas B-18, on 16 August. By 29 August the men were sufficiently competent to make a mass jump before an invited audience, and it was a complete success, which did much to rally support for the idea of parachute troops and led directly to the formation of the first parachute battalion, the 501 Infantry, in late 1940. Training continued steadily throughout the winter, hampered by shortages of aircraft and parachutes, until the following spring when the German successes in Greece and Crete brought about a sharp improvement in the fortunes of the parachutists. But one of the main difficulties was still the shortage of aircraft, for there were only 66 Douglas C-47s in the whole Army Air Corps. Luckily a building programme was under way so that there would soon be enough planes; however, another shortage was parachutes, compounded by the entirely sensible insistence of the War Department that all parachutists would jump with a spare parachute slung on the chest. For many months recruitment was ahead of the supply of parachutes.

Recruitment and Clothing

As in Britain and Germany, the American airborne soldier was a volunteer and well above the average level of mental and physical ability. As the divisions expanded the volunteer element could only be retained for actual parachuting, and the gliderborne men were selected draftees, though as far as possible they were taken from those who had opted for the airborne units. Several attempts were made to give them some sort of distinctive uniform to mark their speciality, but the pressure of uniformity in a rapidly expanding army sharply curbed this. The parachutist of 1940 and 1941 had worn a shiny green overall for jumping and a leather flying helmet, much like the Russians. At first the overall was a version of the normal flying suit, in olive-green twill buttoning at the ankle and wrist. The material was changed in 1941 and soon after the whole idea was discarded when it was discovered that there was in any case no need for any special clothing for jumping out of a plane.

To guard against ankle injuries the parachutists were given special high-topped 'jump-boots' which they jealously preserved, and which stayed with them throughout the war. Unfortunately, they became enormously popular with all soldiers, so the wearing of a highset pair of boots became just as much the mark of an experienced scrounger as of a trained parachutist – though it has to be said that there were some who found it difficult to differentiate between the two. In 1943 a very similar high boot became general issue throughout the army, thus devaluing the parachutist's proud distinction.

Despite the discouragement of special clothing there were three other items which were only issued to airborne troops whether they were parachutists or glidermen. These were the helmet, the jacket, and the trousers. The helmet was the same as the normal GI issue, but had a different liner which allowed two chin-straps to be attached. One of the straps had a moulded leather chin cup, the other had two neck straps attached. Glidermen had the same helmet but not the chin cup. Parachutists invariably released the chin cup immediately after landing and carried it swinging beside their face. It quickly became a parachutist's trade-mark, as it still is today.

The combat jacket was larger than the normal GI issue and had four prominent pockets which expanded like accordions. It fastened with a concealed zip and was meant to be worn fastened up to the neck, which needless to say it never was. The material was fairly robust and when new was slightly waterproof. The trousers were made from the same material and were very generous in cut. There were two more expanding pockets, one on the outside of each thigh and when these were full they gave the trousers an even odder and wider look. Most men carried a large fighting knife strapped to the right calf and tied down with tape to prevent it swinging. Other equipment was often tied down to the left leg, the usual choice being an entrenching tool which otherwise dangled from the belt. All-in-all, a well dressed American airborne soldier going to the wars looked exactly like a military Christmas tree; there was scarcely a part of his body which was not covered by some equipment or weapon, and even his helmet was likely to have a field dressing taped to the front of it.

Training

The parachutist's badge was awarded to all who had passed the training and proficiency tests for parachuting, which meant in almost every case that they had been through the course at Fort Benning, but it could also be gained by making a combat jump without any training at all; a fairly rare occurrence. For every combat jump the man was awarded a metal star which was riveted on to the wings. The 82 Division made four combat jumps, and such was the rate of turnover in the units that by early 1946 when a check was made there were only 12 men still in the division with all four stars.

By the middle of 1941 the state of training of the 501st was still sketchy, owing to lack of practice. There were one or two minor exercises in conjunction with air-landed infantry, but in June 1941 when the US army was close to one and a half million men strong, there was still only the one parachute battalion. From then on things moved much faster. In July 1941 the 550 (Air-landed) Battalion was formed in Panama and was given a company of the 501st to act as a nucleus. On 10 September 88 Infantry Battalion became air-landed infantry, though there were few planes to carry them. At the same time a call was made for gliders to carry the heavy equipment of the parachute units, and trials began in parachuting the 75mm pack-howitzer.

The 502 Parachute Battalion was formed in July 1941, to be followed by 503rd and 504th in August and October, all with the same establishment strength as the original 501st, namely 34 officers and 412 men. Fort Benning Parachute

(Overleaf) 1 August 1940. A superb photograph of a parachutist being dropped from the training tower of the Safe Parachute Company, Hightstown, New Jersey. The open parachute is hauled up to the top of the tower, attached to the ring by clips, and with the parachutist in his harness. At the top the clips are released together, freeing the canopy *(US Army)*

Battle equipment, 1944 style. Four men of the 509 Parachute Infantry Battalion swinging down a road in Southern France after Operation 'Dragoon', 15 August 1944. Notice how much each man carries, and the knives on the shin. Field dressings were carried on the helmet in Northern France, not on the foot and all helmets had camouflage (US Army)

August or September 1940. A posed photograph by men of the test platoon in a civilian DC-3 airliner. The seats have been folded back and a wire strong-point run above the door. The parachutes are probably borrowed from fire-fighting 'smoke-jumpers' and the helmets might be too. The reserve parachute is very loose and would be awkward (US Army)

School was growing larger now and better able to cope with the numbers, though it still took until early 1942 before all four battalions were parachute trained. The training was tough and in parts little short of brutal. The idea was the same as in all the other parachute forces, to weed out the weak, the unfit and the glamour-seekers, and to toughen up those who stayed the course. It was a four-week syllabus, divided into weekly stages. 'A' stage was a physical fitness processing which acted as an effective filter for those who had joined on impulse. 'B' stage was a tangle of tumbling, rolling, swinging, jumping from mock doors and finally 'chute packing. (In the US airborne units you packed your own 'chute, just as the Germans did.) 'C' stage was kinder in that it involved practice on the jump towers, less physical effort but much more nervous effort; it finished with two night drops. 'D' stage was the actual jumping from planes, five jumps in all, one of which was at night; this was followed by the 'Wings Parade' and a memorable party in the nearby

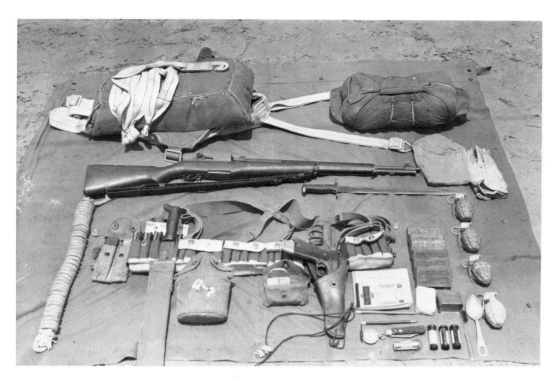

The personal equipment of
a rifleman of the 503
Parachute Infantry
Regiment while training in
Australia, February 1943
(US Army)

town before leaving. Whenever the divisions were static in a theatre of war for long enough, they set up jump schools of their own, miniatures of Benning, and trained those newcomers who had been posted in without the vital qualifications. It was quicker than trying to send them back to the USA, and just as effective.

82 and 101 Divisions

By February 1942 there was need for yet more expansion of the airborne units, and each of the four existing battalions was turned into a regiment of three battalions, thus the 501 Battalion became the 501 Regiment, with 1/501 Parachute Infantry Battalion, 2/501, and so on. The idea was to try to keep the airborne units on the same footing as the normal infantry and avoid having too many special manpower and equipment tables. The regiments had no tactical headquarters, the only central airborne command being the Provisional Parachute Group, still under the control of Major Lee, now promoted to Colonel. The following month this group became the Airborne Command and Lee was again promoted. Even so, this was no way to produce a proper assault force, and in August 1942 the first two airborne divisions were formed. Their basis was the existing 82 Infantry Division, which dated from World War I. It was split in half and formed into the 82 Airborne Division and the 101 Airborne Division and each was given two of the four regiments. Thus started the life of two of the most famous and active US divisions in World War II.

They were smaller versions of the existing infantry division of that time and were meant to consist of one parachute infantry regiment and two glider infantry regiments, but both the 82nd and the 101st were set up with two parachute and one glider regiment The divisional artillery was 36 guns (75mm pack-howitzers) and there were 647 vehicles, which included trailers. The total strength was 8,500 men, against 15,000 in the infantry division. The regiments were each less than 2,000 men, whereas the infantry regiment was 3,000 and the infantry division had over 2,000 vehicles. This organization officially remained in use until December 1944, but in the European theatre it was almost always changed by adding more parachutists and lending artillery units with 105mm guns. The 1944 change recognized the anomaly of the 82nd and 101st and gave each division two parachute regiments and one glider regiment. This increased the total strength to 13,000 which brought it much closer to an infantry division and made it easier to fit the airborne division into a corps or army formation.

Further Expansion

Other divisions were formed soon after the 82nd and 101st: the 17th in late 1942, the 11th in February 1943 and the 13th in 1944. The 11 Division went to the Pacific in May 1944 and stayed there until the end of the war, taking part in the minor airborne operations in the Philippines. The 17 Division arrived in Europe to be

12 May 1943. The cockpit
of a Waco CG-4A glider
(US Army)

(Opposite) US parachutist,
January 1943, ready to
jump. He will carry his
rifle slung over his
shoulder, muzzle
downwards. The small bag
under his reserve carries
rations and grenades. He
has no haversack and extra
supplies would be dropped
in later aircraft lifts (US
Army)

pushed into the Ardennes fighting in December 1944, and later took part in the Rhine crossing. The 13 Division was the unluckiest of the five and saw no actual fighting at all, though it arrived in Europe early in 1945. In addition to these established divisions there were other airborne units which were not attached to any parent formation, a rather unusual situation and unlike the normal tidiness of the US army. The 503 Parachute Infantry Regiment operated in the Pacific theatre, and the 550th and 551st were in Panama until 1944, when they were sent to Italy. Battalions from each jumped into southern France with 1 Airborne Task Force in August 1944 and were then sent to reinforce 82 Division in time for the Battle of the Bulge. But what emerges from this rather confusing account of the individual units is the overall fact that within two years of forming the first airborne division in the US army there were no less than four in existence, with a fifth on the way, and airborne troops in action in every war theatre around the world. In March 1941 there had been less than 600 men serving in airborne units in the US army; by March 1945 there were over 65,000.

A significant feature of the steady rise in effectiveness of the airborne units was the US Army Air Corps. Hand-in-hand with the divisions came the squadrons and wings of transport aircraft and when the airborne divisions in Europe were combined into the XVIII Airborne Corps in August 1944, the associated aircraft were in 9 Troop Carrier Command. The US airborne soldier was unique in that he always had some aircraft within call, though rarely enough for all his needs.

Unlike the huge numbers in the German Parachute Divisions, the Americans were all trained men, fully equipped and capable of mounting an airborne assault at short notice. The driving spirit which had brought about this large and powerful force was largely that of William Lee, who served throughout the war behind the scenes planning, persuading and training. He was fated never to go into action with airborne troops; promoted Major-General in 1943 and later given command of 101 Airborne Division, he suffered a heart attack and had to return to the United States before D-Day. He was not forgotten, and when the 101st jumped into Normandy they went through the door to the cry of 'Bill Lee'.

5 The Pacific 1942-45

The Pacific war was dominated by the sea, and practically all troop movement was by ship. The pre-war aircraft were not capable of carrying any worthwhile load over the huge expanses of water and jungle that are such a feature of the Far East. However, it was always realized that because of these distances quite small bodies of troops could exercise an influence out of all proportion to their numbers, could they but get to the right place at the right time. Ships are slow; overland movement through jungle had to be at walking speed in most of Asia until long after 1945; and the few vehicle roads were easily blocked and watched from the air. The one way of moving troops which offered some freedom from the restrictions of the terrain was by using the new airborne techniques, if only there were aircraft to lift them. If in 1941 there had been an airborne army in Japan on the scale of the German one, and with the aircraft to carry it, then the whole history of the Pacific war might easily have taken a far blacker turn for the Allies right from the beginning.

It is interesting to speculate now on how quickly and easily the Japanese could have pinched out island after island by dropping a parachute battalion into the coast area, seizing a beach-head, landing the follow-up force, and then rolling up the defence in one movement. Alternatively the parachutists could have landed on the usual island airfield as the seaborne landing came in, and destroyed the defending planes before they could get into the air. The possibilities are endless: what, for instance, might have been the effect if the attack on Pearl Harbor had been accompanied by a parachute drop and then an air landing?

At the start of the Pacific war the only airborne force in the Far East was the Japanese. (Its birth and rise are told elsewhere.) Like all the other airborne forces except the German it was hampered by a lack of suitable aircraft and was constantly struggling to justify its requirements against those of the logistic needs of the army. All too often the latter had priority and the tactical force had to wait,

and even when the planes were made available, they were often too few in number and could not be used to fly in a follow-up force. So the Japanese never had the chance to use their airborne troops effectively, which was perhaps just as well from the Allied point of view since there were too few British and American troops in the Pacific in 1942 to be able to offer much resistance to properly mounted and co-ordinated air and land assaults. A few operations like that carried out in Crete would have had a shattering effect on the Allied plans which they might have taken years to get over.

As it was, there were 16 airborne operations of one kind or another in the Pacific area from the time of Pearl Harbor until the Japanese surrender. Most of these were relatively small, but one or two were quite large, though never on the scale of the huge divisional and corps operations which took place in Europe. The Pacific could never muster either the men or the machines for that size of air battle, the emphasis was all on seaborne landings. Once the style of the war had settled there was little sense in changing it to another technique altogether, so the airborne arm remained very much a secondary weapon except for the Chindit's long range raids, where air support and air superiority were vital.

Celebes Islands, Java and Sumatra

The first uses of airborne troops were by the Japanese in the attacks on Java, Sumatra and the Celebes Islands at the very beginning of their widespread invasions. The first operation was a satisfying success; it was the capture of the airfield at Menado in the north-eastern tip of the Celebes. The airfield was held by a small force of Dutch regulars with a much larger force of not very good local native units in support. On 11 January 1942 the airfield was heavily bombed and strafed immediately afterwards by fighters. Before the defenders had time to fully recover, the parachute force arrived and dropped without interruption. The force consisted of three companies of the naval parachute troops and they were dropped without any heavy equipment, but with some air support in the shape of more fighter sweeps. The native defenders fought reasonably well until it was obvious that the Japanese were winning, and then they fled. The small Dutch unit fought with great heroism and tenacity, but was almost wiped out, and the few survivors surrendered.

The battle had taken five hours and although the Japanese casualties must have been heavy – there is now no record of how many men were lost – the result was worth it. It was a good use of the parachute arm, and the effect on the morale of Allied troops in the area was considerable.

Three days later there was another, similar type of attack. This time it involved much larger numbers of troops and aircraft, but was less well co-ordinated. The lack of co-ordination may have been due to the distance from the launching area for the target was the airfield and oil refineries at Palembang in Sumatra, and the nearest Japanese-held airfields were either in Singapore, 300 miles away across the Straits of Malacca, or in Borneo which is even further. This long distance may also account for the absence of fighter strafing before the drop, for the only preparatory air action was a high level bombing attack during the day. The parachute drop did not come in until 1830 hours, by which time the garrison was fully alert and expecting an attack. The 70 aircraft flew in in two waves straight over the anti-aircraft guns heading for a dropping zone about five miles away. Anti-aircraft fire forced them to scatter and drop high and the men were spread around the dropping zone area to such an extent that it took several hours to mount the assaults on both the airfield and the nearby oil refineries. The airfield was attacked by 300 men, and when they failed to capture it a further drop of parachutists was made the next day to reinforce them. They then succeeded, but the oil refineries were held until the Dutch could completely destroy them. It was more than a year before they were back in action. The Japanese lost over 200 men and 16 aircraft in this episode, partly owing to lack of preparation, partly to a complete lack of air support for the parachutists, and partly to an under-estimation of the expected resistance. But they gained the airfield, and defeated a force three times their size. It was a good start.

A week later, on 21 February, the Japanese launched another parachute assault, this time on Timor. The lessons learned at the attack on Palembang had obviously been carefully studied because there was first of all a feint attack by five loads of parachutists on to a position some miles away. The main attack was to establish a block on the Allied lines of communication, and this was preceded by heavy ground strafing which continued until the 350 parachutists were on the ground. The operation was completely successful and was followed up the next day by a seaborne landing which overran the island. This was a proper use of the lightly equipped parachutists which the Japanese possessed, and was an encouraging note to end on. There were no more Japanese parachute assaults until the middle of the following year, by which time the technique had been largely lost.

New Guinea

The next attempt to use airborne troops was by the Allies, and it was an air-landed operation. Wau, in New Guinea, was an outpost for Port Moresby. On 28 January 1943 it was under heavy pressure from Japanese troops and the only way to get in reinforcements was by air. Next day 57 Dakota sorties scraped in under the clouds to land on the tiny airstrip and disgorge two battalions of Australian infantry. More followed on the next two days, and even guns were flown in. The strip was under continual small arms fire, and the first sorties found it easier to keep rolling along as the troops jumped out as this made it more difficult for the mortars to score a hit. The infantry went straight into action as they landed, many of them firing from the moment they left the aircraft doors. The strip was only 1,000 yards long, and the far end was 300 feet higher than the near end, so all planes landed uphill, turned at the top, and immediately took off again downhill. There were no crashes, which speaks volumes for the skill and coolness of the young American pilots. This neat little operation turned the tide of the war in New Guinea and started the long haul from island to island which slowly rolled the Japanese back northwards.

Meanwhile the Japanese were still advancing in other areas and in August 1943 they were pursuing the Chinese Nationalist army in Hunan. In a well planned small operation a blocking force of 60 men was dropped to cut a road, and having done so, it was quickly relieved

5 September 1943. 503 Parachute Infantry Regiment dropping in the Markham valley, covered by a smokescreen (*IWM, London*)

with very light casualties. This was the only Japanese airborne operation in 1943, the main reason being that the small air transport force was fully occupied in supplying the very widespread fighting zones in the Pacific theatre. In fact, the Japanese were now at full stretch, and finding it increasingly difficult to hold on to what they had conquered. The pressure was mounting, and it was increased with the next Allied airborne attack.

The relief of Wau led to a general counter-attack in New Guinea and the first major objective was the town of Lae on the north coast, and the flat land in the valley of the River Markham, which ran into Lae. This valley was one of the few places in northern New Guinea where airstrips could be quickly and easily built, and the next stage in the drive towards Japan was going to need the maximum possible air cover. Speed was essential and Lae was to be taken by a seaborne assault backed up by a large parachute drop in the Markham Valley behind the town. There was intensive preparation for this drop and nothing was left to chance. The troops were 503 Parachute Infantry Regiment,

who had last jumped in North Africa 18 months before, and they were taken to Australia for complete rehearsals. Shortly before the drop they were joined by a troop of 2/4 Australian Field Regiment who were to go in with them. These men had practically no rehearsal at all and were rushed through a one-jump training course before being sent off on their first operational drop! Their 25-pounder guns were equally rapidly converted to air-dropping and were carried in bundles under the Dakotas. The gunners were made parachutable inside two days, an extraordinary performance, the more so when one remembers that the 25-pounder had never been dropped by parachute before, and the method for the drop was worked out on the airstrip by the ground crews.

The Markham Valley drop must have been a clear indication to the Japanese that the scale of the war in the Pacific had changed. Of the 302 aircraft which took part in the drop, 96 carried a total of 1,700 parachutists; the remainder were bombers, fighters and follow-up transports carrying supplies and ammunition in under-wing bundles ready to be dropped once the

Noemfoor Island, 2 July 1944. 503 PIR dropping on to the cluttered and dangerous airstrip *(IWM, London)*

objective was secured. The valley was taken with very little opposition, and immediately the engineers began building the first fighter strip. From then on the main effort in the Pacific went into sea-borne assaults and the transport aircraft were fully committed to simply being load-carriers; but it was obvious that when the need arose the Allies could now mount a very substantial combined air assault which made the earlier Japanese efforts look rather second-rate.

Noemfoor

It will now be convenient to jump a year in the chronology and look at the next airborne operation in the New Guinea area. This occurred ten months later on the island of Noemfoor, just off the western tip of New Guinea. The Japanese had built airstrips on Noemfoor and these were needed by the Allies to extend their blockade of the Japanese supply routes to the south and west. The plan was to capture the main Kamiri airstrip on the island by a surprise amphibious assault, and to reinforce this bridgehead by dropping the 503rd onto the strip. Because the strip was short and narrow the lifts would have to fly in line astern, and the release point would need to be precisely fixed. Three lifts were needed, and it was decided to drop one on each of three successive days.

The amphibious assault went well and the strip was secured. The first lift of the 503rd flew in and it became immediately apparent that there were dangers in not holding proper training and rehearsals. The pilots were unused to dropping parachutists and flew too fast and too low. The navigators missed the release point and men were dropped at all heights from 200 feet upwards on to, into and around the dropping zone. There were many injuries, partly from the concrete-like surface of the airstrip, partly from the many obstacles still littering the runways, partly from landing in tall palm trees and then falling to the ground, and partly from dragging in the strong wind. Next day the second lift dropped with casualties again, and the third lift came in by sea. The regiment then took a leading part in the heavy fighting to clear the island, which continued for the next six weeks. It is difficult to see why it was considered essential to fly in the reinforcements for an amphibious assault which had gone so well, and which had a beach-head where men could be landed, but perhaps it was thought that parachuting would be quicker and easier, and perhaps landing craft were scarce in that area.

Burma

The biggest airborne operation of 1944 was not in the Pacific area at all, but in Burma. This was the Special Force Oper-ation in the rear of the Japanese army, Operation 'Thursday' as it was correctly called, the 'Chindit' Operation as it is more popularly known. Originally General Wingate had intended to train his Chindits as parachutists, dropping them into jungle bases in a fairly random pattern, but the amount of training required dissuaded him from this speciality, and he settled for larger bases with airstrips where he could air-land his forces. He was immediately much restricted in the choice of base because it had to be sufficiently remote from the nearest Japanese units to allow aircraft to land without interference and build up a defensive force. Parachutists could have dropped in, seized an existing airstrip, held it and been reinforced by air-landed troops in the way the Germans had done so successfully in Europe. Without the parachutists the initial danger period after the arrival of the first aircraft became much longer and more acute. It was not possible to capture a working strip, so it became necessary to build a strip in a clearing and, to build the strip, heavy plant and equipment were needed. These could only be taken in by glider, and there were no gliders in India.

Wingate was extremely fortunate in being supported in his theories by General Arnold, Chief of the US Army Air Corps. Arnold saw to it that Wingate got what he needed in the way of aircraft, and he formed a special unit for the Chindit oper-ations, No 1 Air Commando. This was quite independent of the rest of the Air

Burma. A practice 'snatch' of a CG-4 glider by a Dakota. The gliders tow line was suspended between the two poles, and the Dakota flew over trailing a long hook. The hook picked up the line a fraction of a second before this picture was taken and the Dakota is now opening its throttles and taking up the slack. Within a second or two the glider will jerk forward and be pulled off the ground, knocking over the two posts as it goes (*John Topham Picture Library*)

Corps, and was under the command of an intensely lively and energetic young colonel, Philip Cochran. Among the aircraft that Arnold approved for the Commando were 100 Waco CG-4A gliders which were shipped in crates to India. Wingate's outline plan for the fly-in of his troops could now be made; suitable jungle clearings were to be chosen into which his force of gliders could land by night, carrying pathfinders and a small force of infantry for local defence. The pathfinders would guide in the next wave of gliders carrying the bulldozers and the engineers to work them, and then all efforts would be directed to making an airstrip suitable for the Dakotas to fly in and out. This might take a day or two, during which the whole operation would be vulnerable to a Japanese counter-attack, hence the need to be far enough away from the main routes and garrisons. But Cochran could ensure that there was plenty of close air support on call to the defenders.

There was a great deal of training in the weeks before the operation, not least by the Air Commando who experimented with casualty evacuation by light aircraft, close air support controlled by RAF observers with the forward troops, and also double-towing of gliders. Double towing was a favourite idea of Wingate's as he was short of Dakotas, and needed to get the greatest possible loads flown in with each sortie. In the event it was found that it was undesirable to double-tow above quite low heights, and the planes which had to cross the mountain range between India and Burma had difficulties. However, much valuable experience was gained, particularly in night towing and night glider landings. Early in February one of the ground columns was backed up with glider landings when the column reached the Chindwin river, and bridge material was flown into it. It was here discovered that gliders could be put down on quite small areas, provided that they were clear of obstacles, and that supplies could be dropped into clearings no longer than 60 yards and less than 20 wide.

The full story of Operation Thursday is too long to recount here, and it has already been told in great detail elsewhere. The airborne aspects of it are the main concern of this narrative, and the tactical side will be ignored for the sake of brevity. Three main sites were chosen for the first assault. Two, code-named Piccadilly and Broadway were to be used on the first night. Twenty-four hours later the third,

Chowringee, about 40 miles away, would be taken. All three were to be attacked by glider assault, and due to the shortages of tugs all three assault lifts would go in on double tow. Broadway and Piccadilly were to have 40 gliders on each, in successive waves.

Just before take-off of the first lift, at 1630 on 5 March 1944, a last-minute reconnaissance showed Piccadilly to be blocked with felled trees. Wingate immediately shuffled the glider loads, changed the lifts, and sent 60 gliders to Broadway instead. An hour was lost in doing this.

There was now a danger of ground opposition, or so it was thought, but in the event there were no Japanese on the landing zones and the gliders came in safely. There was an interesting variation in the technique of landing. The first wave was released high and came in on a normal approach and touch-down, but the subsequent waves were released at a very low height just short of the end of the strip, using a pathfinder light to mark the release point. They then flopped down as quickly as possible, the idea being not to expose them to small arms and anti-aircraft fire while in the air. It was soon found that there were drawbacks to this system.

The first waves landed easily, but the second waves, which were the ones released low down, could not lose speed quickly enough and two crashed and blocked the runway. Another pancaked on top of them, killing two men. The strip had to be closed for the night and all other gliders turned away. Chowringee was an easier task to prepare. The engineer's equipment was flown in in 12 gliders, and the landing interval between the gliders was doubled with the result that there was only one crash, which destroyed a bulldozer. It was replaced with one from Broadway, using a glider snatch to get it out. Snatching had only recently been invented and practised, and only light loads had been tried, but the need was urgent and it was found that there was little trouble in picking up a fully-loaded glider, though to try it out in a jungle clearing for the first time must have taken cool nerves.

Of the 61 gliders which took off from India, 35 landed on Broadway, 3 of them crashing; 8 were recalled and landed back without trouble; 4 broke loose just after take-off; 4 were brought back because their tugs developed engine trouble; 8 landed in enemy territory in Burma; and

Burma 1944. Men of an Indian Army unit waiting to board a Dakota. This is probably a routine reinforcement move as the men have a good deal of gear, which is all in large kit-bags. Each man has chosen to balance his load on his head (*John Topham Picture Library*)

2 were released short of Broadway and crashed into the jungle. Of the 8 which landed in Burma, 4 crews walked out, 2 crews were captured and 2 crews disappeared altogether. Of the 2 gliders which crashed near Broadway, only 2 men survived. But the 35 gliders which arrived on the strip delivered 400 men, and there were no ambushes and no opposition. The strip was ready for Dakotas by the next evening, and the first one landed at 2000 hours. The build-up had started.

Further strips were built in Burma during the next two months, and the Japanese found themselves faced with substantial enemy bases in their rear areas. They reacted as they were expected to, and wasted much effort and lost many men in attacking these well defended fortresses, but it could not go on for ever. All the bases were utterly dependent upon the air for their supplies, reinforcements and casualty evacuation, and the Japanese quickly mounted heavy strafing attacks on them. It then became necessary to give fighter cover to the Dakotas and the strain on the depleted RAF and USAAF became too much. At the critical time when the impetus was disappearing, General Wingate was killed in an air crash and the entire operation slowed down. On 20 May

No 1 Air Commando was withdrawn to rest and reorganize and the operation was officially declared over on 25 May. It had served its purpose, and shown that large forces could be inserted behind enemy lines and supported for long periods, provided that the conditions were right, and provided that there was sufficient air support of all kinds to sustain and protect the ground troops. But without air supply and without air support such long-range operations could not succeed, and any attempt to have put down strong points and permanent bases would have been suicidal.

Historians will dispute for years whether the Wingate operations were sufficiently valuable to justify the effort and the casualties, and it is very easy to criticize when one has hindsight to see the whole picture. At the time it was important to strike back at the Japanese, and to strike back hard. The Japanese could be hurt most by being attacked where they least expected it, in their rear areas, and for that the Wingate methods were ideal. We now know that in the long run the Japanese were not particularly disturbed by these intrusions, but they lost large numbers of men trying to remove them, even if their front-line units were not affected. For the

(Above) Bringing in a resupply drop. Burma 1943/44 *(John Topham Picture Library)*

(Left) Burma 1944. A resupply drop, south of the Irrawaddy *(John Topham Picture Library)*

Allies, much useful information about glider operations was gained, and the effect on morale was considerable. On balance it must have been worth it.

In the final acts of Operation Thursday a small force of Indian parachutists was dropped in near Mogaung with specialist flame-thrower equipment and a medical team, a rare use of parachute troops in Burma.

After Operation Thursday the fighting in Burma returned to the ground units and there was only one other active use of airborne troops before the end of the war. It will be convenient to deal with it here in order to complete the story of the Burma fighting. In May 1945 the Japanese had been pushed southwards through Burma and were falling back on Rangoon. The city lies 24 miles up a winding river, well supplied with shifting sandbanks and similar navigational hazards. In addition there was known to be a gun-battery at Elephant Point, where it could dominate a difficult part of the river, and where it was virtually immune to an amphibious landing. By far the best solution was to take it by a parachute assault. A mixed battalion of Gurkha parachutists was made up, there being no formed units available, and was quickly rehearsed. On 1 May the battalion flew in and dropped in two lifts on to a dropping zone five miles from the objective. It had a difficult approach to what turned out to be a largely empty enemy strong-point. It was a sad anti-climax to a strenuous and exciting build-up.

Leyte Island

The centre of interest now swings back to the Pacific proper where the war was moving into its last stages. By the middle of 1944 the Japanese were on the defensive and being steadily pushed back, island by island, towards Japan. Neither side used airborne forces, though the US 11 Division arrived in the theatre in May 1944, and kept itself in training for air operations, but it was mainly used as another infantry division. The Japanese had lost command of the air and had too few aircraft for large or sustained airborne assaults and they were forced to confine themselves to what amounted to minor raids. Early in August a few aircraft successfully dropped some agents by night and on 26 November 1944 three aircraft flew over Leyte Island, which was in US hands, to drop parachutists. These men were to sabotage the aircraft based on Leyte so that a Japanese reinforcement

convoy could get through to Ormoc Bay two nights later. One plane was shot down before it reached the dropping zone and all the parachutists were killed. The other two tried to drop on to the dropping zone but were so harried by anti-aircraft fire that they scattered their sticks all over the island and were then both shot down. None of the parachutists succeeded in reaching a single US plane, and all were eventually hunted down and killed.

Ten days later the Japanese repeated the disaster on a larger scale, again with the intention of disrupting US air attacks by destroying the planes on the ground. It is a measure of the desperation of the Japanese command that they were even prepared to consider such a suicidal idea, much less actually try to carry it out. By this time in the war there were virtually no Japanese pilots who had dropped parachutists, nor was there any hope of much rehearsal. Once again the target was Leyte, this time the targets were three airstrips which were to be assaulted in conjunction with a seaborne landing in Ormoc Bay. The parachute troops came from one of the special raiding regiments and the aircraft were originally a raiding flying regiment.

The troops had had fairly extensive ground training for the operation, but it is unlikely that the air side was fully effective and certainly, the intelligence was poor. Two of the objectives were disused airstrips, and the men were wasted; the third was not fully operational and only held light aircraft, a fact that could have been established by air reconnaissance before the drop. Another fact that would have come to light was that the area was well filled with troops, in fact the US 11 Airborne Division was actually responsible for the ground on which the dropping zones were planned. On the night of 6 December the airstrips were bombed from high altitude and shortly afterwards two tight formations of Japanese-built C-47s flew across the strip, in two large vees at about 700 feet. Many of the 300 men dropped were killed before they reached the ground. The remainder landed in widely scattered groups and took time to assemble, using an odd selection of gongs, whistles, clappers, musical instruments and even songs to assist themselves. The amazed Americans stayed in their foxholes and shot down anyone who moved. It took them two days to clear the strip, but little damage was done, and within six days the last Japanese was rounded up. The sea-

borne assault failed, and a co-ordinated attack from the Japanese 26 Division in the mountains of Leyte failed too. The net result of it all was that the US air supply to some of their forward troops was interrupted for a few days, and a number of US troops were casualties in the fighting. The Japanese lost all 300 men and 18 of the mixed force of 51 bombers and transports were shot down. It was the last attempt by the Japanese to use parachutists, and should never have been tried. Without the necessary air strikes to support the parachutists on the ground, it was hopeless to expect them to be able to make any impression on a strongly held island. The Americans did the most sensible thing and sat tight, letting the Japanese do all the attacking, knowing that they could not be reinforced and would quickly run out of ammunition, food and energy. And so it came about.

Luzon

The 11 Airborne Division now took part in the invasion of Luzon, the major island of the Philippines group, and its one parachute unit, the 511 Parachute Infantry Regiment, was dropped on three occasions.

The first time, on 2 February, 511 Regiment was dropped as a reinforcement, but lack of training on the part of the pilots and a misjudgement of the dropping zone by several aircraft caused a very scattered drop and some injuries. On 23 February a company was dropped on to the Los Banos internment camp in a surprise drop at dawn; they overpowered the guards and released the internees within half an hour and a follow-up column of amphibious vehicles evacuated the lot. It was a neat little operation, quickly laid on and carried out without fuss; a good example of a sensible use of airborne troops. Unlike the disastrous Japanese raids of the months before, this one was helped by careful and precise reconnaissance coupled with complete air superiority. The US lost 6 men, the Japanese 247, and one internee was slightly injured.

Corregidor

The finale of the airborne soldiers in the Pacific took place close to Manila, on the island of Corregidor. By the middle of February the Americans were advancing from north and south against Manila, and as soon as Manila was captured the port

Corregidor Island, 16 February 1945. The higher end of the island showing the two dropping zones. The white dots are all parachutes some of which have fallen well short of the dropping zone. A C-47 is making a pass over the right-hand dropping zone (US Army)

was going to be needed. But the entrance to Manila Bay was guarded by the island of Corregidor, a massive tadpole-shaped rock rising sheer out of the water, honey-combed with tunnels and bristling with guns. Indeed the Americans had quite deliberately laid out the defences on the lines of a huge battleship, and the gallant and historic defence conducted by General MacArthur in 1942 showed very clearly how impossible it was to take it from the sea, or to destroy it by bombardment. The Japanese had put a garrison of 6,000 men on Corregidor, though the US army was misled into thinking that there were only 850, and it was obvious that special measures were going to be needed if the island was to be taken by assault. From 23 January onwards Corregidor got a daily pounding from the US air forces to soften it up while the final plans were laid.

Corregidor is so small that there were only two possible dropping zones which were not actually overlooked by pill-boxes. These were a tiny golf course and a nearby parade-ground, both on the topmost height of the island. Each was about 250 by 150 yards which meant that the sticks would have to be very short, and the under and overshoot areas were bounded by 400-foot high cliffs down to the sea. To make matters worse there was a constant wind blowing over the top which rarely fell below 15 knots. This meant that there would have to be a very carefully calcu-lated offset in the release point to get the first and last men on the dropping zone. Only one plane would be able to drop at a time, and each would need three runs over the dropping zone to clear the full load of paratroopers. The flight plan called for each machine to fly in in turn, and between turns to circle in a stacking area. Each jumpmaster was flown over the drop-ping zone and allowed to have a good look at it before the jump, and the operation was controlled by a command C-46 which circled overhead throughout the drop, radioing corrections to each plane as it flew in. Only 51 C-47s were available for parachutists, which meant that only one battalion could be dropped at a time. It was therefore planned to drop the first at 0830 hours on 16 February, the second at mid-day and the third the next morning. No weapons containers were to be dropped, to speed action on the dropping zone, and so the mortars and machine guns were broken down into individual loads and a piece carried on every man. A battery of 75mm guns was to go in with

each lift, this being the only exception to the 'no-containers' rule.

Bombers continued to hammer Cor-regidor, flattening all the barrack build-ings around the parade-ground dropping zone. On the 16th the troop-carriers took off at 0730 carrying the 3/503rd, and as they approached the island a final bombard-ment was just finishing. Dropping began at 0800 hours at a height of 600 feet and in a wind speed of 18 knots. Some of the first load were carried over the edge of the cliffs, though they did not fall into the sea, so the regimental commander in his air-borne command post ordered the remain-ing planes to come down to 500 feet, and the jumpmasters to count six after the green light; this put the majority on to the dropping zones and the troop carriers droned round and round in a steady deli-berate fashion that would have been fatal anywhere else. But the Japanese were below ground and were not expecting such an apparently suicidal attack. They could only bring a few small arms to bear and these caused no trouble to the planes and few casualties to the parachutists. The sur-face of the dropping zone was badly broken up by the bombing and there was a good deal of wreckage lying about, the 18 knot wind left little margin for error and about a quarter of the force was injured on landing. The remainder wasted no time in clearing the bunkers and pill boxes that had survived the bombing and setting up their guns to cover the amphi-bious landing. By 0930 the last man was down and the planes went back to collect the 2/503rd. As they left the seaborne assault went in and was successful. At noon the troop-carriers returned and dropped the 2nd/503rd in a freshening wind, but this time there were fewer casualties on the dropping zone, largely because there were friends about to catch the canopies of draggers.

The island was now clear on the top, though the entire Japanese garrison still survived underground, but the job of the parachutists was done and it was decided to cancel the reinforcement drop by the 1/503rd and bring the battalion in by sea. It then took ten days of bitter and unplea-sant fighting to clear all the Japanese which cost the 503rd a further 850 casual-ties. Only 27 Japanese prisoners were taken out of the 6,000 defenders.

Corregidor was a prime example of the value of a small airborne force of deter-mined men, backed up by adequate air support. Without the parachute drop the

amphibious landing would have been enormously costly, if not altogether impossible. It was exactly what the island was designed to prevent, and it is just possible that the Americans might have had to try some other means of attack such as poison gas or in the last resort, starvation. As it was, heavy preparatory bombing cleared the way for the drop and the drop cleared the way for the landing. It was almost like a larger version of the German assault on Fort Eben-Emael, where the problems were very similar. The meticulous planning was also very similar, and it is probably no accident that both operations were successful.

By June 1945 Luzon was almost all in American hands; only the extreme northeast was still Japanese. Here the enemy was in full retreat towards the port of Aparri, where he hoped to make his escape. There was a need to seal off Aparri and bring the campaign to a decisive end. A battalion-sized task force was made up from 11 Airborne Division and dropped close to the port. 1,010 men took part and the heavy equipment was flown in in seven gliders, the first time they had been used in the Pacific. At 0600 hours on the 23rd the task force took off from the same airfield that the Japanese had used when they launched their unhappy attack on 6

Corregidor. A closer picture of the left-hand dropping zone showing the very small area. Discarded canopies are blowing about in the 18-knot wind (US Army)

75

Opposite: *(Above)* The individual arrival: an Allied parachutist a second or two before landing. This particular man has forgotten his training and still has his feet wide apart and his elbows well out. If the wind is blowing at more than 5–10mph he is in danger of spraining an ankle or damaging a shoulder, or both *(EMI)*

(Below) Arnhem 1944. Parachutists spread along the dropping zone *(EMI)*

December. Precisely at 0900 hours the first plane started to drop, and by 0915 all were on the ground. The wind was 20–25mph which brought about several casualties, but the landing was unopposed and three days later the last Japanese was cleared from Luzon. There were no more airborne operations in the Pacific theatre, and in early August the dropping of the atomic bombs on Japan ended the war.

In summing up the work of the airborne forces in the Pacific it is difficult to avoid leaving the impression that they were unnecessary and a luxury that was nice to have around, but not one which was strictly necessary to win the war. The Japanese showed that with proper planning and careful execution airborne forces were every bit as effective in the Pacific as in Europe, and had they carried on with their attacks through Java and into New Guinea it is perfectly possible that they could have taken Port Moresby, and so cleared the Allies out of New Guinea

altogether. Whether they could have sustained any further-ranging attacks is doubtful, though a quick raid on Darwin would have shaken morale in Australia. One is left with the firm impression that the Japanese lost a superb opportunity in not fully exploiting their airborne forces, the more so since by early 1942 they had shown that they had mastered the elements of successful operations.

For the Allies, it is a matter of regret that 11 Division spent an entire year in the theatre before being used at all, and then not decisively until the very end. The astonishing Corregidor operation inevitably causes one to wonder whether the same technique might not have saved thousands of American lives in expensive seaborne landings on the island 'stepping-stones' towards Japan. But the Pacific was a sea-dominated war, and in the minds of the commanders transport aircraft were for carrying supplies and not for fighting battles.

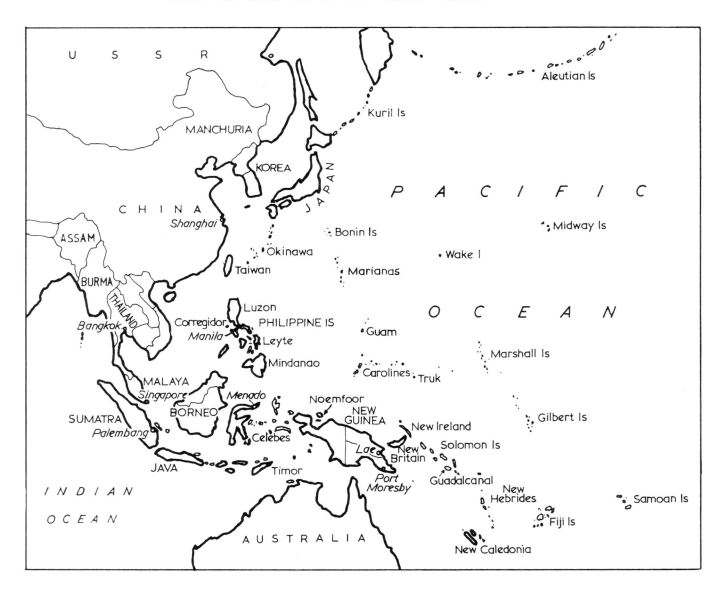

Special Feature: Japanese Airborne Forces

Formation and Training

As with so many of their projects, when the Japanese started to organize parachute troops they did it thoroughly. In the early part of 1940 they set up four training centres at Shimonoseki, Shizuoka, Hiroshima and Hileji at which they ran courses lasting six months. Not surprisingly, the output from these courses was low and German help was called for. Four German instructors arrived in the summer of 1940 and recommended reducing the length of the courses to two months and intensifying them. These early courses had used a scratch collection of equipment to which was allied a very poor appreciation of the requirements of a parachute force. As a result the few manoeuvres which were tried were not at all impressive and there were disturbing numbers of casualties. From the summer of 1940 onwards there was a greater and greater German influence in the training and use of the parachute force, although the Germans failed to persuade the Japanese High Command to see that airborne troops could operate successfully on their own.

With the Germans came improved equipment; the standard Japanese parachute was modelled on the German RZ series, with the same limitations in the way personal equipment could be carried, and the same difficulties for the man on landing. By the autumn of 1941 there were about 100 German instructors in Japan working in nine training centres and over 14,000 men in training split between the army and the navy as both had their own independent airborne units and their own training arrangements. Of the two, the army training was the more thorough and, on the face of it, the safer. Army training was split into five stages, with an assessment at the end of each stage. The general outline followed that of any other training syllabus with great emphasis on physical fitness and running. Stages two and three taught parachute folding, packing and maintenance, stage four was tower jumping, and in stage five the men jumped from aircraft.

The naval course was much shorter, the first ones lasted for only three or four weeks, and it was soon found that the men were dangerously under-trained. The course was then lengthened and became very similar to the army one. Both training systems had features that were peculiar to the Japanese, the chief one being an insistence on jumping from low altitudes. The first jumps were made from 1,000 feet, but each successive one was from a lower

(Opposite) Arnhem Bridge, September 1944. The third day *(painting by David Shepherd—Airborne Forces Museum, Aldershot)*

(Previous pages) Gliders at Caen. 6 Airborne Division: one of the landing zones on the left flank of the beach-head, with shattered Horsas abandoned by their crews. By the time of the Rhine crossing in March 1945, the losses in gliders had been so severe that the US divisions were also using the Horsa, the production of which had outstripped the Waco CG-4 *(painting by Frank Wooton—Airborne Forces Museum, Aldershot)*

A Japanese propaganda picture claiming to show one of the Java drops. It is much more likely to be a training exercise, though it is impossible to say when or where *(Fujiphotos, Japan)*

Japanese naval
parachutists' attack on the
Dutch East Indies (*IWM,
London*)

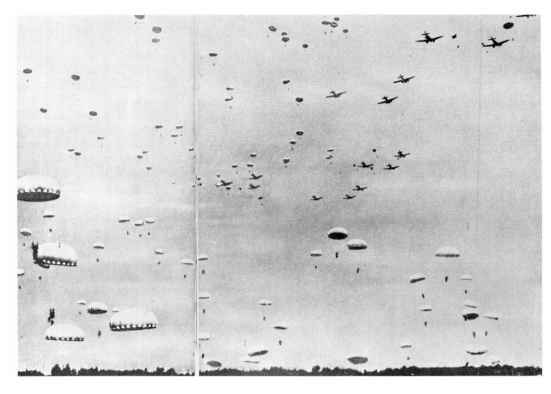

height, until with the sixth and final quali-
fication jump the man was dropped from
350 feet – or so the training schedule
demanded. This is frighteningly low,
though the German RZ parachute would
open quite satisfactorily in such a short
time. However there is some evidence to
show that on exercises in China in 1940
and early 1941 the casualty rate from landings and parachutes that failed to open
caused alarm. This could easily have come
about from the parachutists being deliberately dropped too low for the canopy to
function properly and for the man to have
had time to get over the shock of jumping
and prepare himself for landing. Whatever
the original aims of the training jumps had
been, it seems definite that all the Japanese
operational jumps were carried out from
a height of at least 800 feet, and usually
more.

Another feature, and one to be
applauded, was an insistence on mass
jumping and rallying. The mass jumps
tended to become rather academic exercises in getting men through the door in
the shortest possible time, and again this
can be a prime source of accidents, but
the intention was the perfectly correct one
of getting the jumpers on to the smallest
possible dropping zone without scattering.
Dropping zones in the Pacific were never
luxuriously large. The rallying methods
were crude in the extreme and largely
relied on some sort of noise such as a bell,
but it showed that the Japanese appre-

ciated the need to get parachutists into
formed groups immediately after landing
and on those occasions when they were
properly dropped by their planes they
cleared away from their dropping zones
commendably quickly. The great weakness
of most of the operations was the lack of
suitable aircraft and the fact that the men
were often dropped from the wrong height,
at the wrong speed and in the wrong place.
It takes a great deal of training and initiative to overcome a start as poor as that.

Recruitment and Organization

The men were all volunteers at first, and
all had had at least two years' service before
transferring to airborne units. Later on, in
the last months of 1941 it seems to have
been common to draft men into parachute
units without consulting them first.
Whether this affected the performance of
those units is not clear, though one imagines that it must have done; but there
was always a section of the Japanese High
Command which maintained that it was
not necessary to train men specially for
parachuting, and that there was no basic
difference between airborne and any other
type of operations. No doubt this attitude
was responsible for the compulsory post-
ing of recruits.

The army parachute units were part of
the Army Air Force, possibly a German
idea, and were known as raiding units. At
first they were independent units, mostly
organized under a central command, but

by 1944 they were brought into a proper system of formations. The largest of these was the Raiding Group which had an establishment of 5,575 all ranks and was commanded by a major-general. In the group was a Raiding Flying Brigade which contained the transport aircraft, a Raiding Brigade in which were two battalions, two glider battalions and a machine gun company, an engineer company and a signal unit. Although the intention was to have more than one raiding group, in fact only the 1st was ever fully operational and was held in reserve in Japan for much of the war. A second raiding brigade was formed and put under the direct control of one of the air armies, and this brigade supplied troops for the small operations in China. A brigade consisted of 1,475 men and was tailored to the strength of the Flying Raiding Brigade which could transport it. The raiding regiment was in fact a battalion of 700 men, all parachutists and intended to be transported by a regiment of the flying brigade.

The raiding regiment was organized on very similar lines to a slimmed down infantry battalion with three infantry companies and a heavy weapons company. The major difference was that the weapons were all man-portable and the machine guns and mortars had to be carried in under-wing bundles. The individual soldier carried his personal equipment and weapons in a chest-pack which meant that he could bring himself into action on the dropping zone with minimum delay, but if the containers were dropped wide he lost his spare ammunition and support weapons. Other methods of carrying equipment were tried, including one in which the chest-pack was replaced by a reserve parachute and the man's weapon and ammunition were carried in pockets and satchels slung on either side and down the side of each leg. The raiding force which attacked the airfields on Leyte used this latter arrangement, apparently without much trouble. The great weakness of all the Japanese raiding units was the serious lack of support weapons and the inability of the unit to fight for longer than a day or two without relief. In practice they were well named as raiding units, their whole organization and equipment fitting them only for quick surprise attacks.

The Raiding Flying Regiment was intended solely to carry the parachute troops. It had three squadrons with a total of 35 aircraft, and since these were rarely the same type the carrying capacity varied but it was never adequate for the strength of the regiment it had to lift, so that the theoretical advantages of having a specialist transport force were to some extent lost. However, the idea was entirely correct, and the Japanese were far-sighted in insisting right from the inception of their airborne forces that the fighting units should be under the same command as the transport force. Quite naturally, this transport force was also used for other purposes and one of the weakening factors in the later use of Japanese parachute troops was that the raiding flying regiments had been thinned out and the squadrons reorganized as a result of the losses from US fighters and anti-aircraft fire while carrying out resupply missions.

The glider units were never fully activated although it was planned to have two regiments of 880 men in each raiding group. The reason was that Japan never got large quantities of gliders into production until almost the end of the war, when it was all too late. There had been several good designs in 1941, but it took until 1944 to build them and in the end the only use made of gliders was when a few were flown in to Luzon in 1945 carrying reinforcements. So the entire airborne force throughout the war was parachute delivered, with very few examples of deliberate air-landings as part of the air assault.

The naval parachute units were very similar to those of the army and were again a lightly equipped raiding force designed to assist the seaborne landings by dropping inland of the beaches. In October 1941 there were two such units, 1 and 3 Yokosuka Special Naval Landing Forces. Each had a strength of 844 men, but was apparently intended to be used for certain guard duties or some similar security function. If so it seems an odd use of highly trained men, and there are no actual recorded cases of their being so employed. The 1 Special Landing Force was the parachute unit that took Menado airfield in the Celebes where it showed itself to be well trained and determined; however after that it returned to Japan and was next identified in action on Saipan where it was in an infantry role defending the island, and where it was virtually wiped out.

Uniform

Considerable variety was shown in the uniforms of the wartime Japanese parachutists, though by 1944 there was little difference between ordinary infantry and

A rare, and unfortunately not too clear, photograph of Japanese parachute troops in flight in an unknown plane. They appear to be holding their weapons which are wrapped in canvas. The farthest man on the right is carrying a version of the equipment chest-pack. This is probably a late photograph, though it is not dated. It was found in a newspaper office in Manila in 1945 (*John Topham Picture Library*)

parachutists. In 1940 and 1941 much of the German equipment had been copied and there was a special jump smock very like the 1941 pattern German variety. Some men wore flying suits, and the naval force was fitted out with a two-piece overall in dark green cotton-silk mixture. For winter wear there was a thick overall with a fur collar, but none of these elaborate clothes could survive for long in wartime Japan, and with the increase in the size of the airborne force the distinctive dress was severely pruned down. There were some interesting attempts to settle on a suitable headgear for jumping, and the types ranged from an adaptation of the then current tank crewman's padded

helmet to a specific parachuting helmet derived from the naval helmet. This helmet was virtually rimless, with an ordinary chin-strap and a thin liner. It was frequently worn with a cloth camouflage cover which also had a chin-strap and gave the impression of being a completely different design altogether. However, the force that landed on Leyte was virtually indistinguishable from standard infantrymen in all respects except the carriage of equipment, and it is plain that after the initial experiments the Japanese High Command was not prepared to spend time and money on special clothing and equipment for its little-used parachutists.

6 NW Europe 1944-45

After the Sicily Landings the Allied airborne divisions were pulled back to North Africa to regroup in readiness for the expected fighting in Italy and the ground crews set about repairing and renovating the aircraft that had been damaged in the assaults. Italy surrendered on 3 September 1943 and soon afterwards 1 Airborne Division landed from warships at Taranto. The division was used as light infantry and fought its way up the east coast into and beyond Foggia. Foggia was important to the Allies since it had one of the few good airfields in the area, and bombers could be based on it. Fortunately for the precious parachute brigades the casualties were light although the fighting was sharp and the initiative was kept in the hands of the airborne units. Just as winter was settling in the division was withdrawn altogether and shipped back to England for retraining and reinforcement in preparation for the invasion of North West Europe.

Operation Overlord

The invasion, Operation Overlord, was top priority for the Allies and England was steadily filling up with troops and equipment. The lessons of Sicily had been assessed and digested, and the future of airborne forces was assured, at least for the time being. In September the US 101 Airborne Division arrived in Liverpool from New York, and were put into camps around Newbury. From there they trained hard on the Berkshire Downs and in the West Country. The British had just raised 6 Airborne Division and it was in camps in the Cotswolds where it was training just as hard. 82 Airborne remained in Italy where it was intended that it should support the Italian Campaign by providing parachute assaults from bases in Sicily. After several operations had been mounted and cancelled, two battalions were dropped into the Salerno perimeter as reinforcements and eventually the entire division was committed to the Salerno battle and later sent to garrison Naples. Fortunately casualties had not been heavy, and after a not too strenuous winter the division was sent back to Britain, arriving on 22 April 1944, just in time for the invasion.

By 1944 the output of the American factories was making itself felt and the number of aircraft and gliders was steadily

A Horsa glider, supplied to 101 Airborne Division, after a dawn exercise at Welford in Berkshire, 12 May 1944 *(US Army)*

Overlord: 82 and 101 US
Airborne Divisions, drop
zones

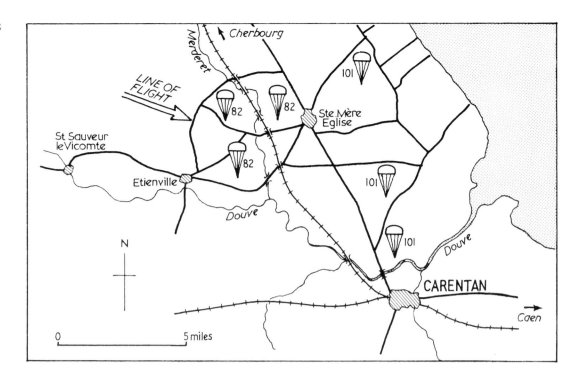

mounting. By January there was enough air lift to move two divisions at one time, almost all of it in C-47s and Horsa gliders. The IX United States Troop Carrier Command had overall control of all US C-47s and by the early spring there were 1,166 machines on its airfields around Southern England. The RAF had a further 150 plus 144 heavy bombers, mainly Stirlings, for glider towing. Between them the Allies had 2,500 gliders, which was rather less than the 3,300 they had hoped for. Most of these were Horsas and Wacos, with a small proportion of the new tank-carrying Hamilcar. The divisions made full use of this unusual quantity of aircraft, and exercises and training went on at full pitch.

The proof of the value of airborne forces was that they were now to be incorporated into the main Allied plan for the invasion. The first intention was to put four infantry divisions onto the Normandy beaches and support them with simultaneous drops by two US airborne divisions just inland and to the west where they would block any German reinforcements coming to the help of the beach defences. The eastern side would be secured by a British parachute brigade dropping and seizing the bridges over the River Orne and the Caen canal to the north of the town of Caen. However, in December 1943 General Eisenhower decided that it would be necessary to take Cherbourg as soon as possible after the landings in order to get a good deep-water

port to supply his armies. To be sure of taking Cherbourg it was necessary to make a landing on the Cotentin Peninsula, and this meant increasing the shipborne invasion to five divisions, which was the limit that the available landing craft could carry.

This western extension of the beachhead altered the picture entirely. The new beach was code-named 'Utah', and it was separated from the remainder by the mouths of two rivers, the Douve and the Vire, both of which effectively cut off any lateral communication until they narrowed down some distance inland. Utah was on its own. Worse still, the ground inland from Utah was flooded and marshy as a result of deliberate inundations by the Germans and there were only four roads leading over them, all four on raised causeways which were easily blocked by quite small forces. To compound the difficulties a tributary of the Douve, a small river called the Mederet, ran parallel to the beach about five miles inland, and it too was flooded so that it was an obstacle to practically all movement. General Omar Bradley took one look at the maps and air photographs and demanded an airborne division to drop and take the causeways. Shortly afterwards he asked for another to drop further south and west and seal off the peninsula from any German reinforcement coming up from that direction. Cherbourg was beginning to affect the whole plan, and it was soon necessary to recast the entire airborne assault.

The British airborne division which was

going to take Caen was shifted to the eastern end of the beach-head to guard the left flank, and the original idea of using small British drops to take isolated gun batteries and strong points was shelved also. Since there were now three airborne divisions involved it became vital that the air lift was increased and the invasion date was put back to 1 June to allow time for the extra aircrews to be trained and the aircraft to be brought in from other tasks. General Eisenhower continued to press the combined planning staffs for more air lift and for simultaneous drops of all three divisions with the fourth in reserve to come in if needed in a second lift. By the end of April the position was sufficiently strong in aircraft and gliders to allow both the US divisions and two-thirds of the British 6 Division to be dropped at the same time. Better than that was not possible unless the Supreme Commander was prepared to wait several months for more aircraft to be built and more aircrew to be trained.

Whilst this build-up period was being pushed forward there was an unwelcome diversion in the form of an alternative plan from Washington. Generals Marshall and Arnold, both experienced and respected commanders, proposed that the airborne army deserved to be used in a much bolder and more sweeping manner which, they affirmed, would bring far greater results. They offered a daring and imaginative idea which had clear origins in the Chindit operations in Burma. The basis was to establish a firm stronghold or 'Citadel' about 50 miles inland and at least half-way to Paris, where it could dominate the crossings of the Seine and attack the German supply lines. It would also divert the German defence in that it would invite attacks on itself and by being heavily supported by fighter aircraft it was confidently predicted that any such attacks would be smashed up before they made any impression. Better still, the concentrations of German troops necessary to contain the 'Citadel' would themselves become targets for air strikes and the German forces would be destroyed before they ever got to battle at all. It was a tempting idea, and might have worked. Equally so, it might not, for the only way to supply the 'Citadel' would have been by air, and to keep a large force of four or more divisions in battle would have taken just about every aircraft that the IX Troop Carrier Command had, as well as almost all the available fighter support. The beaches would have been very sparsely supported and Eisenhower had correctly surmised that the German plan would be to smash the invasion on the beaches before it got inland. So the 'Citadel' would have played into enemy hands and there would have been a distinct danger of both Allied invasions being defeated in detail one after the other. In retrospect this is correct, for we now know that the airborne drops on both flanks were instrumental in the beach-head being held at all, and all the air support was needed to achieve this. The 'Citadel' would have been a nuisance to the Germans, but they could have contained it until they were ready to turn on it and clean it up.

The airborne plan was now becoming clear. On the right flank, or western side, 82nd and 101st were to drop just after midnight onto a series of regimental drop zones with the 101st on the dry ground inland from the causeways and the 82nd further off astride and to the west of the small river Mederet. Both divisions were substantially stronger than their establishment allowed, and they owed this to the experience gained in Sicily. Eisenhower had allowed each to take on an extra para-

Overlord: Short Stirling and Horsa lined up for the take off (*IWM, London*)

Final check before loading for the D-Day drop. The censor has carefully obliterated all the unit insignia, but these men are probably 101 Airborne. The amount of kit carried by each man is worth noting, as is the way it is hung around him. It is possible that these men are not infantry, they might be gunners, signallers or similar specialists (US Army)

chute regiment and had split a glider regiment between them so that they each now had three parachute regiments and a three-battalion glider regiment plus two parachute artillery battalions with 75mm pack howitzers and a glider battalion with 105mm howitzers. 101st was to open the way for 4 US Division which would land on Utah, and 101st would also secure the southern flank of this move and hold off any German attacks from that direction. 82nd was to seal off the western half of the peninsula and prevent Cherbourg being reinforced. It was reckoned that the two divisions would be strong enough to hold the area until 4 Division joined them, particularly if both were delivered at the same time.

On the other flank the British 6 Division could only drop two brigades in the first lift since the majority of the air lift had gone to the 82nd and 101st. To compensate for this to some extent General Gale was allotted 1 (Commando) Special Service Brigade which would land from the sea, but would be on the extreme flank of the beach and would march directly to his divisional area and come under command. 1 Airborne Division would form an

airborne reserve, always an important feature of any operation, and would come in as required, on any beach. Alternatively the division could be used as a quick reinforcement in the same way as the 82nd had been at Salerno. The left flank also had two small rivers cutting off the beach area; here they were the River Orne and its attendant canal running north from Caen, and a few miles to the east the River Dives, also running north. The Orne and its canal were crossed by one road, the Dives by four roads and a railway. The general plan was to seize and hold all bridges and dominate the land in between, thus sealing off the left flank and safeguarding the beaches from attack from that direction. Another task, and a more difficult one, was to silence a battery of four coast defence guns which were sited at Merville where they could sweep the entire eastern end of the beach and engage shipping for several miles out to sea. Bombing could not smash the emplacements and a special task force was set up to make a surprise raid on the battery to ensure that by half an hour before the first landing craft appeared all four guns were out of action. For the Orne bridges General Gale decided on another surprise assault, this time using a silent glider approach in the same manner as the Eben-Emael flight, though from a shorter distance, and to rely on his two parachute brigades for the others.

The British division was short of aircraft. All the IX Troop Carrier Command planes went to the 82nd and 101st, so did all the Waco gliders and some of the Horsas. The division was left with the 150 RAF C-47s, the remainder of the Horsas, the Hamilcars and as many RAF bombers as could be raised. But 6 Division had a special advantage: the RAF aircrews were all highly skilled in night navigation. Also 3 Brigade of 6 Division had had 1 Canadian Parachute Battalion attached to it since August 1943. It had been trained at Fort Bragg and played a gallant part in Operation Overlord and later in Operation Varsity. Its commanding officer, Lieutenant-Colonel Geoffrey Nicklin, was killed and Corporal Frederick George Topham of its medical unit was awarded the VC. Now the troops knew what was required and trained furiously. The special units for the surprise attacks were rehearsed continuously on models and replicas. Meanwhile the Allied air forces mounted fighter sweeps, bombing raids and most important of all from the point of view of the ground commanders, photographic reconnaissance sorties over all the proposed landing areas.

On the German side there was no illusion about the coming invasion. The only unknown factor was the timing – when would it come? And also, exactly where? Field-Marshal Erwin Rommel commanded Army Group B, stretching from Brittany to Calais, with the Seventh and Fifteenth Armies under his command. The Seventh Army faced the invasion beaches, and the Fifteenth Army had the rest of the coast from just east of Caen onwards. Because the invasion was expected somewhere in the Pas de Calais area the Fifteenth Army had been given priority in all defence stores and in tanks and vehicles. On the Contenin Peninsula the majority of the troops were in second-line units and short of transport and tanks.

Rommel based his defence on the idea of a thin, hard crust along the beaches with infantry divisions a short distance behind to deal with any determined landings. About 50 miles inland were the Panzer divisions which would move to counter-attack any penetration of the Atlantic Wall and stop a break-out. In the area inland of Utah Beach 709 Coastal Division was responsible for defence, and its under-strength regiments had spent most of the spring in digging and wiring, so that their training had suffered. On the left flank the 711th held the Orne and Dives area; it too was a poor quality and low-strength formation. On 18 May Rommel set off on a lightning tour of the coast defences, praising, upbraiding, but particularly cursing the slow erection of his special anti-glider landing obstacles. These were long poles dug into the ground on all flat places where gliders might land. They came to be known as 'Rommel's Asparagus' or 'Rommelspargel' and caused much consternation at Allied Supreme Headquarters when they were identified on air photographs.

The Allied air force commanders were pessimistic about the chances of the troop

D-Day. Tarrant Rushton aerodrome. Halifaxes marshalled with their Horsas and Hamilcars (*IWM, London*)

transports surviving the German flak and predicted losses of up to 50 per cent. Unfortunately the leader of this train of thought was the Air Supremo himself – Air Chief Marshal Sir Trafford Leigh-Mallory – and he viewed the impending decimation of his aircrews with marked gloom. To his credit when it was apparent at the end of D-Day that there had been only light opposition, he was the first to congratulate Eisenhower.

Pathfinder techniques had been learned since Sicily, and one other lesson which had been fully absorbed since then was the need for a simple flight plan. For both sides of the beach-head the planes were routed to fly in straight lines along well marked routes using ships as markers where possible. The chances of error were cut down as far as they could be, even though it was known that all aircrew had had to chop and change during the work-up period, doing routine transport flying as well as training for the airborne assault, and this had left some of them less than perfect in the special skills of flying parachutists.

At 2130 hours on the evening of 5 June the US pathfinders took off from near Grantham and flew without interference to their drop and landing zones west of Utah Beach. All dropped on time and all dropped off their planned drop zones by about a mile. One drop zone, the one intended for 501 PIR of 101 Division, was

defended and the pathfinders set up their beacons under fire. An hour later 822 C-47s carrying 13,000 men flew over the west coast of the peninsula, heading east for the drop zones. As they crossed the coast the alerted anti-aircraft gunners opened fire and the tight formations broke up. Pilots began to weave about, which was strictly forbidden, and in many aircraft the heavily laden men who were standing up ready to jump, were flung about and thrown off their feet. Navigators, struggling to identify their drop zone, were confused by the changes of direction, and had to guess where they were. The green jump lights came on anyhow, and some aircraft were actually in cloud when the parachutists were dropped.

101 Division landed in an area about 25 by 15 miles, the 82nd in rather less. There were men all over the Cherbourg Peninsula, a few even landing at Cherbourg itself, 29 miles from the drop zone. About 1,500 men were casualties of one kind or another on landing, and little groups of American parachutists began fighting isolated battles all over the area as the Germans started to round them up. But the very fact that the drop was so scattered helped to confuse the defence, and as always in these circumstances, grossly exaggerated stories began to fly around the German Command structure. The two divisions were not able to seal off the beach as cleanly as they would have liked,

D-Day. The second wave of gliders crossing the beaches (*IWM, London*)

nor could they clear the exits fully, but the confusion that they caused stopped all coherent German movement and allowed the landings to take place on Utah Beach without too much opposition. Contact was quickly made with the airborne divisions and armoured vehicles were pushed ahead to stave off the determined German attacks which lasted throughout 6 June. By the 8th the beach-head was secure, and Cherbourg was captured at the end of the month. The air assault succeeded in all its essential features, even though the execution was scrappy. The plan had been simple enough, for which the lessons learned in Sicily could be thanked, and the use of the two divisions in mass close together in the same geographical area was entirely right and sensible, the more so since 82nd had not really had long in which to work up for the operation. The difficulties had arisen from the poor delivery and indifferent navigation by the aircrews and they once more underlined the terrible dangers of launching a night air assault without highly trained and experienced airmen to fly the troops to the right place at the right time.

On the east flank 6 Airborne Division landed at almost the same time as the Americans and quickly gained a firm grip on its objectives, though here too the night had its dramas. Each drop zone was to have two separate pathfinder sticks dropped onto it, but in each case only one actually arrived. One dropped on the wrong drop zone and its beacon brought in 14 aircraft of the wrong stream before the mistake was realized, otherwise all the parachutists arrived reasonably accurately. The difficulty was that an error of as little as 400 or 500 yards in the high corn crops and thick hedgerows meant that men could become hopelessly lost for an hour or more. Many did not find their way to their rendezvous until dawn, and at daylight came the expected German counterattacks. 3 Parachute Brigade suffered more than 5 Brigade from the problem of collecting the troops partly because their pathfinders arrived late and had not set up their beacons when the main lift flew in. Luckily the navigators were skilled and dropped on their own calculations.

The two bridges over the Orne and the canal were successfully taken by six gliders, three to each, which flew in from a release point over the sea and by remarkably skilled piloting were landed within yards of their bridges. The navigation of these gliders was masterly, and the first one to reach the canal bridge actually crashed through the German perimeter wire around the weapon pits. The bridges were taken within minutes. One glider was somehow directed to a bridge over the Dives, nearly five miles away, and it made an accurate landing alongside an undefended bridge which was promptly secured and held.

Hamilcars coming in to land in 6 Division area. The enormous flaps show up very clearly (*IWM, London*)

The other surprise attack was the Merville Battery which had been most carefully and comprehensively rehearsed by 9 Parachute Battalion and all four companies were involved in the attack together with a glider-borne engineer party. The plan was complicated and relied for its success on several different groups being in the right place at the right time, and on the help of a preliminary bombing of the battery to daze the defenders and shake their morale. Despite the meticulous planning and rehearsal misfortune dogged the entire enterprise, which is something not unusual in airborne operations. The bombing was inaccurate and only succeeded in scattering the reconnaissance party of 9 Parachute Battalion and damaging the village of Merville. The battalion drop was dreadfully scattered. Light flak caused some of the pilots to jink at the last minute and their men were thrown off balance. The sticks straggled out as best they could and the battalion was spread over 50 square miles of country instead of two. The CO collected about 25 per cent of his men and less than a quarter of the special equipment and assaulted the battery. By a combination of luck and sheer nerve they drove out the 130 defenders and put the guns out of action just before the landing craft approached the beach.

The remaining two battalions of 3 Brigade were dropped further east from the Merville Battery with the task of destroying the River Dives bridges and crossings. The drop was scattered, but both battalions found their bridges and then went into the strongest defensive positions they could make to await the inevitable German counter-attacks. In 5 Brigade area around the Orne bridges the battalions closed up and took position to hold the bridges intact against increasing German assaults until the Commando Brigade arrived on foot in the early afternoon, having marched from the beach. Further out from the bridges the battalions were in houses in the villages and their 6-pounder guns held off tanks and self-propelled guns which had come up from south of Caen. Luckily General Gale had flown in the anti-tank guns in gliders, despite the dangers from the 'Rommelspargel', and these saved the day by keeping the German armour at a distance. By early evening the second glider lift came in and in it were the huge Hamilcars carrying 17-pounder anti-tank guns and a few Tetrach light tanks. The eastern flank was then secure, and the bridges were held. Although the battalions were not all in the best possible positions they were able to survive the hard fighting that lay ahead for the next few days. There had been some discrepancies in the operation, but by and large it was a remarkably successful airborne assault by any standards and undoubtedly the finest example of an airborne operation that had been undertaken thus far in the war. The RAF in particular, could take pride in the way that they had delivered the force with commendable accuracy to different drop zones and landing zones, using aircraft of different performance and speeds, and against different intensities of flak and ground opposition.

The planning staffs could take comfort too from the successes of the Normandy assaults. They were proved to have been right to have used the divisions on the flanks and not in front as they had first thought. They were proved right too in keeping to a simple and direct plan, although in 6 Airborne area it was complicated in its detailed execution. They were also proved right in keeping to a simple flight plan and in using pathfinders. All told, the differences between the Sicily operation and the D-Day landings were enormous in the way in which they were carried out and it was apparent that the Allies had forged and almost perfected a most formidable weapon.

The opportunities to use such a weapon were not going to be very frequent in the following months since the one thing that the airborne army demanded was time to prepare and launch anything over a very small force. In the race across France the airborne units were briefed and prepared for one operation after another, but in every case the speed of the ground troops overtook the planners before the aircraft could get away from the airfields. 6 Airborne remained in action until the end of August fighting as an infantry division and advancing as far as the Seine. In that advance more than 1,000 prisoners were taken, for the loss in the division of 4,305 all ranks killed, wounded and missing. Much the same happened on the west flank where the US divisions remained in the line for three weeks after the bridgehead was established and took part in the capture of Cherbourg and the consolidation of the Allied right wing. Then they too were withdrawn back to England to prepare for the next round.

When 1 Airborne left Italy in the autumn of 1943 it left behind one brigade, 2 Parachute Brigade who quickly became 2 Independent Parachute Brigade and operated as a normal line formation in the fighting northwards up Italy. At one time they even had a spell in front of Cassino, but at no time did they parachute or have an opportunity to use their specialized techniques of airborne warfare. The US army also had some airborne units in Italy

and they too were fighting as normal infantry. As the Allied advance swept across northern France, a diversionary invasion was planned for southern France with the intention of drawing off the German effort still further and offering another advance route up the Rhône valley towards the German frontier. The plan called for an assault landing from the sea supported by an airborne landing whose task was to hold off the known large German reserves so that the beach landings could go ahead without interruption. For this an airborne task force was required and during June 1944 all the available airborne troops in Italy were withdrawn and formed into First Airborne Task Force under the command of Major-General Robert T. Frederick, US army.

There were five US parachute battalions from 550 and 551 Regiments, one US glider regiment and 2 Independent Parachute Brigade with three battalions, 4th, 5th and 6th and in support 64 Light Battery and 300 Air-Landing Anti-Tank Battery. The plan called for the task force to seize the area between La Motte and Le Muy, about ten miles inland from the beach-head, and hold it until relieved. The drop zones were known to be rough, but not defended. However, it was expected that the force would be heavily attacked within a few hours of landing.

The air plan allotted aircraft of 51 US Troop Carrier Wing to the operation, with 125 aircraft carrying parachutists and 61 towing the Hadrians and Horsas of the anti-tank artillery. The mounting base was on airfields around Rome and D-Day was to be 15 August. By 0330 on that day the pathfinders had been dropped on the exact drop zones and the main force came in just over an hour later. Unfortunately a thick morning mist obscured the ground and many troops were dropped wide as the pathfinder beacons were not accurate enough at that stage to do more than guide a plane to where it could see the drop zone, and with the mist the navigators were guessing. Some men landed up to 20 miles away, but 73 of the 125 C-47s dropped right onto the drop zone and the task force rallied to find that it was at half strength. Luckily there was very little enemy interference or opposition and the expected attacks did not materialize; the gliders landed without trouble at 0930 and by 1015 all the objectives were secure. The gliders had a longer flight than planned since the mist which confused the parachute aircraft did the same for them, and the glider stream was held over Corsica where it had to circle for an hour. The C-47s towing the Horsas ran out of fuel and had to take their gliders back to Rome for more. At the airfield this was totally unexpected and it took some time for the aircraft and gliders to be lined up and sorted out for another take-off. In the end the Horsas arrived in the afternoon, and it was fortunate that their absence was not critical. The only place where there was any sharp fighting at all was at the holiday resort of St Tropez where some men of the 509th had been wrongly dropped. They stormed the beach defences from the rear and were engaged in some heavy action, after which they took the town and waited for the seaborne landing to come into the harbour and relieve them.

Apart from a few minor local actions against a rapidly retreating enemy there were virtually no other operations in southern France and the task force was soon broken up and its units sent to other formations. The divisions in northern France called it the 'Champagne Campaign'.

2 Independent Brigade was withdrawn back to Rome and waited for the Germans to pull out of Greece. They waited until October and at mid-day on the 12th a company group of 4 Battalion jumped onto Megara airfield to seize it for air-landings. By mistake the company was dropped in a 35mph wind and had 50 per cent casualties on landing. Men were hurt by hitting the ground at high speed, and being hurt could not collapse their parachutes. They were then dragged across the airfield and into rough ground, walls and other obstacles where they were further injured. The remainder of the brigade came by sea or were air-landed. Thereafter they were embroiled in purely ground fighting.

Arnhem

By the middle of September 1944 the Allied armies were all more or less at, or near to, the German frontier. In the south General Hodge's First US Army was actually at the Siegfried Line, in the centre General Patton's Third US Army was already starting to cross the Mosel and in the extreme north General Dempsey's Second British Army was already at the Meuse-Escaut Canal and reaching into northern Belgium. The rush across France had been enormously tiring and expensive in men and machinery, but it now looked as if one more effort would push the crumbling German army right back into

Germany and then to all intents and purposes the war would be over. All it wanted was that last determined push, the Germans were demoralized, or so it was thought, and they were definitely short of supplies and ammunition of all kinds. On the Eastern Front the Russians were steadily pressing in towards the German frontier, and the time seemed right for a spectacular leap forward to catch the enemy off balance. Given time he would collect himself and regroup his forces, and it seemed highly likely that he could gain that time by holding the succession of rivers in front of the Second Army.

Stretching across the British Front were four major water barriers in the next 60 miles. Just beyond Eindhoven, in Holland, was the Wilhelmina Canal. Beyond that, at Grave, was the Maas. A few miles further on at Nijmegen was the Waal and finally at Arnhem the Rhine flowed, having diverted just before Arnhem into the Ijssel which ran off to the north. The ground could easily be flooded so as to stop almost all movement, and then the whole area could be held with comparatively light forces while the remainder were held well back to counter any breakthroughs. For the Allies a purely ground attack would have been doubly difficult as they were now nearly 400 miles from their supply ports and another was urgently needed. Antwerp had been captured, but could not be used until the river approaches to it had been cleared, and the Germans held the north bank of the Scheldt thereby stopping all shipping. A strong drive to 'bounce' the river lines across the front would also cut off Antwerp and allow the approaches to be cleared. So it would fulfil two purposes, and it appeared to be an ideal task for a large airborne operation.

On 2 August 1944 the Allied airborne divisions had been formed into one airborne army under the command of Lieutenant-General Lewis H. Brereton, who had started his airborne career under the famous Billy Mitchell in 1918. Brereton had been the Commanding General of the US Ninth Air Force, and since he was an air force general it was decided that the control of ground operations should be the concern of corps commanders, so two corps were formed. The army consisted of the following forces:

1 US XVIII Airborne Corps, commanded by Major-General Ridgway, newly promoted from command of 82 Airborne Division. XVIII Corps had three divisions, 82nd, 101st and 17th,

Men of 1 Airborne
Division unloading a jeep
from a Horsa during a
rehearsal for Arnhem
(*IWM, London*)

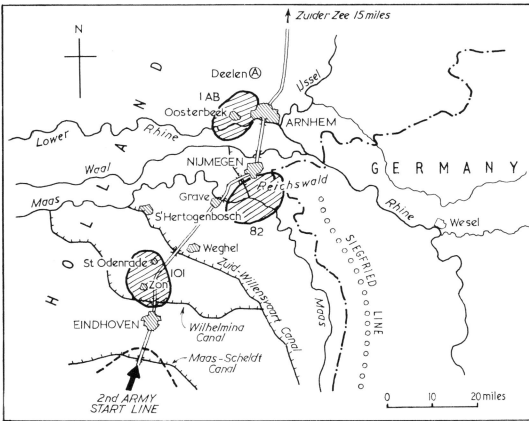

Unloading Horsas at
Arnhem, afternoon,
Sunday 17 September.
Lt-Col W. F. K.
Thompson is carrying two
packs to place in the trailer
(*IWM, London*)

plus some independent support units, particularly engineers, and the promise of 13 Airborne Division when it came to Europe.

2 British I Airborne Corps, commanded by Lieutenant-General F. A. M. Browning, who was also Brereton's deputy. Under command were 1 and 6 Airborne Divisions, 1 Special Air Service Brigade and 1 Polish Independent Parachute Brigade.

3 British 52 (Lowland) Division as the air-landing formation for the army.

4 US IX Troop Carrier Command.

5 38 and 46 Groups RAF, when needed for operational tasks. Otherwise these two groups were employed on other duties, particularly sorties in support of SOE and underground actions in Europe.

In the event 52 (Lowland) Division was never used for air-landing, nor was it used in the other role for which it had trained extremely hard, namely mountain warfare. After standing by for several months it was put ashore at Walcheren Island in an amphibious landing, and far from fighting on mountains or from aircraft, the ground

it actually fought over was below sea level! But this was not known at the time, and the fact that a whole division was allotted to air-landing seemed an indication of a determination to make the airborne method work.

The only criticism of the airborne army came from Air Chief Marshal Sir Trafford Leigh-Mallory; again he was against the IX Troop Carrier Command being a permanent part of First Airborne Army because, he maintained, if the troop-carriers were to carry out their functions correctly they should be under the command of the one air force headquarters. But Eisenhower would not alter the arrangements. He was adamant that the aircraft had to be under the one overall airborne commander, and he pointed out that both Sicily and Normandy had shown how necessary this was. The troop-carriers therefore remained under Brereton, which was entirely right and sensible. Under his enlightened and vigorous leadership the army soon became an efficient and effective force, although there was never complete harmony between Brereton and Browning over how it should be used.

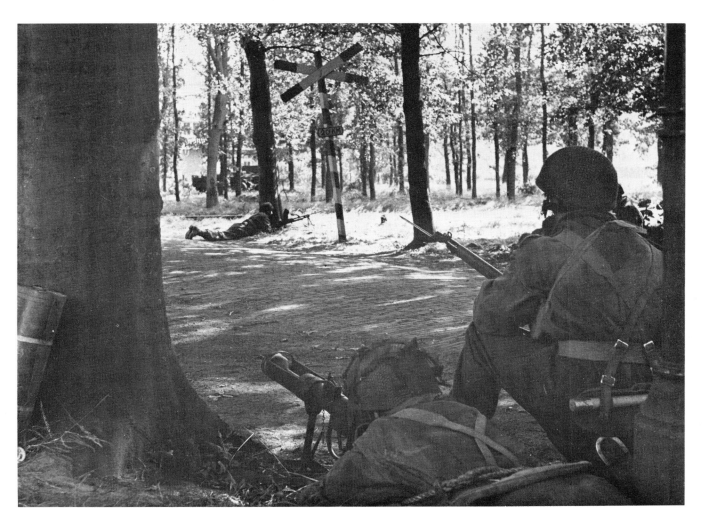

However, the differences were quickly sunk when the planning started for the biggest airborne operation of the war.

This was to be Market Garden, the operation in which the airborne forces were to seize the bridges in front of the Second Army and allow it to push right through to the Zuider Zee to cut off all the German forces in western Holland, outflank the Siegfried Line from the north, and sweep round to the right and down into the Ruhr and the middle of Germany in one huge movement which would bring the war to a close in 1944. It was a vast plan in the best tradition of General Montgomery, who devised it, and based on the experiences of the advances across France during the summer there seemed no reason why it should not work exactly as described. Many German units were undoubtedly demoralized and tired, nearly all were under-strength and under-equipped; and fuel was short for all vehicles and aircraft.

In the Allied forces it was the complete opposite: morale was high, equipment was plentiful, one is tempted to say almost lavish, units (with few exceptions) were well up to strength, and there was a feeling that nothing could stop the Allied war machine. Berlin was nearly in their grasp, all that was needed was a final all-out push and the war with Germany would be over. There was a good deal of substance in that assessment, for at the end of August the Germans had just one division in the whole of southern Holland and virtually no reserves. Their army had just suffered a terrible defeat and had been chased right across France, losing men and equipment all the way. For a space of two or three weeks they were exhausted and shattered, and there is no doubt that one good drive would have cut right through into Germany. But men recover quickly, and by early September the position in Holland was rapidly being put right. Units were being pulled together, reserves were being brought up, order was emerging from chaos, defensive positions were being dug and a general grip and control were established. The opportunity to take Holland was passing quickly.

All was not quite as rosy as it was painted on the Allied side. Although the ground forces had been phenomenally successful and had astonished themselves by

Wolfheze, on the way in to Arnhem. Halted, and covering the road. Loaded PIAT (anti-tank weapon) in the foreground *(IWM, London)*

their summer advances, by late August they were much restricted in what they could do to launch another offensive. All supplies had to come the 400 miles from Cherbourg and until a nearer port could be opened up there was little hope of a rapid build-up for the Montgomery plan. Time ticked away while the convoys of lorries shuttled to and fro along the overloaded roads of France and Belgium, and in Holland the Germans rapidly recovered their composure.

The ground forces were led by XXX British Corps under Lieutenant-General Brian Horrocks, and their part of the operation was code-named 'Garden'. This was the force which was to push through at all costs to the Zuider Zee. The airborne force was a mixed corps made up of 82 and 101 US Divisions and 1 British Division under the command of Browning, a fact that did not please the Americans since they had provided the largest proportion of the troops and were also providing the aircraft. The airborne plan, the 'Market' part of the operation was in general terms as follows:

1   101 US Division was to seize the bridges over the obstacles between Eindhoven and Grave. These were the nearest watercourses to XXX Corps front.

2   82 US Division was to drop in the area around Grave, capture the crossings at Nijmegen and Grave and in addition hold the only piece of high ground in the area at Groesbeek. The Airborne Corps Headquarters would land with 82 Division and establish itself somewhere in the Nijmegen area.

3   1 British Airborne Division, with 1 Polish Parachute Brigade Group under command, was to capture the bridges at Arnhem and establish a bridgehead around them so that XXX Corps could continue their advance to the north.

4   878 US Aviation Engineer Battalion and 2 Air-Landing Light AA Battery RA were to be flown in by glider as the situation permitted, with the task of preparing and defending airstrips on the north side of Arnhem.

5   52 (Lowland) Division would be flown in onto the prepared strips in Dakotas to reinforce the bridgehead and provide a firm base for the launching of the drive to the Zuider Zee and into Germany.

Both US airborne divisions were to be withdrawn as soon as the ground forces caught up with them, but 1 Airborne Division might have to fight on in the ground role. Despite the resources of IX Troop Carrier Command, the whole corps could not be flown in in one lift, and it would be necessary to spread the drops and glider landings over four days, with due allowance for resupply at the same time.

The misfortune about the plan was that it was delayed. The necessary backing for it came too slowly thereby giving the Germans time to regroup in Holland. During the second week of September Colonel-General Student's First Parachute Army was pieced together and moved into the ground just ahead of XXX Corps, blocking the way to the Rhine. II SS Panzer Corps, with two low-strength divisions, 9th and 10th, was refitting in Arnhem and to the north of the town. Although Obergruppenfuhrer Dietrich's Corps had very few operational tanks or self-propelled guns, they had enough to represent a serious menace to a lightly-equipped airborne division. Day by day the picture changed, and it changed for the worse from the Allied viewpoint. They, however, were almost entirely unaware of this shift in the German strength and to some extent were guilty of seeing only what it suited them to see. This was understandable in view of the experiences of the past months, but as always, it is a dangerous habit to under-rate one's opponents and certainly so far as the Airborne Corps was concerned, this was exactly what was done.

When General Browning gave his orders to his divisional commanders on Sunday, 10 September, there were just seven days until the first troops were to drop along the 'airborne carpet' as he termed the assault. It was a desperately short space of time but there had been 17 previous operations since D-Day which had been planned and then cancelled just before they were launched, so there was a good deal of experience and ability in rapid preparation throughout the entire First Airborne Army. Unfortunately there was also a dangerous tendency not to take any operational order too seriously, 'wolf' had been cried too often and now nobody believed it could ever actually happen. The 17 cancelled parachute assaults were a fertile breeding ground for cynicism and the wags were already calling 1 Airborne the '1st Stillborn Division'. More unfortunately still, there were some fatal flaws in the main plan.

The flaws are worth examining because they led to the failure to hold the Arnhem

Dakota and Waco Hadrian, both just airborne, taking off for Holland 17 September 1944 (*IWM, London*)

bridges. The first flaw, and the one which had most influence on the subsequent battle, was the choice of the dropping and landing zones. These were well outside the town to the north and west and were roughly eight miles from the main objective, the road bridge leading back to XXX Corps. The reasons for this choice have been debated endlessly since 1944, and the responsibility for confirming it has been tossed from one side to the other. Everyone now argues with the benefit of hindsight and a full knowledge of the battle, but it is clear that at the time there was some muddled reasoning. The RAF were convinced that there was more flak in the area than there actually was. Furthermore

they were convinced that there were batteries around the bridges. This information came from aircraft who reported being fired upon from near the bridges, yet it was never substantiated by any air photos. However it was enough to ensure that the RAF opposed any idea of landing on or near the objectives, or of flying near the military aerodrome to the north of Arnhem, for this too was thought to be well defended with guns. In fact the ground on the southern bank of the road bridge was perfectly good for glider landings and it is inexplicable that there was no attempt to repeat the *coup de main* landings that had been so spectacularly successful at the Orne bridges; a company

26 September. A survivor. Sgt Bennett, 1 Airlanding Brigade, dressed in borrowed civilian clothes after swimming the Rhine, but still carrying his Sten (*IWM, London*)

could have been put down in five or six gliders and then the bridge would have been secure. Boldness is the great ingredient of airborne assaults, but in many puzzling ways the Arnhem operation seems to lack the essential spark that was so vividly present on D-Day.

The other flaw was the task given to 82 Airborne. The division was given a ten mile sector in which were two large bridges, over the Maas and the Waal, at least two other smaller bridges and the Groesbeek Heights. The Heights, actually a series of low wooded hills, dominated the area south of Nijmegen in daylight and their eastern side ran along the frontier with Germany. Behind the frontier was

the Reichswald Forest where it was known that some German units were resting, hence the Groesbeek Heights could expect to be a battleground soon after the drop went in. It was a tremendous task for the 82nd and when General Jim Gavin assembled his staff and told them to start planning his Chief of Staff, Colonel Wienecke, simply shook his head and said 'We'll need two divisions to do all that'. Gavin had learned some hard lessons in Sicily and Normandy and this time he was determined not to have his men scattered for miles over the countryside, so one aspect of his plan was to ensure that he put everyone down right on top of their objectives, and his priorities for those

D-Day. Pegasus Bridge, over the Orne canal, a few days after the assault. The gliders of the *coup-de-main* party are clearly visible (*IWM, London*)

objectives were the Groesbeek Heights, the Grave Bridge, the Maas-Waal canal bridges, and lastly the bridge in Nijmegen. Browning agreed the order and insisted on the Groesbeek being secure, for if the Germans took it they could control the entire road stretch below Nijmegen. He also agreed to the idea of leaving the huge Nijmegen Bridge to the last, since without the other bridges Nijmegen was useless anyway. Gavin planned to put two regiments, the 505th and 508th onto Groesbeek and the 504th just by Grave, where they could rush the bridges over the Maas and the Canal. Instead of a glider *coup de main* he aimed to drop one company of the 504th near the Maas Bridge to be sure of getting that immediately. Once again there were no direct assaults on the bridges, despite the lessons of D-Day, though as the 82nd had never used gliders in this way in Europe they could be forgiven for not trying it now. However, with so many objectives to take it might have been reasonable to try and put more company parachute attacks onto specific bridges, but Gavin was obviously wary of his aircrew's ability to make pinpoint drops, as well he might have been with his experience. It meant that the Nijmegen Bridge was not even approached until the others were taken, and this could

give the Germans more than enough time to blow it.

The 101st were little better off then the 82nd. General Maxwell Taylor would only have his infantry with him on the first day's drop; his artillery and support troops were to fly in the second lift the next day. His division had to cover 15 miles of the corridor and take two main canal bridges and nine minor ones with three regiments. Like Gavin he had been dropped wide once too often and he aimed for only two main dropping areas; one to the north was for the 501st on their own and they would take the northern bridges around the village of Veghel. The other two regiments, 502nd and 506th, together with the headquarters were to drop close together in the middle of the divisional area and take the bridges south of Veghel right down to, and including, the town of Eindhoven. It was an extremely difficult task, the more so since the regiments would be without any real anti-tank defence and the 506th had an approach march to Eindhoven of at least four miles. A few German armoured vehicles in the right places would play havoc with the timetable, but Taylor was quietly optimistic, and unlike Gavin he only expected to have to take the bridges. There was no German frontier to look after, and no Groesbeek Heights to defend.

1 Airborne Division was to 'capture the Arnhem bridges, with sufficient bridge-heads to pass the Second Army through'. A somewhat broad task, but the term 'bridges' meant first and foremost the main road bridge over the Rhine in the middle of the town. Secondly it meant a pontoon bridge which had been built by German engineers just over half a mile to the west, and it also meant the railway bridge to the west of that. It could be roughly interpreted as meaning that the entire town was to be captured, as well as a lodgement on the south bank of the river beyond each bridge. It was to be an action in which the major part of the fighting would be in a built-up area, street fighting in fact, a type of warfare which mops up men like a sponge mops up water. It is also a type of fighting in which there is less need for heavy weapons and vehicles than in the open country, and this was known in the British army at that time, for there had been enough street fighting in the advances through France and Italy. It was therefore vital that 1 Airborne landed as many men as possible right at the beginning of the operation. Unfortunately the air plan was restrictive and in the event not enough were landed on the first day.

The difficulties with the air plan became apparent the morning after Browning gave his orders. The staff of IX Troop Carrier Command were up all night assessing the requirements for the three divisions and it became clear that the available aircraft could only carry about half of the force in the first lift. Worse than that, the majority of the gliders would have to wait until the next day since there would not be enough daylight to fly two lifts on the first day. The decision to drop in daylight had been taken early on in the planning by Brereton, and it was now too late to change. The actual air lift worked out fairly evenly for all three formations in the end. 101st were given 494 C-47s, 82nd were given 530 and 1 Airborne together with the Corps Headquarters had 519. The US divisions had C-47s entirely, all from the troop carrier command, but 1 Airborne was given a mixture, in much the same way as 6 Airborne had been for Normandy. There were 149 American C-47s and another 130 from the RAF and these were all that were to drop parachutists, so the division was well behind the other two in the number of parachutists who would be carried on the first day. In addition to the C-47s there were 240 RAF bombers

all of which would tow a glider each, but they could drop parachutists if need be, though the numbers they could lift usually ruled this out as being uneconomical. So the divisional staff found that they could lift far more in the gliders than in the C-47s, and the unwritten rule that only C-47s dropped parachutists went unchallenged. A very pedestrian decision was then taken to fly in one parachute brigade and one air-landing brigade on the first day, together with divisional headquarters and a substantial number of jeeps, trailers and equipment, so that 1 Airborne was going to be light in men for the first 24 hours of the battle, whereas the American divisions were putting down three brigades each in the first lift and waiting for their support equipment until next day. They were proved to be right and the British were horribly wrong.

1 Airborne's air plan relied on three consecutive lifts to build up the divisional strength, they were to be as follows:

Sunday 17 September 1 Parachute Brigade and 1 Air-Landing Brigade were to drop and land on a combined drop zone and landing zone nearly seven miles to the west of the centre of Arnhem. The Air-Landing brigade was to hold the landing area and secure those landing zones needed for the drops the next day. All of these were in roughly the same area, to the west of the town, though they were a mile or more away. After that, it moved into the town to reinforce the troops on the bridges. 1 Parachute Brigade was to move directly to the road bridge and seize it as soon as possible; then the brigade was to set up a defensive position around the bridges and to the east of the town. In view of the distance of the objective from the drop zone the brigade was given the divisional reconnaissance squadron, who were carried in armed jeeps, to make a dash for the bridge as soon as their gliders landed. They had over seven miles to go, the first half of it through woodland and the latter part through a straggling built-up area of suburban housing, which thickened up as the town proper was reached and became confined streets with solid buildings on either side. It was all clearly visible on the air photographs.

Monday 18 September 4 Parachute Brigade were to drop onto another drop zone, a mile further from the town than that of 1 Brigade. The remainder of the equipment of 1 Air-Landing Brigade would be landed on another landing zone and finally there would be a resupply drop of con-

tainers onto yet another drop zone, all of them some distance from the original one. 4 Brigade was to move on foot and occupy the high ground to the north of Arnhem.
Tuesday 19 September 1 Polish Independent Parachute Brigade Group was on call to drop onto a small drop zone to the south of the road bridge from where it could be of help if there was any fighting around the bridge. If not, it was to cross the river and link up with 4 Brigade to the north of the town. At the same time there would be another resupply drop in the western area.

Not all of this plan was bad, and in view of the expected anti-aircraft defence around Arnhem it was wise from the point of view of the air planners to take the fewest possible risks, since they had to come back to the same places again and again on successive days. Yet someone might have reasoned that if the dangers from anti-aircraft guns were so great, then there must be men on the ground who were firing them and these same men might play a part in the ground fighting too; but there was great confidence and after all, the other divisions were taking equally great risks, particularly 'Jumping Jim' Gavin and the 82nd who were proposing to fight their way into Nijmegen after giving it plenty of advance warning, and after having fought one or two other battles before-

hand. So 1 Airborne was no worse off than any other part of the corps. But in one particular it was, and this was the fatal failure to put enough men on the ground in the first lift. The other two divisions were putting their infantry in straight away and relying on fighting men on the ground to take the objectives. 1 Airborne was only committing one brigade on the first day and not giving it any reinforcement until the end of the second day, over 24 hours later. One thing that had been learned in Italy and in France was that the Germans always reacted fast. They might not have much with which to react, but whenever they were caught off guard they picked themselves up and hit back almost immediately. They had also shown themselves to be masters of improvisation; all this was known from bitter battle experience and to give away 24 hours in which the enemy could react to a brigade-sized assault on a major communication junction was inviting trouble.

The whole operation started at 1330 hours on Sunday 17 September with a massive artillery bombardment in front of XXX Corps and the first ground troops moved forward. At the same moment the first aircraft were on their way to Holland and as the lifts arrived over their drop zones XXX Corps were making excellent progress northwards along the road. 101

Gliders of 101 Airborne landing near Zon. These gliders were carrying Division HQ and HQ troops (*US Army*)

Arnhem. 22 September 1944. Major-General Urquhart standing outside the Hartenstein Hotel (*IWM, London*)

Opposite: (*Above*) A troop carrier Huey ('Slick') dropping off a reinforcement party on a hill in the central highlands, Vietnam, 1971 (*US Army*)

(*Below*) Vietnam. A typical helicopter landing zone, with Huey troop carriers arriving and departing (*US Army*)

Airborne was dropped more or less accurately and in a short time was moving to its objectives.

The first lift was a massive air effort, with nearly 4,700 aircraft of all types. Preceding the troop carriers were the bombers, 1,400 of them had plastered German anti-aircraft guns and unit positions along the entire Market Garden route. Later in the morning came the troop-carriers, the tugs and the gliders, 2,023 of them in all, filling the sky in huge formations, and protecting the whole enormous armada were 1,500 fighters and fighter-bombers. It seemed to take hours for the planes to pass over any one point on the ground, and the troops of XXX Corps looked up in amazement. So too did the Germans, and not least

Colonel-General Student who had his headquarters between Eindhoven and Nijmegen and so had a ring-side seat for all the air activity. The sight of the endless stream of troop-carriers affected him deeply and in his memoirs he quotes himself as turning to his chief of staff and saying 'Oh, if ever I'd had such means at my disposal. Just once to have as many planes as this!' To which his implacable staff officer replied, 'General, we've got to *do* something!' And they set about planning their counter-attack. Student was astute enough to realize that such a huge force could only be attacking the bridges, but significantly, he never thought they would go as far as Arnhem.

The whole Battle of Arnhem has been

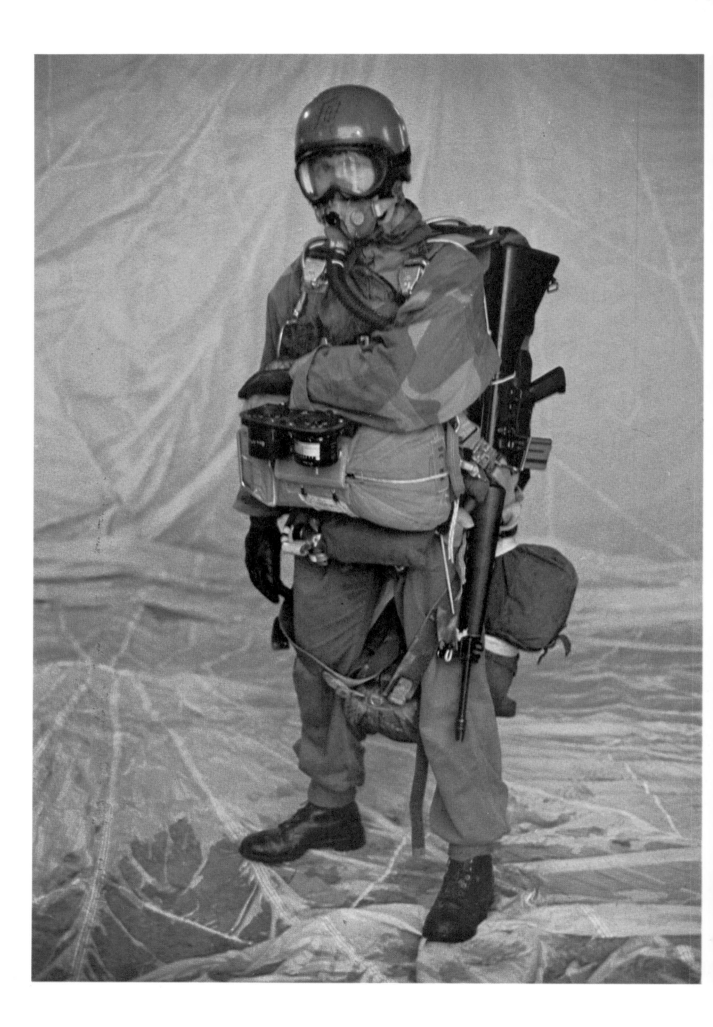

described too often for it to need detailed repetition here and this account will confine itself to the purely airborne aspects of what was predominantly a ground battle, as indeed is every airborne action once it has been delivered. Arnhem was unusual in that the air plan dominated the ground plan to a greater extent than normal, and in that lies its interest. The nearest division to XXX Corps, the 101st, dropped accurately and in a short time was moving on to its objectives. 506 Regiment found that the bridge at Zon had been blown but it crossed the canal and pressed on to Eindhoven where it met with the advancing Guards Armoured Division on the morning of the 18th. 502nd seized the second canal bridge at St Oedenrode within hours of landing and the Guards crossed that too on the 18th. At Veghel 501st had held on to the canal and river bridges against weak German counter-attacks and early in the morning of the 19th the Guards passed through there, moving quite fast, but not up to schedule. 101st now became a flank guard for XXX Corps and took little part in the remainder of the battle.

The Guards were now approaching 82nd divisional area. 504th had seized the Grave and Maas-Waal bridges, though there was still a fight for one of the latter. 505th took the Groesbeek Heights and held off German attacks, which started by evening and were supported by tanks. 508th marched to Nijmegen, but were bogged down in street fighting before they could get to the bridge. XXX Corps arrived that night and next day in one of the momentous and daring exploits of the war, one which ranks with any other for sheer bravery and determination, 3/504 battalion under the inspired leadership of young Major Julian Cook, made a daylight, opposed, river crossing in canvas assault boats and took the bridge. The way to Arnhem now lay clear ahead, but the Germans had had time to prepare, and the defences to the north of Nijmegen were thickening hourly. The operation was already behind schedule and now it began to go badly wrong.

At Arnhem 1 Airborne Division had been dropped accurately onto their drop zones and the three battalions had moved off exactly according to the divisional plan. 1st went north to hold the high ground, 2nd and 3rd went for the road bridge in the middle of the town with 3rd going direct and 2nd veering slightly to follow the river. Only the 2nd reached the bridge, under Lieutenant-Colonel John Frost, and they were immediately confined to the houses on the north side of it. 3rd Battalion was stopped by 9 Panzer Division and bogged down in the town and was soon forced to pull back. Armoured troops now closed in on Frost's force and tried to cross the bridge from the south bank. They were stopped.

The scene was then set for the remainder of the battle. At the bridge Frost and his force were isolated but were blocking the road; to the west the remainder of the brigade was turned back every time they probed forward and slowly the rest of the division were forced into a defensive pocket to the west of the suburb of Oosterbeek, separated from the bridges and the planned dropping zones. Radio communication within and without the division failed almost completely. Nobody, whether in or out of Arnhem, knew exactly what was going on, units were out of touch with each other and with their own brigade, and General Urquhart was himself trapped in a house for 48 hours while going forward to make contact with his forward units. In these conditions commanders returned to the World War I system of runners, and few of these got through. A very realistic replica of the fog of war fell on Arnhem and all the time Frost and his men held on against steadily mounting armoured attacks. This was when the rigid inflexibility of the air plan began to affect the outcome. Browning was near to Nijmegen, and unaware of the true position in Arnhem. There was no effective reserve except the Polish Brigade and the succeeding lifts were mounted from airfields scattered all over southern England. What Browning needed more than anything else was up-to-date information, yet there was no apparent way to get it. Also needed at that moment were sorties by reconnaissance fighters, or light aircraft, or any aircraft that could fly over the battle area and see what was happening. Better still if the aircraft could drop a couple of wireless sets and operators, then another link could have been opened. Nothing like this was done, and the Germans soon brought up enough light flak to discourage later attempts had they been tried. The aircraft only seem to have been used for the purposes of flying men to the area and providing some fighter support during the flight. There was no question of an airborne command post as was done at Corregidor with such spectacular success; the whole operation had a set-piece

(Opposite) A modern parachutist. A British SAS paratrooper fully equipped for a high altitude free-fall drop. He is carrying a small oxygen bottle and face mask, a variety of equipment bundles, a rifle, explosives and other specialized gear. He is wearing conventional parachuting uniform with a special-purpose fibre-glass helmet. He will drop as a member of a small party, probably at night, and perhaps many miles deep into enemy territory *(Photographers International)*

Arnhem. Glider pilots
street fighting (*IWM,
London*)

air of finality about it, and nowhere was this better exemplified than in the way that the resupply aircraft continued to drop containers on to drop zones that had been held by the Germans for days.

On Friday 21st, Frost was finally overrun at the bridge. His small force of highly trained and splendidly determined men had fought for three and a half days, having come prepared for a 48-hour battle. Within the narrow perimeter of the northern end of the bridge they had carried out the main task allotted to the entire division, and now they were reduced to an exhausted and bloodstained remnant, out of food, water, ammunition and medical aids. The German self-propelled guns and tanks from 9 and 10 Panzer Divisions finally overcame them by systematically shelling every house to ruin before the infantry moved in. About half the force were killed or wounded, Frost among them, and the other half were captured when they tried to make a fighting withdrawal; the very few who escaped were sheltered by the Dutch resistance and helped across the river during the next few days.

The turning point in the Arnhem battle was probably Tuesday, 19 September, when fog blanketed the English airfields where the Polish Brigade was waiting to emplane for Arnhem and caused a postponement for 24 hours. However on that day a Polish glider-borne anti-tank contingent landed west of Arnhem, onto a defended landing zone, and had no option but to join the divisional perimeter at Oosterbeek. The worst setback of that day was a resupply drop by 163 aircraft of 38 and 46 Group who flew with incredible bravery through heavy and accurate flak to drop 390 tons of badly needed ammunition and supplies onto a drop zone which was firmly held by the Germans, because the radio messages had failed to get through giving the position on the new drop zone.

The Polish Brigade, the only reserve force for 1 Airborne, had to wait for three agonizing days before they took off, and then it was in heavy cloud and rain. About half were turned back, but the other half dropped south of the river, in a hail of fire, and were unable to make any impression on the battle since there was no way for them to cross. By the 24th the position was impossible; XXX Corps had barely reached the Pole's perimeter and the decision was taken to pull out the survivors of 1 Airborne, if it could be done. The evacuation started the next night by which time some assault boats had been brought up and the last organized party crossed under sporadic fire just after dawn on the 26th. The front stabilized north of Nijmegen and there was no advance into Germany for another four months. The losses had been enormous. 1 Airborne was almost completely destroyed, and lost 7,578 out of a total strength of 10,005. 82 Airborne lost 1,432 and 101st 2,118. In the entire operation, including losses from ground troops and aircrew the number killed, wounded and missing was 13,974 while the Germans probably lost much the same number. It was, as Browning had presciently remarked to Montgomery on 10 September, 'A bridge too far'. It need not have been a bridge too far; the plan almost worked, and it could have been successful but for some unexpected and still largely unexplained failings. The plan was bold, and it was a time when boldness could still pay, though only if everything went right, for the German strength was rapidly growing. The weather played a significant part in delaying aircraft and obscuring the ground from those that did fly. The intelligence should have been better, and there is some evidence to show that there was such optimism that hard facts about German troops in the Arnhem area were disregarded. But the two crippling blows to the entire operation in Arnhem were firstly the failure to land enough troops on the first day, and secondly the inexplicable and totally frustrating loss of all radio communication. Without communications the British side of the battle was even slower than Blenheim or Waterloo and commanders at all levels were helpless. But despite the losses and the failures, it was the biggest air operation the Allies had mounted and it had worked. It proved that the airborne theory of warfare was effective and that big airborne operations were actually worth the enormous effort involved in mounting them. Arnhem was the apogee of the Allied airborne operations of the war, it was the biggest, the one which lasted the longest, and the one which got the most publicity – both then and now. It deserves it.

Battle of the Ardennes

Early in the morning of 16 December 1944 the Germans launched their last full attack on the Western Front, the Battle of the Ardennes. Late the following night the last German airborne assault of the war was dropped. When the Ardennes Offensive was being planned Colonel-General Student demanded to have a part

in it with his Parachute Army. After some prevarication he was given eight days in which to prepare a one-battalion parachute drop onto a cross roads eight miles to the north of Malmedy, where he was to open up a route for the advancing German army and also to block the road and hold off any attempt by the US army to reinforce to the south. The cross roads was on a high marshy heath known as the Hohes Venn and Student found that at best he could not expect to be able to fly more than 1,200 men to the drop zone. There would be no anti-tank weapons beyond the hand-held rocket launchers and Panzerfausts, and no heavier support weapons than could be packed into a container. It was expected that the relieving force would reach them in 24 hours, which gave them a good chance of being able to hold the objective by relying on the element of surprise to still be in their favour. If anything went wrong with the timetable the outlook was not good for the parachutists, since they would not be able to hold off a properly co-ordinated attack using infantry and armoured vehicles. However, there was much confidence on the German side that the timetable would not slip, indeed it *could not* be allowed to slip as it was crucial that the armoured columns reached the crossings of the Meuse before the Allies had sufficient time to react.

Student nominated one of his most experienced parachute commanders to lead the assault, Colonel von der Heydte, who had commanded 1 Battalion, 3 Regiment in Crete, but his men were rather less reliable. Hitler had taken a hand in their recruitment and had ordered the commander of every parachute regiment to send his hundred best men to von der Heydte's special battalion. The results were predictable and resulted in all the 'Bad Hats' and doubtful characters from the Parachute Army arriving at the same time. However, 250 men of von der Heydte's own regiment volunteered and joined him of their own volition. He did his best to lick the battalion into some sort of shape. The aircraft were 100 Junkers 52s who had last seen action at the Battle of Stalingrad. They were old, tired and not too reliable and their pilots were mainly young and inexperienced. The original plan was for a day drop, which at least gave some sort of chance that the aircraft could keep together and arrive at the drop zone at the same time, but von der Heydte was put under the command of General 'Sepp' Dietrich, commanding the Sixth

Bastogne. A supply glider in a bleak landscape (IWM, London)

Panzer SS Army and Dietrich insisted on a night drop on the first night, at a time when the Americans opposite would be alerted, and when the untrained force stood the least chance of success.

To compound the difficulties the weather worsened to strong winds and snow flurries. Nevertheless, with as much cheerfulness as they could muster the men went to their aircraft and took off from two airfields, Paderborn and Lippspringe, and flew west with the intention of converging over a large hill just ten miles from Malmedy. To help the green pilots there was a searchlight route marked in the moonless sky; even so a few managed to get lost, but after crossing the lines the straggling became appalling and planes were weaving and dodging about, being blown by the high winds and wandering off course through bad navigation. Von der Heydte's pilot was the one who had flown him into Crete, and his plane arrived over the drop zone on time, to find the flare markers exactly in place, having been dropped a few minutes before by a Messerschmitt fighter. About 15 Junkers followed their commander into the drop, though several failed to drop accurately. The drop zone was strewn with parachutists, many of them hurt, and three hours later there were no more than 100 at the

rendezvous. By morning about 350 had been mustered, and that was the total. There were no support weapons and no radios, as the signal platoon had all been dropped miles away. There were parachutists all over the American back areas, some as far as 20 miles away, and many were injured by dropping onto rocks and trees. Some were not found for months until the thaw revealed their bodies.

Undeterred, von der Heydte did what he could with his tiny force, but there was no question of holding up reinforcements or blocking the road. He split his men into small parties and laid ambushes or raided small units, but they were all rounded up after a few days and their actual contribution to the German offensive was very small. However, the scattered nature of the drop acted in the German favour in just the same way as the scattered drop in Normandy had done for the Americans, and the whole rear area was thrown into a state of alarm by exaggerated stories of parachutists dropping everywhere. For the second day of the offensive the US headquarters was in some doubt as to whether another airborne invasion had been launched on the same scale as Crete or Holland.

These invasion scares held up the reinforcing units who were made into a mobile reserve to combat the parachutists, but

30 December 1944. A crashed C-47 shot down while dropping supplies to the besieged 101 Airborne in Bastogne (*US Army*)

when it was seen that the menace was by no means as bad as expected, the men were released again and the gain to the German formations was only slight. Far more confusion was caused by the 30 or so men of Otto Skorzeny's Special Force who dressed in American uniforms and rode in jeeps around the US rear areas. Their reputation became so powerful that there was near panic and movement was continually held up by the need for perfectly bona fide troops to identify themselves.

When von der Heydte was captured it was the end of the German parachute operations. What had started with such a magnificent flourish and such overwhelming promise nearly five years before had withered away almost to nothing and in their final scene the last of the *fallschirmjaeger*, dirty, tired and cold, were led into captivity with hardly a whimper.

The only other airborne operations during the offensive were some particularly gallant American resupply drops and glider flights into the perimeter of Bastogne. The drop and landing zones were marked by pathfinders who parachuted in carrying beacons and despite losses from German flak the C-47s and Wacos kept the garrison supplied until the counter-offensive moved down and relieved them.

After the defeat of the Germans in the Ardennes it was necessary to keep the pressure on them to prevent them reorganizing and forming yet another coherent defence. On all fronts the Allied troops pushed steadily forward throughout the winter, and in the north the Reichswald Forest and the land up to the banks of the Rhine were cleared. It was from here that Montgomery proposed to make a bridgehead and sweep into Germany. By March 1945 there were 4,000,000 men in the Allied Expeditionary Force, and five Armies, one British and four American, lined up waiting to cross the Rhine. By a brilliant stroke First US Army took the Remagen Bridge, and so gained a bridgehead, but all the others were going to have to fight to cross. The main thrust was to be in the north, with Second British and Ninth US Armies, using the town of Wesel as the chief objective. The two armies could dispose of a huge force between them; it was no less than six armoured divisions, 17 infantry divisions, one specialized armoured division, equipped with such vehicles as mine-clearers, five independent armoured and one infantry brigade and a commando brigade. Despite this apparently overwhelming might Montgomery considered that he needed to use airborne troops to assist in the crossing.

Artillery men of 17
Airborne Division fitting
parachutes at Mourmelon
before taking off for the
Rhine crossing, 24 March
1945 *(US Army)*

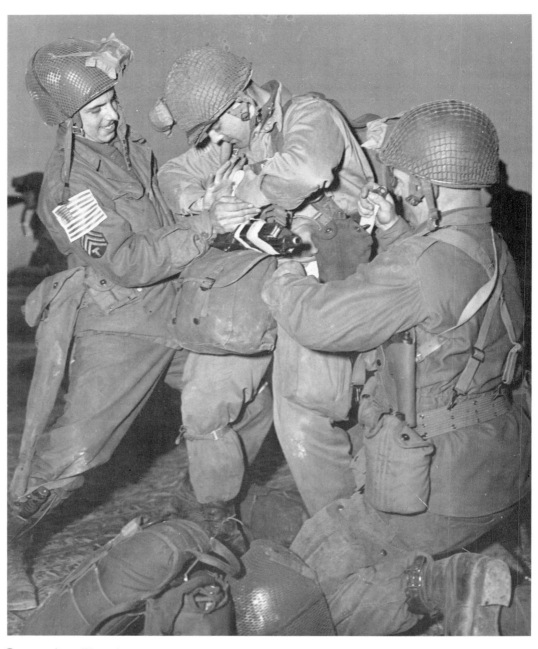

Operation Varsity

The responsibility for the airborne plan lay
with First Allied Airborne Army who gave
the task to XVIII Airborne Corps, commanded by Lieutenant-General Matthew
Ridgway and consisting of 6 Airborne and
17 Airborne Divisions. First Army then
set up a most comprehensive and elaborate
set of planning teams and staffs. The result
was the complete opposite to Market
Garden in almost every way. 'Varsity' as
the operation was called, was the best
planned and best executed airborne operation of the war, and perhaps it is no accident that it was the last. Indeed, it was
so well done that there are some who
maintain that it was not necessary at all,
and that the generals had been frightening
themselves with exaggerated ideas of the

German opposition to the crossing. But in
fact they had not, and the flak barrage
alone is sufficient indication of the prepared defences on the far banks, though
it was afterwards found that all the German units around Wesel were well below
strength and most were only at 30 per
cent. The general airborne plan was for
the two divisions to be dropped at the
same time on the far bank of the Rhine
and the task given to the Corps was 'To
disrupt the hostile defence of the Rhine
in the Wesel sector by the seizure of key
terrain, by airborne attack, in order to
deepen rapidly the bridgehead to be seized
in an assault crossing of the Rhine by
British ground forces, and facilitate the
further offensive operations of Second
Army'. To achieve this aim the Corps was

17 Airborne Division
assembling by their Curtiss
C-46 Commandos. Rhine
crossing, 24 March 1945
(*IWM, London*)

to seize the high, wooded ground immediately opposite the landing places.

There were various features of the plan that merit a quick survey, if only to show how clearly the lessons of Market Garden had been assimilated. The first and most important one is the time given to planning and the issuing of orders – in all it was about a month and it was remarkably thorough. Next, all the landing and dropping zones were to be within range of artillery sited on the west bank to obtain immediate support. Troops were to be dropped or flown on to their objectives, there were to be no long approach marches, nor any fighting through one objective and on to another. It was decided on a daylight drop and the glider troops were to be flown in onto battalion landing zones right alongside their particular target. Parachutists were to be dropped onto brigade drop zones actually on the objective. This would mean that the entire corps was proposing to land on defended landing and dropping zones, and in order to give the defenders the least possible time to react both divisions would be dropped simultaneously in one lift, with the least possible time between aircraft. Since the C-47 only carried twenty men this meant that there was going to be a very large number of planes in the air at the same time which it was hoped would swamp the anti-aircraft guns. These guns, and it was known that there were many

in the Wesel area, were also to be dealt with by counter-battery fire from the artillery and by continuous and spirited fighter ground-attack sorties right up to the moment when the transports were overhead.

After the landings the fighter support would continue, with forward air controllers on the ground with the airborne units, using aircraft radios to talk to the planes – a common enough practice now, but fairly new then. Resupply would be immediate and on to the same drop zones as the brigades had dropped on to, but careful radio arrangements were made so that any alterations of subsequent resupply drop zones could be passed to the squadrons well before take-off. Finally, and most importantly, the link-up with the ground forces would be on the same day.

The plan actually worked on these lines, and on 24 March 1945 the assault went in. It was a fine spring morning and almost 19,000 men were delivered on to four drop zones and four landing zones within the space of 40 minutes. 541 paratrooping C-47s took off, together with 1,050 glider tugs towing 1,350 gliders (300 of them were on double tow). Opposition was strong, the anti-aircraft guns that were undamaged after the preliminary strafing were able to open fire as the transports flew overhead, and all the landing and drop zones were covered by fire from concealed positions. Fifty-three aircraft were

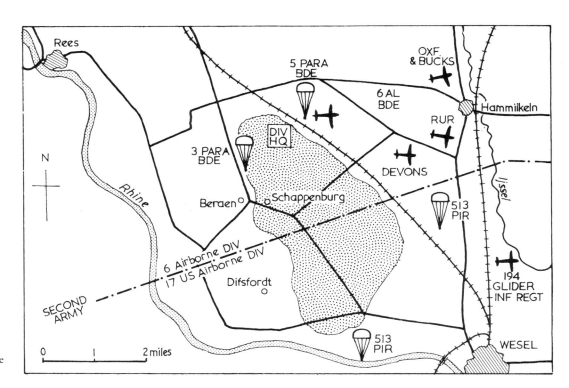

Rhine crossing 1945.
Caught in trees, a
paratrooper of 17 Airborne
Division *(US Army)*

shot down and a further 440 badly damaged, but all units reached their objectives, all the communications worked, and the losses were far lighter than had been expected. By 1500 hours the ground forces linked up and from then on Varsity ceased to be an airborne operation. The divisions passed under the command of the Second Army and fought on foot for the next few weeks in the rush across Germany.

One useful lesson that came out of Varsity was that a daylight assault against defended landing and dropping zones was possible provided that the landings took place in the shortest possible time, and were well supported by fighters. A number of lessons were learned about rallying and organizing troops on the drop zone when under fire, and it was found that the private methods of rallying so beloved of some commanding officers, such as blowing hunting horns or bugles, were quite useless because of the sound of firing and that smoke or flares were far better. It was also found that to try to rally on a prominent landmark such as an isolated wood or hill was inviting trouble as the enemy always knew the range to it and could bring artillery on to it with no loss of time. The losses in glider troops were heavy in some places, and it was concluded that the casualties were far less from parachuting onto defended areas than from landing

gliders. The moment a glider landed it became the target for every machine gun that could see it, and many were shot up before anyone could get out. Others were lost in the air as they flew in and several blew up when their petrol loads were hit by tracer bullets. Eight Locust light tanks were landed from Hamilcar gliders, but only two got into action in full working order. One was lost over the channel when its Hamilcar broke up in mid-air due to turbulence in the slipstream, one overturned on landing, one was set on fire and one was knocked out. Four reached the rendezvous, but two went little farther. It was the second time that tanks were actually flown into battle.

When the war with Germany ended 1 Airborne was reforming in England and was sent to Norway to take control of the country and disarm the German troops there. They returned to England in August and were disbanded on 15 November 1945. 6 Airborne went to the Middle East and then on to Palestine where they stayed until the withdrawal in 1947. The USA kept 82nd and 101st in Europe for some months, and they played their part in the operations in the closing stages of the war. 82nd finished up policing Berlin, and gradually all the other divisions were disbanded and absorbed into 82nd.

A Browning gun team crawling forward under fire on the drop zone. Rhine crossing (*IWM, London*)

Special Feature: British Airborne Forces

Less than three weeks after the evacuation from Dunkirk and the collapse of France the British Prime Minister, Winston Churchill, directed the War Office to investigate the possibility of forming a corps of at least 5,000 parachutists including a proportion of men from all the Dominions and some from France and Norway. He was anxious to take advantage of the summer to train these men so that they would still be available for Home Defence in the event of invasion.

Formation

It is usually thought that this historic minute is the basis for the British airborne force which still exists today, but in fact Churchill was 24 hours behind his Director of Military Operations who had opened the Central Landing School at Ringway in Manchester the day before, 21 June 1940. The school was asked to investigate the problems involved in the carriage of troops by glider and also in parachuting both men and equipment. Shortly after this the Air Ministry and War Office agreed to build four prototype gliders and conduct flight trials, after which they would select the most suitable. Parachute training started in July and on 6 August Churchill was told that 500 men were under training, but that there were no suitable aircraft for them to use. It was to become a familiar cry, heard with varying intensity for the next 30 years. In 1940 the school at Ringway had to be content with six Whitley bombers, obsolescent, uncomfortable and slow.

The Air Ministry was not convinced that parachuting was the best way to send troops to battle, and leant strongly towards gliders, though they had some naive ideas on the piloting of them. In assessing the type of operation that airborne forces were best suited to they decided that the proportion of parachutists to glidermen should be about one to nine, so only one-tenth of the force need be dropped, the remainder flying in in gliders. Quite what prompted this leaning towards gliders is no longer clear, but there was a definite feeling that unarmed transport aircraft should not drop parachutists, and the numbers of parachutists were therefore related to the armed bombers that could be spared to fly them. It was quickly discovered that bombers were almost useless for parachuting and those that had to be used were heartily disliked by all. The difficulty was that there was no suitable British troop transport and with the aircraft factories working flat out to build fighters and bombers there was no hope of there ever being one. Obsolete bombers were usually good enough for glider towing, though not all were even capable of doing that, and the British airborne forces had to wait until mid-1942 before the first American Douglas C-47 Dakotas arrived with the US army. The Dakota was ideal, a civilian airliner with plenty of space for 19 or 20 men, a good range, good speed and climb and both rugged and simple to maintain. It was a godsend, but it was also a bone of contention since there were never enough Dakotas to go round and the US formations rightly and properly looked upon them as their own. The major restriction on the size of the British airborne arm throughout World War II was the availability of transport aircraft. This is still a problem today. In 1940 and 1941 it was a constant complaint of the fledgling British airborne units, and it encouraged a steady trickle of querulous minutes from Churchill.

By the end of 1940 the 500 parachutists were still under training and were not expected to be ready until the following spring. No arrangements had been made to train any more parachutists, no role existed for them, no units had been allotted as glider troops, and so far there were no gliders. This was hardly surprising, for the danger of invasion still existed and priority in manpower and material was very much directed towards defending the United Kingdom. There was in fact no real idea as to how these airborne troops would or could be used once they were trained, and this problem was to remain unresolved until late in 1941.

But, while the staffs deliberated, the

training went on. The first parachutists were introduced to their new element from a small platform which replaced the rear gun-turret, at the extreme end of the Whitley. Standing on this flimsy piece of plywood, battered by the freezing slip-stream, the unhappy pupil was plucked off backwards when his instructor reached out and pulled his ripcord for him. From this terrifying beginning the class went on to jump through a hole in the floor of the plane, as this was the only practical way to get a man out of the cramped fuselage, because the door was far too small. Landing training used the same forward roll as did the Germans, simply because no-one had time to think of any other method. Luckily the professional physical training instructors quickly devised what has now become the standard parachute landing fall all over the world in which the shock of landing is absorbed over the side and back by rolling sideways and round in a controlled fall. The injury rate went down noticeably.

Selection and Training

The selection system was very similar to that used by any other nation, though in the early days of 1940 there was only the German pattern to follow. All men were volunteers and came, not without protests from their commanding officers, from any unit of the army. All were sent to what soon became the Depot of Airborne Forces, Hardwick Hall, near to the Parachute School at Ringway. At Hardwick Hall the volunteers underwent two weeks of intensive, almost harsh, physical training with the simple object of weeding out the weak and poorly-motivated. The failure rate was always quite high at this stage, but the standard was never lowered, despite one or two attempts to do so from various directions.

After Hardwick Hall the next stage was the actual parachute training at Ringway. Ringway was the pre-war aerodrome for Manchester and most of the training took place in converted hangars. Unlike many other countries the British parachutist never packed his own parachute, and so the training course could concentrate on the techniques of jumping, controlling the canopy in the air, and the landing. Two weeks was all that was needed for this and it was very nearly as strenuous as the time at Hardwick Hall. One piece of apparatus which often failed otherwise good men was the fan. The fan was a mock jumping tower about 30 feet high set up in the hangar against a wall. The pupil climbed up

Two Whitley sticks being inspected. Late 1940 or early 1941. The men are wearing ordinary battle-dress, high boots and leather helmets, though some have ordinary boots and gaiters. The shrouded tail-wheel of the Whitley can just be seen (*IWM, London*)

117

One of the first parachute exercises, late 1940. Unloading a container (*IWM, London*)

and stood on a tiny platform above the ground, and hooked on a skeleton harness. From the harness ran a wire, up over a pulley and down on to a small drum where it was wound on by the instructor. There were small paddle wheels on the axle of the drum and it was perfectly free to revolve; the only braking effect which slowed the man's fall was the air resistance on the paddles. At first sight it looked dangerously inefficient, but it was perfectly safe and lowered the heaviest man quite gently. However, the newcomer had no way of telling that and to step off into space was a test of nerve that some found too much for them.

The jumping programme started at the end of the first week with two balloon jumps and was followed in the second week by five aircraft descents, two with a weapon or a leg-bag and one, at least, by night. After that the pupil was a trained parachutist and qualified for a small increase in pay together with the right to wear blue and white cloth wings on his right sleeve just below the shoulder.

Ringway was not the only training centre, though it was the largest and the most famous. The statistics of training at Ringway are remarkable, over 400,000 descents made by parachute and just over 60,000 men trained between 1940 and 1945. There was another and very similar centre at Kabrit in Egypt where 6 Airborne Division trained its local recruits, and another in India at Chaklala. Neither of these subsidiary schools achieved any-

thing like the output of Ringway but they served to keep men in practice and to provide a steady flow of trained recruits to the divisions.

By the end of 1940 just over 2,000 descents had been made at Ringway using the six Whitleys, but it was obvious that this was too slow a pace. In April 1941 the peculiarly British invention of balloon jumping was introduced. By taking five men and a despatcher in a car below a large balloon the training could be speeded up enormously, and the flight instruction could be much more personal since the pupil could hear his instructor shouting from the ground. The method is still used in Britain, though no other country has seen fit to try it. Those who can afford to, or who enjoy reasonably settled and predictable weather, prefer to use aircraft.

Clothing and Equipment

Throughout this early formative period there was much experimenting with clothing and equipment, most of which was patterned on that of the Germans. The first trainees wore leather flying helmets and a copy of the German overall. After a few weeks the helmet was changed for a strange-looking canvas helmet with a thick pad of sorbo rubber round it. This was extremely comfortable and effective, but was useless in battle and in time a rimless pot-shaped steel helmet was made, held by a three-point leather strap with chin cup. Even so, the sorbo headgear continued to be used by trainees. The

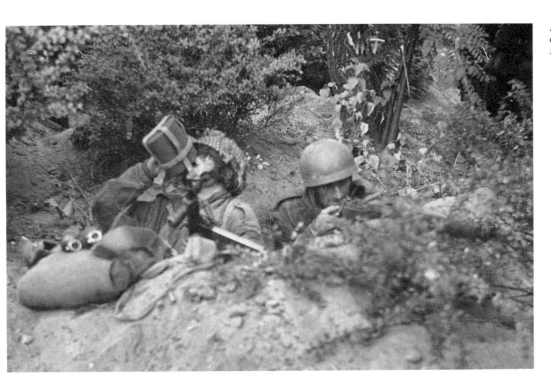

Arnhem. A position on the edge of a wood (*IWM, London*)

German overall with its shaped legs and snap fasteners was not replaced until November or December 1941 when the familiar and still surviving Denison smock became standard airborne issue. Even the German idea of using side-laced boots was tried, and immediately dropped. From then on British airborne troops wore the same boots as the rest of the army though they gave precious little ankle support for hard landings.

One great problem was how the man could carry sufficient equipment, since he had to drop through a hole only three feet in diameter in the floor of the Whitley and when wearing a parachute there was little room for any other bulk. One idea was to do without the conventional webbing equipment and carry everything in the smock pockets, and to this end there was an experimental issue of trousers with leather-lined pockets which were meant to be strong enough to take ammunition. Weapons had to be dropped in containers carried under the wings, and it was already obvious from Crete that the delay in collecting a container could be fatal to the entire unit, but until the Dakota became a reality in 1942 there was no other way of getting weapons larger than a pistol or sub-machine gun down to the dropping zone. With the Dakota came the introduction of door-jumping and immediately a completely new horizon was opened up. One interesting change was that the number of refusals in training went down sharply; it was far less frightening to jump

through a door than to drop through a little hole in the floor. The next change was that the man could carry much more equipment with him, and from 1943 onwards it became commonplace to take kitbags as well. By 1945 the British parachutist was carrying heavier loads than any other in the world, though he may not have been particularly happy doing it.

Organization

The first parachute unit actually appeared at Ringway in the middle of 1940. This was No 2 Army Commando and all men in it who had accepted parachute training were fully trained by the start of 1941. In August the unit became a battalion, and in September 1941 was named 1 Parachute Battalion, and incorporated into 1 Parachute Brigade. The idea of enlarging the airborne troops into brigades originated in May 1941 when it was decided to form two of them, one in the United Kingdom and one in the Middle East, together with a glider force sufficient to lift 10,000 men and their equipment. The RAF agreed to provide ten bomber squadrons for troop transport and glider-towing. The gliders were to be made by civilian non-essential industry so that they did not interfere with the vital flow of aircraft from the factories of the established makers. By mid-1941 the trickle of trained parachutists was gathering impetus and the lesson learned in Crete had changed the views of many of the sceptics. From now on fewer and fewer obstacles were put in the way of the

The discomfort of war. A group of 2 Para Regt having an early morning shave on a Tunisian hillside. December 1942 (*IWM, London*)

A contrast in styles. Watched by a well-wrapped Montgomery, Major-General Matthew Ridgway congratulates Brigadier James Hill after presenting him with an award for his part in the Rhine crossing (*IWM, London*)

Rhine crossing, 1945. Pulling a 20mm AA gun away from a wrecked Horsa. This picture brings out vividly the dangers which faced the pilot and co-pilot in any crash landing (*IWM, London*)

new airborne ideas: confidence was growing.

In October 1941 1 Air-landing Brigade was formed from a brigade which had just completed mountain training, and so was accustomed to moving with lightweight equipment. There were no gliders for this brigade, and the concept of its use foresaw that the troops might just as often be delivered by aircraft landing on an airfield as the Germans had done, hence the name 'Air-landing' rather than 'Gliderborne'. It was a substantial force, with four infantry battalions and supporting arms and from the start it was realized that there would never be enough aircraft to carry all the units in one lift. One question that needed investigation was the best way of delivering such a force in successive groups, and how best to organize those groups. At this time the War Office still thought that there would be little difficulty in flying troops into battle as air-landed units, and that very little special training would be needed. To some extent this was true, and still is today, but while it may make only small differences to the job of the individual infantryman, air-landed operations make a tremendous difference to the way the force is supported and supplied. Artillery support may be only minimal, and ammunition may run short. There is no line of communication up which more men and more ammunition come, and down which the wounded and the tired go. The fighting is on all sides and movement is rarely any quicker than that of a marching man. All of this was dimly realized, but nobody had actually examined it or tried to work out how to overcome the difficulties.

Further Developments

With two parachute brigades being formed and an air-landing brigade already in exist-

ence there was an obvious need for some higher formation to look after them and control them, and on 29 October Major-General F.A.M. (Boy) Browning was given command of all airborne forces, and his headquarters was designated as 1 Airborne Division. In the following month another significant step occurred. The US Military Attaché in London was a close friend of Major-General Browning and showed the new divisional commander the latest plaything which the US army had sent over. It was the first jeep ever to arrive in England. Two days later it was being loaded into a mock-up of a Horsa glider at Ringway. To everyone's relief it fitted, and Browning knew that his division could be mobile on the ground.

By December 1942 1 Airborne Division was just about up to strength and had tried some small operations, notably the Bruneval raid in February. But despite the steady recruitment when 1 Parachute Brigade was sent to North Africa in September, it had to be made up to strength with cross-postings from 2 Parachute Brigade. The first Horsa gliders appeared in spring 1942 and the summer was spent in learning how to load and fly them. The RAF were particularly anxious to find a suitable towing aircraft since the Whitley could not manage a loaded glider. The Air Ministry and the War Office had settled on two types of glider. The smaller one, the Horsa, carried 28 fully equipped men or a jeep and a 75mm gun, or similar trailer load. It was ugly, ungainly and rather heavy, but it performed magnificently in all weathers from Norway to India and was even used by the US airborne forces on some occasions. With the next glider the British scored a notable triumph. This was the Hamilcar, the largest wooden aircraft to be built during

World War II and the only glider ever to go into service anywhere in the world that could lift an armoured fighting vehicle.

Development after 1942

The development of airborne techniques became so rapid during 1942 that it cannot be covered in detail here. By 1943 the Glider Pilot Regiment had been formed, with the express intention of providing the pilots for the air-landing units. There had been much experimenting with dropping techniques, though the variety of RAF aircraft did little to help this sort of research, and the personal equipment and armament of the individual men had been settled upon. The airborne units began to look more professional and complete and the air of improvisation that had been present in 1941 and early 1942 largely disappeared. Recruitment was not as fast as had been hoped, and the standard of the volunteers was rather low, but the strength of the units steadily increased and expertise improved.

Despite the shortages and difficulties, the chiefs of staff considered that airborne divisions were worthwhile and on 23 April 1943 the formation of another division was authorized to be known as 6 Airborne Division. The 6th was to become as well known as the 1st, and more than made up for its late birth. It was formed by an inspiring and talented leader, Major-General 'Windy' Gale and got off to a flying start with 3 and 5 Parachute Brigades and 6 Air-landing Brigade. It was intended to be the Middle East Division, though in fact it spent the major part of the war in

Europe and only went east as a division in 1945.

The 50 Indian Parachute Brigade had been formed at Delhi in October 1941 and by 1943 was well up to strength, but with no aircraft available to carry it the brigade was committed to land operations in Burma in 1943. Early in 1944 it was decided to expand it to a division, and 44 Indian Airborne Division was formed with two parachute brigades and one air-landing brigade. It was never to operate as a division in the airborne role, although there was an idea in 1945 to form an airborne corps with 44 and 6 Divisions in readiness for the expected campaign to force the Japanese back to their homeland.

These divisions were not the only airborne troops serving in the British army. In addition there was the Polish Parachute Brigade, which fought magnificently at Arnhem and the Special Air Service Brigade which included, besides two British SAS regiments, two French battalions, a Norwegian, a Dutch, and a Belgian parachute company. In all the brigade contained about 2,000 men and was rather more mobile than a normal parachute battalion, though not so well supplied with heavy weapons.

By 1945 the three divisions and the independent brigades and units totalled just under 40,000 men most of whom had been delivered to battle by air at some time or other. A year later that total strength was halved and 18 months after that it was halved again. By 1950 it was down to about 3,000 each in Britain and India. It stayed at that for the next 25 years.

Modern British paratroops. A mass drop by the Parachute Regiment on exercise 'Deep Furrow' in Turkey, September 1973 (*Crown Copyright*)

7 Far East 1950s

Vietnam

It is not too much of an exaggeration to say that the country we now know as Vietnam has been the cradle of the post-war theory and practice of the air-mobile and airborne operation. This trend started in the late 1940s with the French use of air-transported troops and continued through the late '60s and '70s when the US army brought in the true air-mobile division and its helicopters. The reason for this concentration of innovative effort is that Vietnam has been almost continuously at war since 1940; first it was the Japanese, then the French, then the Viet Minh or Vietcong, then the Americans. Whoever the enemy, the result has been sickeningly familiar: a devastated country, a shattered government and a scattered and demoralized population. This unhappy process continued with increasing emphasis after 1945, by which time the Viet Minh, or communist movement, had gained most of the support in the country and had set up a form of government. This was all knocked on the head when the French returned and took control of what they considered to be their rightful colony.

The Viet Minh objected and the differences soon came to be too deep to be settled by other than fighting and the Viet Minh took to the hills and became a guerrilla force, working with the support and encouragement of Red China, just across the northern border. The French army in Vietnam was poorly supported from home and was at all times short of essential equipment and supplies. The numbers of actual Frenchmen in the ranks was never much higher than 30 per cent, the remainder being locally recruited Vietnamese or foreigners serving in the Foreign Legion. In 1950 the proportion was 65,000 French in the Expeditionary Force whose total was 152,000, with a further 120,000 locally recruited Vietnamese units. By 1952 the French figures were 51,000 out of a total of 192,000, and early in 1953 the French government imposed a cut of 20,000 on the Expeditionary Force bringing it down to just over 170,000 at which

it stayed until the end. The navy and air force are included in the numbers of Frenchmen, so that the army share was even less than appears at first glance. The quality was therefore variable, but at the core of the army were the French Mobile Columns and the parachute battalions, though many men in these were foreigners too. The French government never allowed French conscripts to go to Vietnam, and the war was fought on a shoestring. As can be imagined, this did little for good morale among the rank and file.

The parachutists were all regulars and almost without exception they were veterans of World War II from the Free French units in the British army, or, as has often been hinted, from men who had served in the German *Fallschirmjaeger* and who had joined the Legion because they could find no other way to earn their living. Certainly German was a common language in the Legion at that time, but it had always been fairly common even before the war, so this may not be as powerful an indicator of nationality as some have tried to imply. The fact is that whatever their background, the men of the parachute battalions were tough, well trained, professional fighters. But they were inadequately equipped and only barely adequately armed by the standards of the day. Support weapons were few, signals equipment and radios were elderly and not entirely reliable, and worst of all the aircraft were not only few but also antiquated. The best that the French could muster were some Junkers-52s seized from the Germans in 1945, and these they positioned at Hanoi. It speaks volumes for the Junkers that these planes kept going, despite the fact that most of them had already fought one war and must have been at the limit of their designed life.

The load-carrying limitations of the Junkers were so severe that for most of the parachute operations the troops had to jump into action with only very light scales of weapons and ammunition, but fortuna-

Opposite: (*Above*) British parachutists in a C-130 Hercules. The white nets are part of the safety harness holding the man into his seat (*COI*)

(*Below*) German parachutists in 1977. Men of 272 Fallschirmjaeger Battalion of 27 Luftlande Brigade (*Photographers International*)

A reinforcement drop in the hill country north of the Hanoi Plain. A stick coming out of a C-47. The drop zone beneath them is marked with abandoned canopies blowing in the wind. About 1950 (*Établissement Cinématographique et Photographique des Armées*)

A typical para machine gun post. This could be anywhere in Indo China, and could be any time during the French occupation. The man with binoculars is wearing canvas jungle boots, which were not normal issue in Indo China, and the man well down in the pit is carrying a packet of cigarettes in the strap of his helmet. The weapons are a mixture of French and American (*EC et PA*)

tely in a guerrilla war this was all that was needed in the early stages. Most of the action in the first two years took place in the northern part of the country within easy range of Hanoi so that the JU-52s could fly to and from the drop zone without refuelling.

With so few troops the French were hard-pressed to contain a guerrilla war and they quickly adopted the technique of fortifying selected strong points and patrolling from them. The Viet Minh easily by-passed these firm bases and controlled the outlying countryside, particularly at night. As time went on and the Viet Minh grew stronger they picked off the smaller posts one by one and ambushed the roads. The French were increasingly pulled into a war where the initiative lay with the enemy and most of the fighting took place on ground and at times chosen by him. It is all very similar to what happened fifteen years later when the US army found that it had committed itself to the same course, with similarly predictable consequences. The parachute force was used to reinforce the small garrisons that were attacked, and to extricate them if the battle went against them. They also jumped in to mount counter-attacks, or in rare cases to make surprise sweeps into the middle of a Viet Minh-held area.

The French airborne troops were used in almost exactly the way that the US army used its air-mobile formations in the later war, with one vital exception; with their helicopters the Americans could extricate units which were in trouble. For the French parachutists the only way out was on foot.

French Operations in Vietnam

There is no point in attempting to recount all the actions in which parachutists were used during the French Indo-China War. The French records show that there were in all no less than 156 separate and identifiable operations ranging in size from a small patrol to a brigade, but it will help to catch the flavour of the type of war that was fought if we briefly examine a few of the occasions when the airborne arm was used. The first use of a battalion was on 27 May 1950 when one was dropped to recapture the small outpost of Dong Khe which had been taken by a surprise assault the day before. The drop zone was a large jungle clearing on top of a hill out of range of Dong Khe and there was no opposition as the drop was totally unexpected. Rallying quickly the battalion assaulted the post and after a fierce fight recaptured it before nightfall. A mobile column moved quickly up the road and relieved them within 24 hours. The next large operation was in October of that year when the guerillas under General Giap launched a large assault on several points along the Cao Bang ridge, north-east of Hanoi. They took two key posts and the garrisons were

A much larger drop, probably a battalion operation. The drop zone has been secured by an earlier drop, and the men in the foreground arrived with that and took up positions around the edges. Red River plain, 1950 (EC et PA)

127

Opposite: *(Above)* Dien Bien Phu. Shellfire. Running for cover *(EC et PA)*

(Below) The seizure of Dien Bien Phu. A paratrooper carrying his MI carbine walking past the bodies of Viet Minh soldiers on the edge of the drop zone *EC et PA)*

forced to retreat in some disorder, closely pursued by six elated Viet Minh battalions. One parachute battalion was hurriedly alerted and dropped in the path of the Viet Minh to allow the garrisons to get clear, which they did, but the parachutists lost 80 per cent of their men, a virtual wipe-out of a complete unit. A few days later another battalion was dropped as part of the same rescue operation to clear a road in front of the retreating force, and this they managed to do without too many losses.

For the next year the battalions were continually in one action or another, most of these being pure reinforcement operations, but on 14 November 1951 there was a genuine brigade-sized offensive assault. This was the seizure of the town of Hoa Binh, which was a route centre in the middle of a flat plain 20 miles in front of the French fixed positions and a commanding position from which the Laotion border could be controlled. The brigade was flown in and dropped as close as possible to the town and with a quick assault the surprised defenders were pushed out and fled into the fields. A strong ground column moved up later in the day and relieved the parachute brigade, which then became part of the garrison. This was unfortunate because many of the parachutists were still in Hoa Binh when it was invested by the Viet Minh some months later, and a large number were lost in the stiff fighting which followed the forced withdrawal of the French garrison.

By 1952 the aircraft position improved, but it was not before time since the Junkers were by then on their last legs and becoming highly unreliable, not least from shortage of spares. There were now some ex-World War II C-47s from the USA and in late 1952 the French were able to buy a small number of new C-119 Flying Boxcars. At no time did the transport force exceed 75 machines, and for much of the war it was about 50. These were flown unceasingly, supplying the distant posts in hostile territory, running a shuttle service to those with an airstrip, and launching the various air assaults. The French aircraft industry had still not recovered from the effects of the war, and practically every other available transport plane was involved in Korea. The Korean War badly affected the supply of modern equipment to the French, and this was no more acutely felt than in the provision of aircraft; the USA was not keen to support what it considered to be a colonial war and

it was some time before it was realized that both the UN and the French were fighting the same enemy. By then the commitment to Korea was too deep to allow much more than a trickle of supplies to Vietnam. In fact the Viet Minh were supplied by Red China with more up-to-date US equipment, captured in Korea, than the French could get legitimately from the United States.

In the middle of 1953 there was one highly successful airborne raid which helped to restore the rather flagging morale of 'Les Paras' and also the planning staff. 'Operation Hirondelle' was what the US army later came to call a 'search and destroy' mission into the high ground to the north-east of the Red River delta. This was the area that had been lost to the Viet Minh three years before in the action along the Cao Bang ridge, and it had bitter memories for the survivors. Three battalions were dropped close to Lang Son where there were substantial stocks of supplies, weapons, ammunition and fuel stored in caves and quarries in the hills. These dumps were all completely destroyed and so were some vehicles. The brigade then made its way back to the coast, clearing the ground of any warlike material as it went, and was picked up by coastal boats of the navy two days later. It was a well planned and well executed operation undertaken with the primary objective of disabling another Viet Minh offensive, but with a secondary one of demonstrating to the Americans that the French forces were capable of decisive action and therefore worth supporting with arms and material.

By this time there were some helicopters in Vietnam, not many, but sufficient for minor operations and one valuable use of them was to act as an airborne reconnaissance patrol for road convoys. Helicopters were good for spotting ambushes ahead of the convoy, though there were so few that this task was often done by light fixed-wing aircraft too. The Viet Minh were now so strong that they virtually controlled all the roads outside the actual French garrison areas, and any military movement was likely to be ambushed at any time.

The Siege of Dien Bien Phu

Unfortunately, just as the French were beginning to receive sizeable supplies of American aid and were being accepted as co-fighters in the struggle against communism the whole French military effort

was brought to its knees by the siege of Dien Bien Phu. This isolated town was captured by a brigade drop on 20 November 1953 and quickly consolidated by a ground force. It was then fortified and the Viet Minh slowly closed in, cutting the roads and forcing the garrison to rely on air supply. However, as there were two airstrips the French were not worried and in fact they hoped that the Viet Minh would batter themselves to pieces in making frontal assaults against their dug-in positions. But the Viet Minh were more skilful and mounted a series of diversionary attacks all over Vietnam, exhausting the French and wearing out the mobile reserve. Meanwhile they steadily brought artillery in from China and dug the guns into well concealed positions overlooking the garrison. Worse still, they brought in whole regiments of anti-aircraft guns of all sizes, and prepared to isolate Dien Bien Phu from the air as well as the ground.

By January 1954 the French air force in Vietnam still had only 75 transport aircraft which were totally committed to supplying 15 garrisons, three of which were entirely dependent on the air for all supplies and reinforcements. Chief among these three was Dien Bien Phu where the pressure was mounting and though 25 more planes arrived in February the transport fleet was still dangerously overextended. American aid was sent in the form of extra maintenance staff and equipment, but this was only a partial relief and all aircraft were worked to the limit. As Dien Bien Phu became invested the airstrip came under fire; by mid-March the only way to send in supplies was to use parachutes and on the 14th a battalion jumped in to reinforce. Another arrived by the same route on 4 April and a third on the 7th. By that time the perimeter was so small that about 20 per cent of all resupply drops landed among the Viet Minh and there was no way of getting the wounded out as even the light aircraft could no longer come in through the anti-aircraft barrage.

Desperate to hold on to what was now an obviously doomed garrison the French continued to drop battalions into the perimeter. Two companies were dropped on 11/13 April and the remainder of that battalion on 2 May. On 7 May it was all over and the Viet Minh accepted the surrender of the garrison; 11,000 men went into captivity, 30 or 40 per cent of whom were parachutists. It was the end of French rule in Vietnam, and all but the end of the parachutists. There had never been more than 12 battalions of parachutists in Vietnam at the best of times, and it was generally eight. Seven of these were sent into Dien Bien Phu, and none came back. It says much for the morale of the troops that of the few who remained most went to

Dien Bien Phu, the siege. Reinforcements being dropped into the shrinking perimeter, anxiously watched by the defenders. The C-47 circles in the distance to come in for another pass *(EC et PA)*

Algeria and joined the battalions there to fight a similar sort of war in a very different environment.

The French used their airborne troops in Vietnam with considerable skill and ruthlessness. The casualties were always heavy, but this was not allowed to make any difference. Had there been more fighter and reconnaissance aircraft it is very likely that the parachutists would have been even more successful and certainly their losses would have been lower, particularly in the fighting retreats and counter-attacks where they were so frequently used. The final sacrifice at Dien Bien Phu must not be allowed to cloud the picture since it was completely against normal French tactics to go on reinforcing failure to that extent. Unfortunately it became a political fixation and once past a certain point there was no way out at all. On the credit side it was clearly demonstrated how quite a small transport fleet could make an enormous difference to the mobility and capability of an army, and that light aircraft and helicopters were essential for reconnaissance. Later, in Algeria, these airborne methods were refined and adapted to make greater use of helicopters, but it was also shown in Vietnam that lavish supplies and support are not necessary for an airborne war against guerillas, though they do make it easier. For a demonstration of economy, thrift and quick planning the airborne operations in Vietnam are hard to beat. The pity is that they were in the end unsuccessful.

Korea

The Korean War began in 1950 and it was not long before the US army found it necessary to use airborne troops, and employed them in the traditional and correct way. After the initial invasion of South Korea by the North, and the retreat of the South Korean army, there was a turn-around and the United Nations forces — which at this stage were almost entirely American and South Korean, surged northwards over the border and on the Yalu river. From there they had to retreat once again and come back to the south of the original border. However, on the way to the Yalu, with spirits high and visions of chasing the North Koreans right out of the country, there were several attempts to use parachute troops in front of the UN advance to disrupt the North Korean lines of retreat. The largest drop was in October 1950.

The 11 Airborne Division was moved to Japan as soon as the war started and when the operation was planned they moved across to Korea to hurriedly prepared mounting bases on dirt airstrips where they waited with their tactical transport aircraft for the word to go. The 187 Regimental Combat Team was chosen for the drop and at that time it was about 3,500 strong. A regimental combat team (RCT) was roughly equivalent to a brigade, having three infantry battalions and all the supporting arms and services to enable it to act independently of its divisional headquarters for quite long periods. The idea had originated in World War II and was retained for some years afterwards. Indeed it still exists under another name for practically all airborne brigades in all armies are well able to operate on their own, just as the regimental teams were designed to do.

On 22 October 187 RCT was dropped on to two separate drop zones about 25 miles north of Pyongyang, the North Korean capital, and astride two main roads and a railway line. Tactically the operation was not decisive, though it was in the proper tradition for parachute forces, but the advance was so rapid that the troops were scarcely in position before the ground elements caught up with them. However the actual airborne side was impressive. It was the first time that the C-119 tail-loading aeroplane had been used operationally and it was the clearest possible case for scrapping all the old side-door aircraft straight away. The US air force had been steadily re-equipping with the C-119 for some time before 1950 and for the Pyongyang drop they were able to muster

Korea. November 1957. A C-54 Globemaster being refuelled. C-119 Fairchild Packet flying overhead. This machine had become the standard parachuting aeroplane of the US forces by the time of the Korean war (*US Air Force*)

131

80 of them. These 80 carried all the men
and to supplement them there were 40
C-47 Dakotas whose job was to drop
ammunition and supplies only. The drop
went down with copy-book precision and
the aircraft returned for a second and third
lift in which they dropped twelve 105mm
howitzers, four 90mm guns, four 3-ton
trucks, 39 jeeps, 38 trailers and 584 tons
of assorted ammunition on to the two drop
zones before the end of the day. It was
a staggering display of the advances in airborne techniques since 1945, and it was
the first time that such quantities of heavy
support weapons and vehicles had been
parachuted in one operation. Naturally
there was no opposition from the North
Koreans throughout this display of aerial
might, either on the ground or in the air,
and the troops could take their time in
clearing the drop zones of the piles of
ammunition and supplies that were
stacked on them.

Next year the 187th repeated the operation in another part of Korea during a
brief northward push by the UN. The pattern was the same, as were the results.
This time no less than 3,300 men were
dropped together with weapons and
ammunition in the same quantity as the
year before. Once again C-119s were used
to fly the men, and once again the older
wartime aircraft were used to carry the
ammunition and supplies. This time the
C-47s were missing, perhaps because they

were needed elsewhere, or perhaps because
they could not carry enough. In any case
this drop was unusual in that C-46 Curtiss
Commandos were flown on the supply
missions in what must have been their last
operational use.

The only other use of airborne troops
in Korea was the dropping of small parties
of sabotage troops who cut railways or shot
up designated enemy troop centres on
much the same lines as the SAS had done
in the Western Desert or the SOE had
done in France. Unfortunately these small
raids were not particularly successful as
the Koreans were not much concerned by
having a railway line cut. They merely set
several hundred coolies to work to rebuild
the line so that it was generally working
again within 24 hours; meanwhile the
sabotage party was being vigorously pursued. The country was so inhospitable, as
were the inhabitants, that very few of these
small parties survived and the idea was
dropped as being uneconomical.

Malaya

At the same time, the early 1950s, the
British army was fighting a long and tiring
campaign against communist terrorists in
Malaya. These terrorists lived in the
jungle and the British used the same techniques as the Chindits had used in Burma
in 1944. Long-range patrols walked into
the jungle and took the terrorists on at
their own game on their own ground. The

Korea. October 1950. Men
of the 187 RCT boarding
a C119 for the drop behind
North Korean Lines. The
personal equipment is little
changed from 1945 except
for the frame carriers slung
under the reserve
parachute. The man
struggling up the ladder
has a 3.5in rocket launcher
(*US Army*)

A Browning machine gun team, from a locally recruited parachute battalion, on guard at the edge of a village in North Indo-China. They have a mixture of French and American weapons (*EC et PA*)

Opposite page: (*left*) An Italian parachutist about 1941/42. He is wearing a pot-shaped helmet covered in camouflage scrim and attached by a copy of the German three-point strap. His long overall is a fairly close copy of the German design also, although the thin leather belt and fighting knife are typically Italian. His Baretta submachine-gun would be carried in a canvas weapon container when jumping and he would probably wear thin rubber knee-pads.
(*centre*) An officer of the Folgore Division, dressed in much the same way as the trooper behind him

(*right*) A Sergeant of the Folgore Division, wearing a M 1943 field uniform, here worn with regimental collar patches and cuff band which reads, *Per L'onore d'Italia (Painting by Mark MacGregor from* Naval Marine and Air Force Uniforms of World War II *by Andrew Mollo—Blandford Press*)

(*below*) Japanese parachutist, about 1942. He is wearing a cloth covered helmet with characteristic full-covering sides and chin strap. His long overall is inspired by the German original and he wears special high leather jump boots. His bandoliers of ammunition would be packed in to a chest pack for the actual descent, as would be his folding rifle. In the latter years of the war the distinctions in the parachutist's uniform largely disappeared, to the extent of even wearing canvas jungle boots for jumping (*painting by Mark MacGregor from* Army Uniforms of World War II *by Andrew Mollo— Blandford Press*)

Re-supply drop, Indo-China 1953 (*EC et PA*)

137

patrols were supplied by air drops and casualties were evacuated by light aircraft when a suitable strip could be found. When the Special Air Service appeared in Malaya they perfected the use of the parachute in placing patrols far into thick jungle and then walking out or attacking the terrorist camps from an unexpected direction. Parachuting into jungle had not been used before because of the danger of being caught in the 200ft high trees, but the SAS evolved the use of climbing ropes and lowered themselves and their kit down to the ground without coming to any harm. The parachutes had to be left in the trees, but they were surprisingly difficult to spot unless one was directly underneath them and specifically looking for them. Later heli-

copters were used and greatly improved the flexibility of the operations since they could pick up a patrol from one area and move it to another, whereas previously the parachutists had had to walk out.

The wars in Korea, Malaya and Indo-China were all over by 1955, and from then on there was virtually no use of airborne warfare in the Far East, though the area was far from peaceful. Malaya settled down to build up its rubber and tin trades and take full advantage of the boom times that were foreseen, but had not yet arrived. North and South Korea were left with an uneasy peace and a grumbling border heavily defended and manned. Indo-China seethed with political unrest under weak government.

Korea, 7 March 1957. Final touches to a parachutists static line before a training jump (*US Army*)

8 Middle East and the Congo 1950s and 1960s

After 1945 the Mediterranean area was comparatively calm for several years, though there were the usual minor riots and disturbances that had always happened along the North African and Eastern Mediterranean coasts. In 1951 Mossadeq, Prime Minister of Iran, seized the oilfields in Abadan, and the British 16 Parachute Brigade was sent out to Cyprus to be ready to intervene should it be needed either in Iran or in any other country in the area. After three months the local Egyptians in the Suez Canal Zone rioted and attacked some British shoppers, and the brigade was moved into the zone. It stayed there for the next three years, acting generally in a ground role and on one occasion even moving up to the frontier with Egypt in preparation for a move to Cairo. But apart from these alarms there were no serious breaches of the peace and the brigade exercised and trained in uncomfortable camps and became bored with the sight of sand. In 1954 everyone was delighted to pull out and go home.

Suez

Suez, that unpopular military 'police action' against Egypt, was precipitated by the Egyptian government seizing the Suez Canal in the middle of 1956. Both the British and French felt that they had more right to the canal than President Nasser and both countries prepared to invade and re-take the canal. Britain positioned 16 Independent Parachute Brigade in Cyprus yet again, and the troops moved into familiar tents and huts and prepared to go back to Egypt. France sent 10 Airborne Divison from Algeria. Both countries flew in all the transport aircraft that they could spare, which was not many in either case, but noticeably few on the British airfield. Cyprus was also filled up with large amphibious, naval and conventional ground forces of both nationalities. They had about a month in which to get to know each other and rehearse.

Meanwhile the Israelis took matters into their own hands. Sensing the danger of allowing Egyptian domination of the Canal they chose to strike first and eliminate the

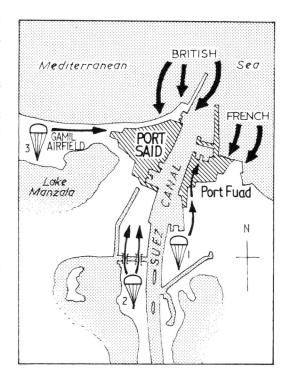

bulk of the Egyptian forces in the Sinai Peninsula before they could be reinforced. The campaign started at night, and on the evening of 29/30 October 1956 16 C-47s flew low over the desert towards the Canal heading for a vital point in the road link from Suez with the main garrisons in the Sinai. There are low sandy hills to the east of the Canal and the Israelis were planning to occupy the Mitla Pass where the main road crossed them. If this could be held it would paralyse the Egyptian communications. There had been no initial air strikes, no warnings, no reconnaissance of the drop zone – nothing indicating the possibility of an attack. The Dakotas flew low to avoid radar, and their escort fighters flew with them. The 16 troop-carriers had just 395 men of 202 Parachute Brigade in their cabins and it was necessary to put them down accurately on the target as they were too few and too lightly equipped to be able to fight a battle to take the Pass.

Egyptian fighters were on an airfield only 40 miles away, but they received no alert and at 1730 the Dakotas pulled up to 700 feet and out jumped the 202nd.

The British on their way to Suez. Brigadier M. A. H. Butler DSO, MC, Commander 16 Independent Parachute Brigade nearest the camera and men of his headquarters in flight to El Gamil airfield in a Hastings *(John Topham Picture Library)*

Suez, the heavy drop comes in while the men of the first drop hurry off the drop zone. As was the normal French practice, some loads were dropped on a cluster of time-expired man-carrying parachutes, and others were dropped on a few large canopies. The rate of descent was the same, and the cost of the smaller canopies was much less as they had already had a useful life, but the complications of the multiple opening were greater. In this picture however there have been no failures and all the loads are coming down well. They appear to be jeeps. The small canopies are the extractor parachutes which have pulled the main chutes out of their containers *(EC et PA)*

They were three miles from their drop zone, but by 1930 they had taken the Pass and were dug in ready to hold it. At 2100 hours the Dakotas returned with jeeps, 106mm anti-tank guns, medium mortars and ammunition. At the same time the remainder of the brigade set out in vehicles to link up with the Pass. The Egyptians reacted quickly, but with daylight came the Israeli fighter cover and heavy strikes against the Egyptian airfields. The Mitla Pass held, the brigade linked up and the Israelis swept up to the banks of the Canal itself, to remain there until 1973. This action was another example of the Israeli readiness to use unconventional methods coupled with considerable boldness, to throw their Arab opponents off balance. The risks in launching the parachute assault were daunting, but it was worth trying and it came off. Sadly, neither the French nor the British would have dared do the same.

Two weeks later two Israeli parachute companies from the same brigade were dropped at the lonely outpost of El Tor, 130 miles to the south of the Mitla Pass. El Tor was an Egyptian isolation prison with a barracks, a small oil well and an

airstrip. The Israelis wanted the airstrip for an airborne attack on the southernmost point of the Sinai, Sharm el Sheikh. The two companies jumped on to the airstrip and seized it while an infantry battalion was rapidly flown in using Dakotas, Noratlas transports on loan from the French and even a civilian airliner pressed into service use. Aircraft were in short supply in Israel and the demands were heavy, anything that could carry troops was doing so. Sharm el Sheikh fell a few days later to a combined land and air assault in which helicopters were used to fly in some of the air-landed troops, a tactic copied from the French Algerian experience.

After some time-wasting preliminaries the Anglo-French assault on Port Said was finally fixed for 5 November. The French parachutists had too few aircraft to lift more than one battalion at a time, but they had the advantage of some helicopters and all arms had had recent experience in Indo-China and Algeria. They were not restricted by cautious ideas and were convinced of the need for rapid and bold strikes. The British were heavily restricted by their aircraft, none of which were tail-

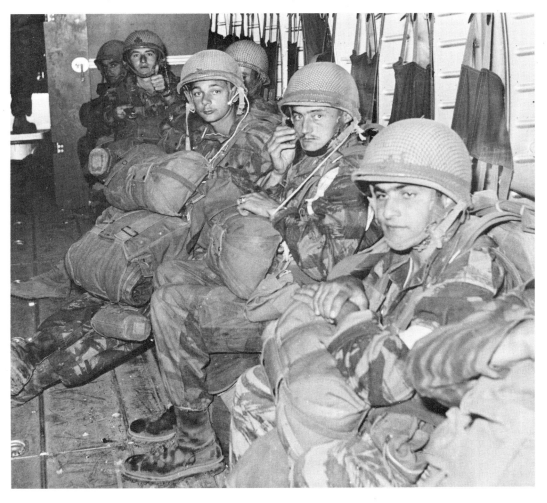

En route to Suez. French paras in their Noratlas have plenty of room to stretch out. Notice that every man has his helmet tied to his equipment with a piece of line, so that if it is blown off in the slipstream it will not be lost (*EC et PA*)

141

The French load into their
Noratlas planes on
Tymbou airfield, Cyprus.
They are well laden, but
not excessively so, and
seem to be able to get up
the steps reasonably easily.
The jumpmaster is
standing at the top, giving
a hand when needed. Each
man's static line is neatly
secured on the top of his
pack, so that he does not
have to worry about
pulling it out by catching
it on anything while
climbing in. Compare this
with the more untidy
arrangements made in
other armies *(EC et PA)*

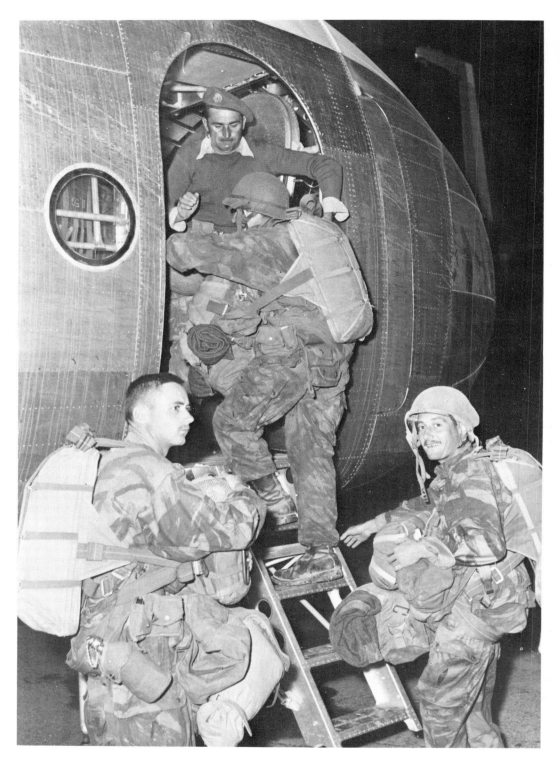

loading so that all heavy loads had to be
underslung in the same way as they had
been in World War II. Indeed, the differences between the British drop at Suez in
1956 and any drop in 1945 are very slight
and the men's equipment and weapons
were almost identical.

In the early dawn of the 5th two formations set out from Cyprus, one French and
one British. The French one consisted of
17 Noratlas carrying 2 Regiment Parachutiste Coloniale and some men of 11 Demi-

Brigade Parachutiste de Choc. Their drop
zone was a tiny strip of sand alongside the
canal to the south of the town. The actual
drop zone was only 500 yards long and
200 yards wide, with no room for under
or overshoots; men who missed would go
into a deep saltmarsh. Because they were
using the American parachutes which
opened quickly the French could afford to
fly low, and in order not to drop men off
the drop zone the commanding officer,
Colonel Chateau-Joubert ordered the fly-in

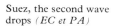

Suez, the second wave
drops *(EC et PA)*

to be at 300 feet. The Noratlas pilots put on a superb display of precision flying and ran in in two lines only 90 feet apart with 300 feet between each pair in the line. The drop was perfect, but was resisted by dug-in Egyptian infantry and the drop zone quickly became a minor battle-ground. Originally it had been hoped to put the troops down in helicopters, but luckily this was vetoed on the grounds that the anti-aircraft fire was too heavy. In the event it is doubtful if helicopters would have survived for more than a few minutes. After two hours of sharp fighting 2 Regiment gained its objectives – two bridges over a waterway – and the second lift was flown in.

The second lift was dropped south of Port Said on the opposite side of the canal and moved quickly into the dock area, effectively isolating the two parts of the town from each other. The entire operation took less than ten hours and gravely distracted the Egyptian defenders who were looking seawards and not expecting an attack in their rear.

There is one feature of the French assault that was novel and interesting and which had been evolved in Algeria – the airborne command post. The commander of the French Demi-Brigade was installed in a specially equipped Noratlas which circled above the drop zone and battlefield for several hours. It carried a complete tactical headquarters and plenty of radios and was in continuous touch with the force

on the ground, the ships offshore, and the base in Cyprus, as well as the supporting air effort. The result of this was that the commander was fully aware of all that was happening at all times, and had instant and clear communication to his subordinates on the ground. He could if necessary actually see what was happening below him, yet he was sufficiently detached to be able to think and plan in reasonable freedom. It is tempting to think that the later American flying headquarters with their elaborate operations rooms had their origins in this Noratlas at Suez, but that would be taking supposition a little too far.

The British drop was on the El Gamil airfield, two miles west of Port Said and on a thin strip of hard ground that allowed no room for ground manoeuvre. The force was 3 Parachute Battalion Group, carried in 18 Valettas and 14 Hastings – just about all the transport aircraft that could be mustered. The drop started at 0715 and was over in 15 minutes. It is memorable for one reason only. By 1956 Britain had adopted the NATO ruling that all military parachutists must jump with two parachutes, the second being a reserve carried on the front of the harness. Everyone in 3 Parachute Battalion was carrying cripplingly heavy loads and many men jumped with belts of Vickers gun ammunition draped round their necks and tucked under the parachute harness. The drop height was going to be low, almost too low to allow time to pull a reserve, so

143

Lieutenant-Colonel Paul Crook took a deliberate chance with his battalion group and ordered all reserve parachutes to be left behind on the mounting airfield. It was the last time that British soldiers jumped with only one parachute. There was fierce opposition by the Egyptian army and the force had a tough fight to get to Port Said by nightfall, but there was close liaison with naval fighter ground attack planes who were used in the classical way as heavy artillery and anti-tank support. In fact the air support was the best part of the assault, setting aside the fighting qualities of the troops.

The planning was timid and tied entirely to a seaborne attack, instead of making use of the flexibility and range of the airborne units. Furthermore, having captured an airfield it was never used! It seems incredible that no attempt was made to air-land any troops after 3 Parachute Battalion dropped, but such is the case, and valuable reinforcements came ponderously in by sea the next day. They could easily have arrived by noon on the 5th. Nor was there any need to restrict the air assaults to the top end of the canal. A battalion on Ismailia, in the middle of the Canal Zone, would have brought results out of all proportion to its size. But caution and a fixation with sea landings ruled the day and apart from the expertise of the French, Suez was not a notable operation nor one that is remembered with much pride.

The only good to come out of it was that the British had it brought home to them in stark terms, how, eleven years after the end of World War II, the transport aircraft of the RAF were laughably inadequate. A little more money was then put into building some, but in comparison with the parachute armies of quite small countries, the British were even then totally inadequately supported. The Hastings and Valettas were designed in 1946 and had the old two-wheeled undercarriage layout which made it difficult to load them internally and impossible for them to parachute any form of heavy load unless it was carried slung underneath between the undercarriage legs, where it hung in the slip-stream and ruined the aircraft's performance. For Suez the anti-tank guns had to be slung on loading beams dating from 1945, while the French could carry everything inside their Noratlas and parachute heavy loads over the rear door-sill. Admittedly the Valetta had disappeared by 1960, but the Hastings remained. The new aeroplane was the Beverley, a roomy and adequate load-carrier, but designed for short-range use in Europe only. It was a tactical transport of some value, but the world was turning towards larger and larger scenes on which to act its military tragedies, and the Beverley soon demonstrated its failings.

The Lebanon and Jordan

In the summer of 1958 there was a civil war in the Lebanon and more trouble in Jordan. The United States and Britain co-

Port Said. French parachutists moving into the town from the south. They are all carrying the special folding version of the MAS 36 rifle and appear to be relatively casual in their approach march (*EC et PA*)

Suez 1956. Lt-Col Paul Crook, commanding 3 Bn Para Regt walking off the drop zone at El Gamil, with his signaller on his right. The British airborne troops have always spurned the wearing of helmets except for the actual parachuting and in this photograph men are actually pulling on their red berets while under fire

operated to quell the insurgent risings by sending troops to support the government forces in each country. The United States chose to support the Lebanon and sent marines from the Sixth Fleet, but she also sent 2,000 parachute troops from Southern Germany. The significant thing about the parachutists is that they flew direct from their German bases non-stop to Beirut where they could have been dropped and from where the planes could have returned to Germany without needing to stop or refuel at any point on the entire journey. This was a masterly demonstration of the strategic use of airborne troops and it could only have been done with the new Lockheed C-130 Hercules freighter which the Americans were using for the first time. Once again the US Air Force was ahead of the world in regard to transport aircraft, and from then on she has remained in front. The British were using the Hastings and the new Beverleys. In order to carry a reasonable load, and not be forced to use the payload for fuel, the operational range of the Beverley was restricted to about 600 miles. Luckily Cyprus could be used for a mounting base, but without Cyprus there would have been no hope of getting men to Jordan other

Suez 1956. Men of 3 Bn Para Regt on the edge of the drop zone.

Opposite: (*Above*) Suez. A machine gun covers the open ground while Port Said burns in the background (*EC et PA*)

(*Below*) Congolese paratroops in training, 1961. The Congo had one battalion of paratroops, but relied on aircraft from other nations. These men are training for a river crossing. They are equipped with a miscellany of styles. Their clothing is French, the webbing equipment looks British, and the nearest man is holding a WWII MK2 Sten sub-machine gun (*John Topham Picture Library*)

than in small numbers in the Hastings, mounting from Malta, or perhaps by using a few requisitioned civilian airliners.

It was all quite extraordinary, for even in 1958 Britain had widespread overseas possessions which she needed to protect, and also had treaties with a number of countries, such as Jordan, to whom she was bound to give assistance if they asked for it. One would have thought that Britain above all other nations had a pressing need for long-range transport aircraft capable of carrying large loads over several thousand miles, and indeed she had, but nobody was prepared to recognize it or do anything about it. One stumbling block was the Royal Air Force which was living on memories of the Battle of Britain and despised the idea of becoming a force of 'truck and taxi drivers' as one of its members put it. Transport Command was considered inferior, and all effort, money and kudos was directed towards the fighters and bombers. It was a short-sighted policy and rebounded on their heads in the next decade.

Kuwait

Peace, of a kind, descended on the Middle East as the 1950s faded out and no airborne forces were needed to demonstrate their abilities to intervene in tense situations, except when the troops themselves were used in more or less conventional ground roles. Britain could fly to all the Middle East countries from Cyprus, and kept a strong air force base there for that purpose. In the early 1960s the ruler of Kuwait asked for military help from Britain and a battalion of parachutists was sent for a short time to make gestures at the threatening Iraqis. The battalion soon withdrew and took post on Bahrain Island, in the Persian Gulf, from where it could move within two or three hours to any of the Gulf States. During the next six years Bahrain became the main mounting base for the Middle East, though Cyprus was always available. A transport squadron was moved into Bahrain and rigging facilities for heavy dropping were put in on the airfield. The resident parachute battalion was rotated annually and the force became a battalion group with all the necessary service and support that it needed. The group was kept in a high state of readiness and flew up and down the Gulf on frequent airborne and ground exercises, partly to 'show the flag' as a political gesture, and partly to keep everyone on their toes. The presence of this force, together with its air-

craft, was a steadying influence in the Gulf during a period of considerable turbulence in the local political scene. The group never actually had to fight, but it was used as a reserve for the Aden garrison, and at the end of the time in Bahrain the troops were spending more time in Aden than in the Gulf.

The United States had no need to station troops in any of the Middle East countries, though it might have done no harm if she could have found one who would have allowed it. The constant presence of the Sixth Fleet and the knowledge that the C-130 force in Germany could bring a brigade to any part of the area within six or seven hours was sufficient, though it was all a rather distant threat. The British were always moving about and were very much seen to be there, and that is much more effective when keeping the peace.

The Congo 1964

In the Mediterranean relative calm ruled, but things were anything but quiet in the rest of the world, and in 1964 there was a particularly unpleasant episode in the Congo. The Congo had been in a turmoil for three or four years, but by 1964 the civil war was to all intents and purposes over and the United Nations troops had withdrawn; but there was continual trouble in the country and the government did not by any means have overall control. The insurgents, if they can be called that, were little better then bloodthirsty bandits and in November 1964 they occupied the town of Stanleyville and held hostage about 1,300 white people – mostly Europeans, but with some Americans among them. Government troops promptly began a vigorous drive towards Stanleyville, and the insurgents let it be known that the safety of the hostages depended upon the withdrawal of government troops. In other words, the hostages were being used as a bargaining counter, and the threat of massacre was clearly made. What was needed was some way of rescuing them without warning. In a way it was a similar situation to that of the Los Banos prisoner of war camp in Luzon in 1945, and it was solved in the same manner.

The United States, Britain and Belgium were perfectly willing to do whatever was wanted and in the end it became a combined Belgian-United States operation. The US Air Force provided twelve C-130 transports and a further four C-124s, Belgium provided its Regiment Para-

Commando under the command of Colonel Laurent and both parts of the force met at Kamina where the operation was mounted. The plan was to drop parachutists as close to the town as possible and rush the guards. An airfield was also needed so that the hostages could be flown out and the parachutists provided with a means of retreat. There was an airfield two miles from Stanleyville, which was not ideal, but it had to do. At least it possessed the advantage that it was far enough away from the centre of the town for it not to be defended, and so it proved to be.

The first lift arrived over the airfield at 0500 hours and dropped 300 men from seven Hercules aircraft. Immediately patrols set out to clear the roads to Stanleyville and when the follow-up planes arrived 20 minutes later they were able to land and unload their troops and jeeps. The Belgian parachutists quickly routed the insurgents and escorted the hostages back to the airfield, but not before 60 of the unfortunate people had been murdered in the town square in Stanleyville, and the Belgians had suffered seven casualties themselves. By late morning it was all over. There was a similar though smaller operation two days later 200 miles away that rescued a further 300 hostages for the cost of six Belgian soldiers killed and wounded. These two airborne interventions completed the Congo operations, but they were striking examples of the way in which airborne troops can be used. For instance, the aircraft came from bases in the United States, and the troops from Belgium; the operation was in Africa. It would be hard to find another example where three continents were involved in the mounting, and where sheer distance apparently counted for so little. The aircraft flew right across the Atlantic just to get to the mounting base. The troops flew from Europe to Africa for the same reason. Both returned afterwards whence they came. Ordinary ground troops could never have done it. Air-landed troops might well have carried out the Stanleyville operation, but certainly could not have done the second because the insurgents were more alert and surrounded the airfield and fired on the drop zone. A stationary plane would have been a sitting duck, but parachutists could clear the insurgents off. Helicopter-borne air-mobile troops could certainly have done the job, and probably more effectively than parachutists since they would have been able to land nearer the centre of the towns and take immediate

action, but there were no helicopters in the Congo at that time, and helicopters cannot yet fly the Atlantic. The Stanleyville rescue was a shining example of the classic value of airborne troops, in the role of long-range strategic intervention, and as such it deserves more prominence than it gets.

The Middle East 1967

As always, peace was short-lived in the Middle East and by 1967 war was in the air again. The United Nations had persuaded the Israelis to pull out of the positions they had gained in the Western Sinai in the 1956 War, and as a result the Egyptians were once more at Sharm el Sheikh, overlooking the approaches to the Gulf of Aqaba and the Israeli port of Eilat. In spring 1967 the temptation became too strong, and rather unwisely the Egyptians closed the straits to Israeli shipping and any other shipping destined for Eilat. It was more than any nation could be expected to stand for long, and when the Egyptians brought the Arab League into the picture and began to make noises about a total blockade of Israel the response became obvious and imminent.

By this time Israel had a sizeable airborne strike force and some good ideas on how to deploy them. There were sufficient Israeli Noratlas planes to lift a battalion with its jeeps and anti-tank guns and also sufficient troop-carrying helicopters of both American and French extraction to lift another battalion. There were two full-strength parachute brigades in the order of battle, a regular and a reserve, and both were trained in parachute assaults as well as helicopter operations and it was intended that the troops could be switched from one kind of aircraft to the other without any loss of time, or indeed with scarcely any change of plan.

The state of training of these men is perhaps best illustrated by a different happening at a different time. During the tense time which followed the 1967 War the first aircraft hijackings began. One of the more dramatic hijackings was the seizure of an Olympic Airlines VC 10 and its forcible detention on a deserted airstrip in Jordan. The plane was taken over after it had taken off from Beirut and the total flying time from the moment that the pilot announced that he was hijacked to the moment when it landed on the desert airstrip was about 40 minutes. In that time the word was passed to Tel Aviv. Tel Aviv alerted the stand-by company of parachutists that is apparently permanently ready for this kind of emergency and a rescue operation was planned. The company boarded the helicopters and flew to the airstrip intending to land before the hijacked plane and surround it as it stopped. They were just too late; as they approached they could see the VC-10 landing, and to try any heroics then would have meant the death of some or all of the passengers, so the helicopters returned to base, albeit reluctantly. One wonders how many other countries have a force at permanent readiness such that they can turn out within minutes and can fly over 60 miles within three-quarters of an hour of getting an alert. In most armies it takes an hour to even get a helicopter off the ground, much less fly it on an emergency mission.

But to return to the theme. Despite the preparations and the training the war of 1967 made no real demands on the Israeli parachutists except that one of the battalions re-took Jerusalem in a purely ground role, but a gallant and imaginative one nonetheless. In the Sinai one battalion was used as an air-mobile force to take out a potentially troublesome Egyptian position near El Agheila, in the north. A small pathfinder force was landed by night behind an Egyptian gun position and marked a landing zone. The guns were kept busy by Israeli attacks along the front, and the noise of firing drowned the arrival of the battalion in several lifts. When all were present the battalion rushed

the guns and silenced them and then swept along the infantry positions from behind. There was complete surprise and the Israelis suffered only light casualties.

At Sharm el Sheikh a similar type of operation on a much larger scale was planned. It was necessary for the Israelis to take the position with as much dash and show as possible because this was the place that had started the war, and the Israelis had to show that they could finish it in that spot. They intended a large combined sea and air assault with a full battalion dropping to link up with a marine force and a helicopter force. The boats got there first and found no opposition so they went ashore and found the Egyptians had fled. The helicopters then arrived and put down their troops, and finally the frustrated parachutists were flown in and landed on the undamaged airstrip where they unloaded their planes with a rather bad grace. It was a punch that met empty air, but it was a punch all the same.

There were several other helicopter operations during this war, many of them along the Northern Front on the Golan Heights. In these actions the tactics were usually similar, a short approach flight to a point behind, and out of sight of, the objective, the troops landed quickly under cover of Israeli artillery fire, and a quick rush on to the objective. A dangerous game, but immensely effective if successful and always economical in lives and time.

9 Vietnam

The Background

The campaign in Vietnam presented the United States with a series of different challenges and problems which made it far more complicated and difficult than most of the other post-war counter-insurgency campaigns and also made it misleading and confusing to try and draw parallels. It is common to compare the Malayan and Vietnamese campaigns, and to conclude that the US army was less than effective or efficient in dealing with their opponents whereas much smaller numbers of British troops using less sophisticated and less expensive equipment soundly defeated the Malayan communists in similar conditions. Many American soldiers have thought so too, but they and any others who try to read across from Malaya to Vietnam, or indeed from Borneo to Vietnam, or even from the French wars to those of the present day, are failing to see the essential differences between the Vietnam campaign and those that had gone before. The fact is that in practically every other counter-insurgency campaign the Western nation, usually Britain or France, was fighting in a country that they had governed for many years. The internal structure, the police, the government, the telecommunications, road works, every facet of life had been laid down by the westerners, and there was a central core of them who ran the country. At the same time there was always an ex-patriate element resident in the country with a tradition of service to the colony, and the majority of the local population were educated in western schools and universities. Both sides could speak each other's language. In Vietnam, French was the language of commerce and government, and to the Americans it was a foreign country.

Most of the previous campaigns had been an internal problem and the Western nation had been able to fight on ground that was both familiar and broadly friendly, but this was not so in Vietnam. The whole position was complicated by the fact that the country had been split in two after the French withdrawal in 1954

and the North was a hostile and active enemy. This had also been the case in Korea, but in Korea there was no sympathetic movement supporting the North among the southerners; in Vietnam there was. In Malaya there was no external enemy, but there was a well-organized guerilla army operating with the sympathy and support of part of the population. In Vietnam there was both, and there were further complications which arose from the way the country was governed. The government of the Republic of Vietnam controlled part of the country from its capital, Saigon; in this it was supported by massive aid from the United States and had its own army, known as ARVN (Army of the Republic of Vietnam). Where the government writ did not run, and this soon became a major part of the country, there was rough and ready rule by the Vietcong guerillas who lost no opportunity to make capital out of the weak and ineffective democracy in Saigon. Finally there was the communist North, offering a way of life that on the face of it looked more promising than the corruption of the South. There was also a regular Northern army, called the People's Army of Vietnam, or the PAVN.

The North and South were not at war with each other, yet the North repeatedly invaded over the frontier with both irregular and regular forces, whilst fomenting trouble among the civilian population and aiding and encouraging the Vietcong guerillas who were operating all over the southern states. Thus the ARVN had not only to deal with actual incursions into its national territory, but had also to contend with an indigenous guerilla war. It was both counter-insurgency and conventional war at the same time, and no other country had tried to fight against those odds. The sad part of the story of Vietnam is that both the ARVN and the Americans concentrated too much on the conventional war with the PAVN and the guerillas, leaving the communist National Liberation Front to flourish almost unchecked in the Republic, and so the war was lost

(Opposite) A C-130 dropping 155mm howitzer ammunition into a forward camp *(US Army)*

from inside the country long before it was lost on the battlefield.

Use of Airborne Troops

At first American aid was confined to equipment and air support, with the ARVN providing all the fighting men; indeed in the very early years the few American servicemen in the country were forbidden to go into action with the troops they had trained, but this soon changed after 1962 and 1963. The ARVN were taught to operate from firm bases and to venture out only in offensive sweeps, in much the same way as the French had done. With the American aircraft the ARVN were highly mobile and where the French had slogged out on foot ten years before, the ARVN went in aeroplanes or helicopters. But helicopters had not yet made their mark, although the swamps and paddy fields of Vietnam were teaching the US advisers a good deal about air mobility. The ARVN therefore used parachutists as a rapid reinforcement and in the early 1960s they kept a battalion group at permanent readiness to jump in to anywhere in the country at one hour's notice to move. With average luck and good communications it was expected that the battalion on duty could arrive on the drop zone within two or three hours of being called for.

An innovative idea was to plan for airborne briefings so that no time was wasted before take-off in giving orders or going over air photographs. The enemy was familiar to all and the only briefing necessary before boarding the plane was to give the troops the roughest idea of the sort of operation they were going to be involved in, and get them moving to the aircraft. Meanwhile a reconnaissance party had taken off in faster aircraft and was flying to the scene of the operation. Here they looked for a drop zone and prepared to mark it. At the same time a squadron of fighter ground-attack aircraft were scrambled and flew around the drop zone shooting up any likely trouble spots and enemy movement. The reconnaissance aircraft told the troop-carriers by radio what the ground looked like and gave an up-to-the-minute report on the ground fighting, all of which was passed on to the parachutists. As the troop-carriers came in sight the reconnaissance aircraft dropped smoke markers on the drop zone and controlled the drop from the air. Once on the ground the force was continually supported from the air and was generally decisive in

removing the enemy. The troops then had to be extracted, which obviously took much longer, and was not always possible by air, so the men had to walk out.

These reinforcement operations were effective enough, but they did not deny the ground permanently to the enemy, and he merely reoccupied the battlefield after the ARVN had left; however, he generally retreated from the actual battle, and his losses mounted. The first time the airborne readiness force was actually used was on 24 March 1961 in the Plain of

Reeds, to the west of Saigon in the Mekong Delta. The 2 Battalion of an ARVN regiment had been sent to sweep through a large area and clear out any Vietcong. They were only 270 strong, about one-third of their full strength, and early on the 24th they were ambushed by a full Vietcong regiment and pinned down. By 1000 hours they were surrounded and called for help. The decision to jump the readiness force was made at 1145, which seems a long delay, and the aircraft were called for while the battalion was warned.

Two and a half hours then passed while the force was got ready, and one suspects that what had been learned in training was not being applied with much vigour. However, the first plane took off at 1415 and dropped at 1450. The C-47s then went back for a second lift to complete the battalion strength on the ground, and that lift dropped at 1610. The enemy withdrew at 1640 leaving over 200 dead behind. There were about 30 casualties among the airborne battalion, and 30 more in the surrounded 2 Battalion. Whilst not a deci-

Men of 101 Airborne running to their 'slicks'. Fire Base 'Saber' Vietnam, 1969. The men have removed their hats to prevent them being blown off in the downwash. Helmets are no longer worn (*US Army*)

153

Infantry of 1 Brigade, 25
Infantry Division moving
towards the edge of their
landing zone, while still in
the downwash of the
rotors, Vietnam, May 1966
(*US Army*)

sive action in itself, it well illustrated the usefulness of the airborne reinforcement method, which was kept in use until after 1 Cavalry came into the country in 1965, when their helicopters enabled the concept of air mobility to be fully and properly employed.

1 Cavalry

When 1 Cavalry did move in, the war had become very close to an actual conventional conflict as we understand it today. The PAVN had moved at least two full infantry regiments into the Central Highlands and had set up firm bases and rest areas. From these they attacked the outpost of Plei Me, but air-lifted reinforcements and fire-power forced them to withdraw. The withdrawal was the opportunity that 1 Cavalry had been waiting for and a battalion was flown by helicopter to ambush the line of retreat. This it did most successfully, one feature of that success being the fact that all units except the USAF fighters were actually under the command of the division and could be directly and effectively controlled from the one headquarters – the ideal arrangement for the complications of airborne warfare, as we have seen elsewhere. But the PAVN learnt fast, and the vulnerability of slow flying helicopters to ground fire soon forced the machines up to heights of 1,500–2,000ft. Consequently the element of surprise was lost and it became difficult for the air crews to locate small bodies of men on the ground. The reconnaissance helicopters and their protective gunships found that they had to fly low down if they were to do their job, and losses quickly mounted up among the aircrews who often flew only a few feet above the ground. Often the only way to find out if anyone was hiding among undergrowth was to hover above the spot and literally beat down the vegetation with the down wash from the rotors.

The traditional way to mark a landing zone was to fly gunships to it before the troop-carriers ('slicks') arrived and 'prep', or 'prepare' the surrounding areas by fire, to clear out any lurking Vietcong. 1 Cavalry soon found that this method merely advertised to the Vietcong where they were going to land, and he immediately left the area, so that when the troops arrived there was no enemy to be found. A better method was soon found to be to land a pathfinder group on another spot, up to two days march away, and leave them to find and mark a suitable landing zone. The slicks then came in without any preparatory fire, and little loss of surprise. Variations on this method were used throughout the remainder of the Vietnam war, and the only exceptions to the rule were hurriedly prepared operations where there was no time for pathfinders.

In 1953 one marine battalion was moved by helicopter in Korea, and it caused a minor stir among thinking military men. By the end of the Vietnam war, just 20 years later, staggering quantities of men and war material were being shifted by helicopter as a routine matter. As an example of what could be done with the helicopters within the establishment of 1 Cavalry alone, in one period of six days there were 4 battalion assaults, 11 moves of artillery batteries, and supporting fire from gunships for all moves. In another 18-day period when the division was engaged in a massive search and destroy operation 15,000 troops were moved (many of them several times over), 33 unit operations were mounted, 7 artillery batteries were moved, all of these operations were carried out by helicopters. The divisional aircraft, both fixed and rotary wing fired 27,000 rounds of ammunition and dropped or fired 1,000 tons of bombs and rockets. With such lavish air support one might well wonder how it came about that the US forces did not simply walk right over the Vietcong and the PAVN too. The answer to that question is more than this book can discuss, and it is something that will be debated and argued over for many years to come, but in essence it stemmed from the attitude of mind that failed the French in their campaign in the same place: it is no good living in a firm base and leaving the whole country to be occupied by the enemy. Despite the overwhelming air strength of 1 Cavalry and the other divisions, the Vietcong controlled the outlying villages, and controlled almost all the country once night had fallen. Like true guerillas they moved away from the offensive sweeps and rolled back again once the helicopters had gone home. No army wins against those tactics.

After 1 Cavalry the 101 Airborne Division was moved into the country, in its new role as an air-mobile division, and after that the numbers of helicopters of all kinds grew rapidly until the great majority of troop movements were by air. The Vietnam war became the helicopter war and the cost and complexity were amazing. The large bases, such as Dah Nang, had huge concrete aprons full of helicopters, with

An AH-IG 'Cobra' gunship lifts off at the start of a fire mission. Under the starboard weapon rack is a cluster of 2.75in rockets and a 7.62mm mini-gun. In the chin turret is a 40mm automatic grenade launcher *(US Army)*

25 Infantry Division helicopter landing reinforcements in operation 'Wahiawa', Vietnam 1966. Just visible in the after part of the cabin is the machine-gunner who provides local protection for the machine both in flight and on the ground *(US Army)*

acres of sheds for maintenance and small armies of mechanics supported by electric generating plants, radio workshops, and fuel dumps fed from oil tankers moored offshore. It was the equivalent of a small manufacturing town, and cost every bit as much, but this is the price of modern war and it impoverishes all but the largest nations.

It remains to quote General Moshe Dayan, that imaginative and successful Israeli commander who visited Vietnam as a freelance journalist. He summed up the contribution that 1 Cavalry had made to warfare when he wrote: 'American warfare in Vietnam is primarily helicopter warfare. The 1st Cavalry Division is the organizational and tactical expression of the imaginative use of the helicopter in battle.'

Special Feature: The Air Mobile Division

The Air Mobile Division is a peculiarly American invention, although several other armies are looking at the idea and weighing up the pros and cons. It is a little difficult to describe in a few words without being misleading, but it is probably fair to say that it is very similar in concept to the old-style World War II Airborne Division using helicopters instead of transport aircraft and parachutes. The Air Mobile Division operates over a shorter distance, but faster; in fact, if the parachute units are strategic air mobility, then air-mobile units are the tactical mobility. The difference is rather greater than it appears at first sight for the strategically mobile airborne unit may be flown anywhere in the world and dropped by parachute straight into a war zone where, in the worst case, it will have to fight on its own deep in enemy territory. Here of course it will soon be met by the advancing ground troops and withdrawn, or at worst left to fight as infantry alongside the link-up force.

The air-mobile force acts rather differently. No one imagines that large helicopter forces are going to be able to fly over enemy-held territory to land large bodies of troops in the same way as the parachute units can do. It may be possible to make short forays ahead of the forward defended localities, but for the most part the air-mobile force moves rapidly about its own areas, keeping its vulnerable helicopters well back from the enemy anti-aircraft fire, and shifting troops and equipment to threatened areas or to exploit success, or anywhere else that extra effort is needed. The essence of the Air Mobile Division is rapid short-range movement, where short range is a range measured in scores of miles. The key to the Air Mobile Division is the helicopter, and whilst the helicopter is an almost unbelievably versatile machine, it is also enormously expensive. In fact the helicopter is one of the most expensive pieces of modern army equipment. It is not so much the cost of the machine itself, but of the the complicated support equipment and manpower that is necessary to service, repair and

generally keep it in good condition so that it is able to fly at all times. There is also fuel; helicopters are most inefficient users of fuel. They consume enormous amounts of it, and because they have only a short range they need to be continually topped up. Behind every military helicopter there is a long line of maintenance men, repair men and, above all, men producing fuel. They comprise what is called the 'logistic tail' and this tail is greedy for skilled men and specialized vehicles and space in which to put both down. It is a high price to pay for air mobility, but for those who can afford to pay it the advantages are well worth the cost.

The US army enthusiastically pays that cost, and gains by it. Aircraft have been integrated into the US Infantry Division since the end of World War II. In Korea a few helicopters were added and by 1962 there were no less than 97 of them. If all of them were flown at the same time, they could between them lift one of the battalions, and this brought about the realization that the time had come to look properly at the idea of helicopter-borne infantry. At the same time as this idea developed, the strategy of nuclear warfare in Europe, and 'strikes' all with low-yield weapons, the supreme military threat of the 1950s, was seen to be useless against the Soviet threat of massive conventional war. One way of improving an army's capability is to increase its firepower, another way is to increase its mobility. The US army set out to do both. Luckily there were sufficient far-sighted generals who could see what was needed, and there was also an energetic and able Secretary of Defence, Robert McNamara. He called for a complete reappraisal of the mobility of the army and set up a special investigatory Board under General Howze. The Howze Board came out strongly in favour of the helicopter as a battlefield vehicle and recommended the formation of special 'Air Mobile' divisions with light scales of equipment supported by armed rocket-firing helicopters instead of conventional artillery and their guns. A partial return, in fact, to the techniques of the 1940

blitzkreig where Stuka dive-bombers took the place of support artillery.

1 Cavalry Division (Air Mobile)

The concept was tried out between 1963 and 1965, by when 1 Cavalry Division (Air Mobile) was formed. 1 Cavalry was, and still is, an infantry division, and one of the oldest formations in the US army; in 1965 it became the most up-to-date formation in that army. It is organized on exactly the same general lines as all other infantry divisions and consists of three brigade groups of three infantry battalions each and supporting arms and services. The total strength is 15,787 men, 1,700 jeep-type vehicles and 434 helicopters. The majority of the helicopters are the well-tried Bell UH-1 medium load carriers, or 'Huey's as they are called. The Huey can lift ten armed men or a huge variety of loads to the same weight. It can also be fitted with rocket racks, machine guns and a whole family of specialized weapons such as guided anti-tank missiles. The Huey became as common in Vietnam as the jeep was in World War II and the peculiar thumping beat of its two-bladed rotor could be heard all over the country both by day and night. It is reliable, robust and

Tay Ninh Province, Vietnam. Skytroopers of the First Air Cavalry Division (Air Mobile) load burlap sacks of enemy rice which was found in the jungles of northern Tay Ninh province, 3 March 1970 (*US AAF*)

William Henderson who is with the 1 Battalion 6 Infantry, 3 Brigade, 101 Airborne that operates out of Mai Loc, refuels his AH-IG Cobra after returning from a mission. The Cobra provides cover for advancing troops making sweeps in the field. 16 October 1969 *(US AAF)*

effective and for this the US army is prepared to overlook its more obvious faults, though it is now all but obsolete.

Among the remaining helicopters are 48 twin-rotored CH-47 Chinook heavy load carriers, each capable of carrying 40 armed men, or the same weight in weapons or equipment. This machine has a rear ramp-door and can be loaded with light vehicles or guns, though it usually carries artillery pieces by slinging them beneath the fuselage on a single wire. This external carrying method is often much quicker than landing the helicopter and loading inside, also it needs less ground space for loading and unloading and in the Vietnam jungle this could be a vital factor. The Chinook is also a general load carrier, humping ammunition, rice, stretcher casualties and particularly fuel, this being carried in flexible bags on the floor. Both the Huey and the Chinook were developed from earlier models that were flying in the 1950s so that they were proved and reliable.

Reconnaissance is also carried out from the air, using two- or three-seat helicopters. The first ones were two-seater Bell OH-138s, using a piston engine, but a contract of 1968 gave Bell the task of providing a military version of the Jet Ranger, a five-seater known as the Kiowa. It is still the standard observation helicopter of the air-mobile divisions but is supplemented by the Hughes OH-6A which is smaller but has roughly the same performance. Both of these light machines can be fitted with a variety of armaments, including the 7.62mm mini-gun.

The troop-carrying helicopters are capable of lifting one brigade at any one time, assuming that all machines are airworthy and that the air base is close enough. Under these conditions the brigade can be lifted from any convenient piece of flat land and flown away in less than half an hour. It is a sobering sight to see the huge flock of helicopters lining up in the sky to drop down in succession, pick up their loads and pull away with a tremendous roar of engines and rotors. In Vietnam the load-carrying helicopters usually flew in loose columns very like naval convoys with sections peeling off to their particular landing zones, or in some cases the entire column flying in to one place. Although the whole arrangement appears at first sight to be very little different from moving troops in trucks or armoured personnel carriers, there are in fact a number of differences and not a few difficulties. One is concealment. As Vietnam showed, it is

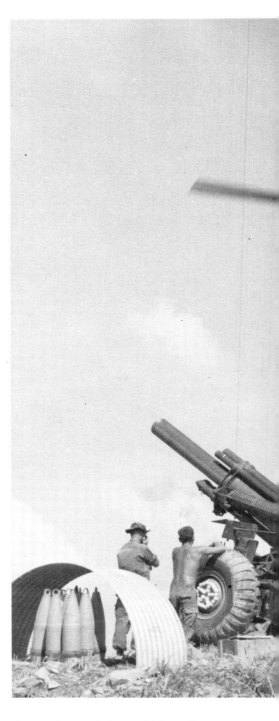

almost impossible to hide a long column of helicopters when they are in the air and in a European battle radar will quickly pick up an air mobile force on the move. However, nobody believes that helicopters are going to be used over enemy lines in a sophisticated war. They are going to move troops rapidly from one part of the front to another well back behind the forward areas, and they will only come forward in small numbers, contour flying and taking every advantage of the cover provided by folds in the ground and trees. After all, a helicopter flies just as well 10ft from the ground as it does when 100ft

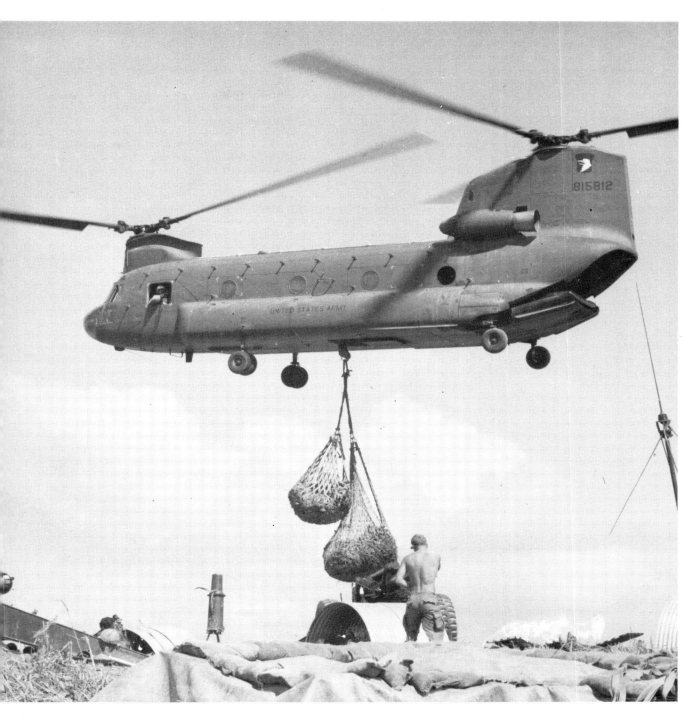

Mai Loc, Vietnam. Ch-47 'Chinook' helicopters from the 101 Airborne Division, bring in supplies to Mai Loc. In the background is a 150mm towed howitzer. 16 October 1969 (US AAF)

from it and it is surprising how hard it is to spot a low-flying helicopter from a mile or more away – even the engine noise is misleading.

The Gunship

Protection for these air armadas is provided by the gunship, a sort of rotary winged fighter. The original idea is now well lost in history, but it would seem that the first practical attempt to put substantial firepower on to a helicopter was made in the late 1950s when the French fitted the SS-11 missile onto their Alouette machines. The US Air Cavalry took it

several stages further, particularly in Vietnam where troop-carriers were always vulnerable to small arms fire from the ground and where the landing zones were as often as not under fire too. The first move was to put a machine gun in the door of a Huey and use it rather like the rear gun on the old two-seater fighters. This was not bad, but it was not effective enough and the next move was to fit outriggers and hang one or two guns on them. The pilot now flew in exactly the same way as a fighter and pointed his machine at the target. This had the advantage that he presented a smaller target.

163

An OH-6A light observation helicopter from the 101 Airborne Division lands on a temporary pad at Fire Base 'Victory'. 16 October 1969 *(US AAF)*

From then on it was simply a matter of adding bigger and better weapons, finally ending with a whole selection of rockets, guns and bombs. Finally the TOW missile was clipped on and was tried out in great secrecy in Vietnam in 1972. The results exceeded all expectations and it was found that with a stabilized sight which cut out all the helicopter movements and gave the gunner a steady picture, the accuracy of the missile was remarkable. Perhaps the best performance was in Kontum where a heavy machine gun crew was in a sandbagged enclosure on the top of the town water-tower. A Huey carrying TOW missiles calmly shot away the legs of the tower, one by one, so that it toppled over! And this was done at a range of 2,200 yd (2,000m).

The Armed Attack Helicopter

But load-carrying helicopters carrying weapons on outriggers were not the complete answer, though they have to suffice for the European nations who cannot afford a specialized machine. The US can, however, afford such a machine, and the result is the Armed Attack Helicopter (AAH). It arrived as a concept in Vietnam when it was found that the columns of troop-carriers needed to be protected in flight. The converted load carriers with the outrigged weapon loads simply did not have the speed to move around the

column, engage targets, and then catch up again, or go off to investigate suspicious signs. So the logical thing to do was to build a special machine for the job, and give it the necessary speed, lift and weaponry. This is the basic idea behind the AAH, though it has other uses too, mainly as an anti-tank weapon carrier. It is the artillery, the support machine gun, the medium mortar, in fact the entire family of support fire weapons for the air-mobile force and can move over any country at 150mph (240kph).

The standard AAH in the Air Mobile Division at the moment is the Bell AH-1G Hueycobra, a streamlined version of the Huey using the same engine and rotor, but only 36in (0.91m) wide across the fuselage. The two-man crew sit one behind the other, protected by armour, the gunner in front. He has a small turret below the nose controlled by his sight and containing a fast firing mini-gun or an automatic grenade-launcher capable of throwing 150 small shells a minute, or some combination of the two. Little stub wings carry the external loads, and there are four load points. A typical load could be 76 2.75in rockets, or up to eight TOW missiles in two pods. The gunner fires all the armament, and the turret follows his flexible sight as he turns it to track targets. On a mission of 60 mile (96km) radius the Cobra can reach the target area in half the time taken by a Huey

(Opposite) Vietnam. An AH-IG 'Cobra' gunship from Btry 'B' 2 Bn, 20 Artillery, joins the 'Nighthawk' search ship, to support ground units of the 1 Cavalry Division (Air Mobile). 1969 *(US AAF)*

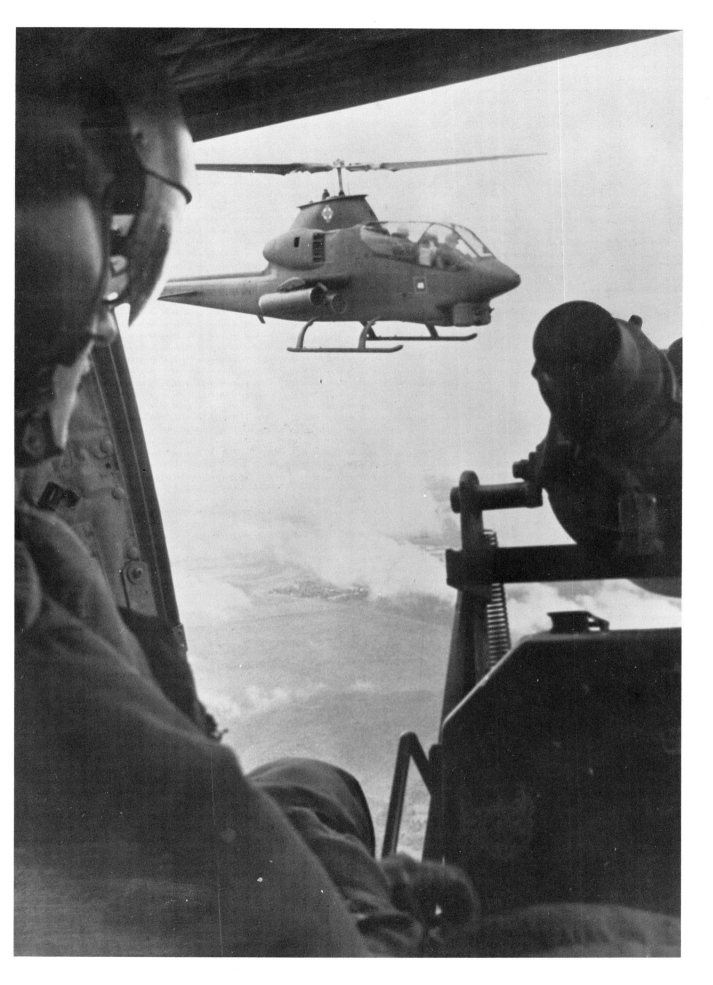

and can stay there for three times as long.

The AAH can provide enormous firepower for a restricted period, but in order to be effective it needs a continual supply of ammunition and fuel. A platoon of AAH consumes fuel by the ton and ammunition by the tens of tons when in action so that there has to be a Forward Rearming and Refuelling Point (FAARP) fairly close to the front, and a steady flow of Chinooks to and from it carrying up fresh stores. However, the returns for this logistic effort are impressive. The Cobras are a highly mobile reserve of firepower that the commander can rush to any threatened part of his area, or can use to follow-up a successful attack and turn a minor thrust into a full-blown assault within minutes. The flexibility and speed of response are something quite unknown until the last two decades and the old ideas of tactics look extremely pedestrian in comparison. A small force with an air-mobile reserve becomes equivalent to a much larger force of conventional troops because it can cover the same area of ground using its helicopters to put men down at threatened points. The possibilities are endless, and it will take time to explore them all in all kinds of warfare. Vietnam was a good beginning, but it was only a beginning.

In addition to 1 Cavalry Division, the US army now has another air-mobile division. The 101 Airborne went to Vietnam as airborne infantry to carry out any parachute operations that might be needed, but in early 1972 they were turned into an air-mobile division, with one parachute brigade. Even that has gone now, so that the 101st is a pure air-mobile division. It was an easy change to make, since the equipment and general attitude to war are so similar and the difference is not great once the loss of the parachuting element is accepted. In other armies the idea has been accepted with enthusiasm, but the expense has been daunting. The West German army uses helicopters for troop movements, but not in the full realization of the air mobile concept. However, the need to shift troops rapidly from one part of the front to another is obviously strong in Germany where the main Soviet thrust is expected to come. France has always used helicopters imaginatively and aggressively, but she too cannot afford to have fully equipped air-mobile divisions, though she does have some smaller units which are helicopter-borne, using the Franco-German types such as the SA-321 and SA-330.

The obvious question which everyone asks is whether the helicopter-borne air mobile formation will replace the conventional parachute formation, and the experience of Vietnam seems to show that there is now no place for the expensive, tactically immobile parachute unit on the battlefield where a helicopter unit can literally run rings round it. The answer will take some time yet to emerge, but the fact is that with the present helicopters, whose range is restricted, whose operating hours between overhauls is short, and who depend on large and well-equipped bases for their maintenance and repair, there is undoubtedly a place still for the long-range strategical parachute force. Vietnam was a large tactical battle, the next one may not be so straightforward.

Republic of Vietnam. UH-ID helicopters of the 1 Battalion, Cavalry Regiment, 1 Air Cavalry Division (Air Mobile) come in for a landing during an assault mission 20 km east of An Khe. 28 December 1965 (US AAF)

Special Feature: NATO and Warsaw Pact Airborne Forces

On paper both NATO and the Warsaw Pact countries can dispose formidable numbers of airborne troops, but in fact it is highly unlikely that any of them, apart from the Soviet Union and the United States, could actually launch more than a token force into battle.

Warsaw Pact Forces

The largest airborne army east of the Iron Curtain is obviously that of the USSR and even now there is some doubt as to the actual number of men who can rightly be considered to be airborne, but there is no doubt at all that the Soviet Union takes the matter of air movement very seriously indeed, and frequently practises the techniques. It is generally supposed that the Soviet army has a total of seven airborne divisions. Each division contains approximately 7,000 men and so the airborne force is 50,000 strong. These divisions are organized in the same way as the more normal infantry division but have lighter scales of equipment and so are smaller in total numbers of men, guns and vehicles. There are three regiments in each division and a fairly strong element directly under the control of divisional headquarters. This element contains the anti-aircraft battalion, the engineers and some of the artillery. There are 45 self-propelled guns

of either 57mm or 85mm actually in the divisional organization but larger armoured vehicles and even tanks have been seen carrying the insignia of the airborne troops. These are air-landed from the big transport aircraft, and air-landing plays a large part in the Soviet tactical doctrine.

This enormous airborne force is kept well out of sight in central Russia and only brought out on show when it suits Soviet government policy. From time to time the Press prints photographs of exercises, though it is significant that few of these ever seem to take place in Eastern Germany or anywhere else where they could be observed by the West's military attachés. It is known, however, that there is a very large fleet of transport aircraft capable of lifting the airborne divisions and all told it seems likely that there is sufficient lift for three divisions to be carried at any one time. This would probably require a great effort, but it does mean that at least one division of 7,000 men could be picked up at very short notice and dropped several hundreds of miles away without difficulty. In fact, the modern Soviet transport aircraft are little different in performance from the American ones and the assault could easily be flown up to 2,000 miles (3,200km) without a refuelling stop. The standard transport plane is

Soviet military parachutists before emplaning. Static lines have been led over the right shoulder and tucked under the harness for convenience (*Novosti Press*)

the Antonov AN-12, which has a payload of 20 tons or 60 paratroopers. There is a rear loading ramp and heavy loads can be dropped over the rear door-sill in the same way as from the C-130. From time to time there are photographs in the Soviet military magazines showing these loads being parachuted. But despite the expense and value of this large number of men and aircraft, the Soviets have not used their airborne troops operationally since the end of World War II. Their experience in

World War II was undoubtedly enough to put anyone off the whole idea since each of the three operations which they launched was a total failure and resulted in the loss of virtually every man.

After 1945 Soviet airborne troops took part in several of the post-war military invasions in the Eastern bloc, but they always did so in the air-landed role, they have never been seen to parachute. Probably the most famous operation was the invasion of Czechoslovakia in 1968 when

A Soviet sports club climbing into an AN-12 allegedly for a group accuracy jump from 1,000m. Here again every man has a static line as well as a rip-cord, and none wears a protective helmet. The large clumsy reserve parachute must be a nuisance for competitive jumping and it is not used by the national teams (*Novosti Press*)

a complete airborne division was used, but it landed on the tarmac of Prague airport and there was not a parachute in sight. This leads one to ask whether the Soviets do not look upon their airborne army more in the nature of a fast-moving reserve rather than as a long-range assault force. Such an idea, however, is not in keeping with the published doctrine in which the Soviets maintain that airborne forces should be used in their traditional role. Nevertheless, whatever the projected use

of these troops, they constitute a constant threat to the Western nations and to the neutral countries too.

The position of the other Warsaw Pact countries is much nearer to that of the NATO Alliance in that most of them have a small airborne force, but all of them are short of transport aircraft in which to fly them. Poland, for instance, claims to dispose of one division but has less than 100 transport aircraft of all sizes so that even with the maximum possible effort on the

Soviet Infantry boarding MI-4 'Hound' helicopters during an exercise (*Novosti Press*)

(*Opposite*) A British landrover dropping on a medium-stressed platform. The three large canopies are assembled in separate segments, partly for ease of manufacture and partly to allow the air to escape and so prevent oscillation. The heavy loads must not swing, or they damage themselves on landing. The suspension lines to the platform are clearly shown, and the shock-absorbing bags underneath show up well (*Crown copyright*)

part of the air force it is unlikely that more than two or three battalion groups could be lifted at one time, and it would be more realistic to say one battalion group with a good follow-up force. Czechoslovakia claims to have a brigade and Rumania two regiments, and once again the air lift is insufficient for any but a proportion of the total number of men.

NATO forces

On the NATO side the numbers appear to be disturbingly low, and the balance of effort would seem to lie heavily in the favour of the Soviets. The United States has 82 Airborne Division permanently based on Fort Bragg and the Special Forces Groups as well as 173 Independent Airborne Brigade. For these there are enough tactical transport aircraft to lift at least one of the brigades at one time, and by making a special effort and withdrawing some routine supply flights another brigade could probably be lifted simultaneously, but that is all. The heavy equipment and vehicles can be flown and parachuted over the same distances as the men, and this is frequently practised all over the world. Although the US airborne division does not apparently carry quite the same weight of equipment as the Soviet (there are no self-propelled guns for example) what it has got can all be parachuted on to the drop zone, and it does seem that here it is more flexible than the Soviet division, which looks as though it has to rely on capturing an airstrip to air-land its equipment, much as the Germans did in 1940. Another distinct advantage for the

US division is that it has a long history of success behind it, and whatever may be said about the uselessness of tradition, it does matter that the planners of an operation should have confidence in the methods they are using, and the US army has got plenty of confidence in the use of 82 Airborne.

Britain has one regular parachute brigade and one reserve brigade, but the regular brigade is now much reduced in effectiveness by a 1976 decision to have only one battalion at a time in the parachute role, one in reserve, and the third as normal infantry. The reserve brigade continues in the parachute role but is soon to be cut, and the transport aircraft fleet is now so reduced that it can only lift one battalion at a time in its C-130s. Hence, if the British were to try to launch anything more than a battalion-sized operation they would be forced to use US aircraft again as they had to in World War II, or fly the force in a succession of lifts.

France has had a small but effective airborne element in its army since the end of World War II and has also striven to have sufficient French aircraft to be able to lift all the men and equipment. She now has one parachute regiment and an airportable division in the Strategic Reserve in France and the colonial parachute troops, who were once known as the Foreign Legion, in the Mediterranean. To carry this force there is a mixture of aircraft with the C-160 Transall forming the backbone of the fleet. The air-portable division has its own helicopters in the organization, but can also call on the heavy

June 1973. Greek paratroops dropping during exercise 'Alexander Express' in northern Greece *(Crown Copyright)*

(Overleaf) French parachute troops making a training jump from Transalls of the French Air Force. Each plane is dropping two sticks at once, jumping simultaneously from the side doors just behind the prominent undercarriage bulges. The Transall is a good example of a modern turbo-prop troop transport. It can carry 81 parachutists in a pressurized compartment to a maximum range of 2,800 miles *(Aerospatiale, Paris)*

lift machines in the Air Transport Command of the air force.

West Germany has taken to the idea of air-portable and airborne troops with enthusiasm, as one might expect from the country that started it all. There are two airborne brigades in the Bundeswehr and a growing force of helicopter-borne troops, though they are not yet sufficient to be formed into an actual air-portable division in the same way as the US army can do.

There is sufficient airlift to carry at least one battalion group of parachutists and to follow it up with resupply drops and reinforcement, but the German army does not see itself fighting outside its own country, so the general idea behind the use of airborne troops is that of rapid reinforcement of threatened areas and quick follow-up to successful attacks. Hence the need for long-range independent operations is not so pressing.

A heavy drop during the UK joint Airborne Task Force exercise 'Ruby Signet' in Denmark (*Ministry of Defence*)

Italy has a battalion group of parachute troops, largely equipped with US equipment, but well trained and experienced. They lack transport aircraft and also heavy drop gear, so that their main use would be likely to be as a rapid infantry reinforcement on the battlefield. Turkey has two parachute battalions, US-trained and equipped, and probably sufficient somewhat elderly transport aircraft to be able to lift one at a time, but little experience or equipment for the task of heavy dropping the support weapons. Finally there is Belgium, with one battalion of Parachute Commandos who showed their capabilities in the Congo and earned great praise for their fighting abilities.

When seen as a matter of numbers alone there is not the slightest doubt that the Soviet Bloc has an overwhelming superiority in airborne forces and in the aircraft to carry them. By comparison the NATO formations appear tiny, scattered, and diversified and to some extent this is true, but it must not be forgotten that the Soviets appear to be equally overwhelming in practically every other area, yet we do not believe that they will necessarily win the next war. It is not only a matter of quality against quantity, it is also a matter of experience against inexperience, and in

this respect the Western nations have a strong lead. After World War II there were practically no airborne forces at all in Russia and it was not until 1956 that they started to build up the divisions. Despite the many opportunities when airborne troops could have been used to some advantage, the Soviets saw fit not to use them, and this must affect not only the morale of the units, but also their expertise. The invasion of Prague was a golden chance to drop troops all round the city and elsewhere in the country too, yet all that happened was that they were flown into large civil airports or driven over the frontier in lorries. This is no substitute at all for an actual airborne operation. So, with little practical experience to guide it, it is likely that the Soviet army will use its valuable airborne troops rather conservatively and cautiously, instead of boldly and decisively; but this does not mean to say that they will not be used in great strength, they undoubtedly will, and it is perfectly possible that they will be more than strong enough to overcome whatever defence is against them, unless that defence can gain the upper hand by skill and guile, and against inexperienced troops this is still possible.

Soviet military parachutists waiting to board their AN-12s. These men are equipped with static line parachutes but seem to have a rip-cord also, leading over the top of the pack. All wear cloth helmets, unlike western parachutists who have head protection (*Novosti Press*)

10 Into the 1980s

Not everyone agrees with specialized ways of fighting wars; every service in every country has its core of hard-line conventional thinkers who believe that all wars are won by the continuous pressure of the lowest common denominator, and to a great extent they are right. The point is that it is the specialized forces who create the situations where the continuous pressure can have best effect. Ever since the beginning of airborne warfare there have been those who would sooner be without it, for a variety of reasons – jealousy for one, envy for another, but more often, and more powerfully, a firm belief that it is simply not worth the enormous expenditure in aircraft, in trained men, in installations and in special equipment – all of which have to be provided at the expense of the conventional forces. So far, however, these critics have had only partial success and it is a fact that there is scarcely a country in the world today which does not claim to have some sort of airborne or parachute force, no matter whether it is only one battalion, and no matter whether the men are trained or not. Airborne forces are fashionable in a way that they have never been before. But sooner or later all these protagonists are going to have to answer one simple and crucial question: Will the airborne method of warfare solve the military problems of future wars? In other words, is there a future for airborne forces?

Everything changes, and the methods of World War II will no longer work, except in very special circumstances. In the sort of future war that seems likely to happen in Northern Europe or in any similar civilized and highly populated area of the world there is no place for huge streams of troop transports cruising in over drop zones marked by pathfinders, nor is there much hope of resupplying any soldiers who are dropped, nor of giving them any continuous meaningful air support. The combined effects of radar, missiles and supersonic fighters will always be too much for any repetition of the Arnhem type of operation behind an enemy's lines, and the same defences are going to keep out any helicopter assaults of the Vietnam type too. But warfare is no longer the prerogative of the rich countries, it breaks out anywhere – Nigeria, Cyprus, Lebanon or Guatemala – and these smaller wars are fought with simple weapons and unsophisticated equipment.

Conventional parachute operations are extremely attractive in these little wars. There is no great need for an expensive transport fleet, a few civilian airliners can carry enough troops to seize an airfield. Two jumbo jets can lift a battalion, four ordinary airliners such as Boeing 707s can do the same, and there are plenty of 707s flying the air routes of the world. For a small country intent on a *coup de main* at the start of a campaign it would not be difficult to scrape together enough aircraft to lift three battalions, fly them into the opponent's airspace and put them down on his main national airport. Such airports are usually near enough to the capital city to make it possible for the force to rush in and either seize the seat of government, or destroy a centre of communication, or deliver any other unexpected blow that more or less ends the war before it ever starts. The Germans tried to do it in Holland in May 1940, and only failed because the Dutch were prepared for airborne attacks and had troops deployed everywhere around the capital and had road blocks on all approaches. Without these Queen Wilhelmina and her government would almost certainly have been captured within a few hours of the frontier being crossed, and Dutch resistance would have ceased. It could easily happen again, and the Israeli raid on Entebbe airport and the Soviet landing at Prague have shown how difficult it is to detect a really determined enemy who is prepared to use all the modern deception techniques to get his aircraft into the airport.

For the large power trying to stop a war between two small countries the airborne method is even simpler and more attractive. Nowadays a parachute assault can be launched from 2,000 miles away, and a quick parachute drop to seize an airfield, followed immediately by a massive air-

(*Opposite*) A mass drop in Turkey by a British parachute battalion. The equipment containers can be seen hanging beneath many of the men, who are using the new British PX parachute (*Crown copyright*)

179

landed force would be enough to paralyse any country starting a war. If only the Americans could have done this on Hanoi in 1966 or 1967 it would have stopped the Vietcong while they still only had comparatively lightly equipped forces. Three years later it was too late, and this emphasizes the other aspect of the airborne method, the timing is critical; too early can be a complete waste of effort, too late can result in a disastrous defeat. Choosing the right time is generally not difficult militarily, but the politics will rarely coincide so that everything becomes a compromise. Luckily for the hostages in the Congo in 1964 the politicians were entirely in agreement and the military could move with no restrictions.

Power in many countries is held by a small group only – the leader, his immediate cabinet, the senior police officers, the radio station staff and, of course, the senior army officers. Apart from some police and army who have to be out in the countryside because of their duties, the remainder tend to stay close to the person of the leader, for power flows in a limited circle of élite men. These are ideal conditions for a quick and savage blow. Once the centre of power is held the country is all but impotent, and the more egocentric the leader, the easier is the attack. It is a situation tailor-made for an airborne strike. So it will pay any country to keep some conventional airborne force in hand and in training. Their role will be much more that of a light intervention force and the days of divisional drop zones are long past. These light forces must be backed up by air-landed formations with the support weapons and equipment, though here again there is probably no need for more than one division of air-portable units. Any operation that requires more than a division to be put down on the ground is too big and is highly unlikely to last for longer than a day or two because it will demand such a huge tonnage of supplies. The airborne operations of the future must be both light and fast; a rapier thrust not a blow with a bludgeon.

General and Limited War

The main preoccupation of the Western powers is 'general' and 'limited' war. General war is a euphemism for all-out nuclear conflict, with no holds barred and both sides using all the tricks in the book. Limited war is a euphemism for war just short of general war, another name for it is 'conventional war', as if any war is ever

conventional except in so far as it destroys and impoverishes. In general war it is very difficult to see exactly how airborne forces could be employed with advantage, but it is equally difficult to see how any military forces can operate in such a situation and the answer has to be that the opportunities will depend upon the changing circumstances, which effectively says nothing. One often-quoted use for an airborne force would be the rapid reinforcement of an area devastated or cleared by nuclear weapons and for an air-landed formation this could be possible. To do it effectively, however, would require that there had been enough time for advance planning in order to make sure that the aircraft were on hand and ready for loading. Even then the troops who arrived first would only be lightly armed and any enemy who fires a nuclear strike is going to be well prepared to follow it up instantly and swamp the area with armour before anyone has a chance to react; if he does not, then he has wasted a valuable strike and the opportunity it creates. The amount of time available in which to get the airborne holding force into the area is therefore extremely tight, so much so that it looks impossible by ordinary standards.

The very nature of general war makes the possibility of a large offensive airborne operation even more remote because such an operation relies on an airhead for its supply and support. The lifeline of aircraft runs to one or more landing zones or drop zones in the enemy territory that can be wiped out by a single nuclear strike. Limited war offers other opportunities, particularly for rapid reinforcement. There will always be a need for troops to be shuffled from one area to another, and sometimes the time available will be so short that the only practicable way to move them will be by air. When the distances are more than a helicopter can manage, and that is not very far at the moment, the move becomes an airborne operation of one kind or another.

Attack Helicopters

One of the essential requirements of any force in a future war is going to be the ability to bring decisive firepower to bear against enemy armoured units. When discussing Soviet tactics this means massed armoured units, because the land battle will be decided by armour, backed up by massed artillery. There is only one way to stop tanks, and that is by knocking them out: all other means such as mines and obstacles will only slow them down temporarily; if they are to be brought to a halt it must be by firepower. To stop a mass attack requires massed firepower, and massed firepower tends to be expensive, difficult to move, and even more difficult to hide. One solution is to put the firepower on helicopters, or more specifically, on 'attack helicopters'. Only two nations can afford these machines, the USA and the USSR, but they are the weapons of the future battlefield and in the 1980s and '90s the US army will be equipped with the next generation of attack helicopter, the AH-64.

AH-64 is twin-engined, and apart from the advantages that this gives it in speed and rate of climb, it also has much greater *agility*. Agility is a new word in helicopter language and it is fairly self-explanatory, an agile helicopter is one which can bob up and down quickly, or swing from side to side, ducking and weaving like a boxer on his feet. Agile helicopters will survive on the battlefield, sluggish ones will either have to restrict their operations, or run the risk of being shot down, because agility is the attack helicopter's defence. By continually moving it tries to defeat the enemy's return fire while still keeping the target in view so that its own projectiles or missiles can be launched or guided. For the next few years, and perhaps right through the 1980s, the US attack helicopters are going to be using some sort of wire-guided missile which needs a human operator to guide it to the target. The operator looks through a stabilized sight, so no matter how the helicopter jerks about in the sky the picture remains steady and unchanged. For the operator this is an upsetting experience, his stomach and all his other instincts tell him that he is being thrown about the sky, but his eyes tell him that the complete opposite is the case and it takes some getting used to. However, it does mean that the pilot can twist and evade while a missile is flying, and provided that the target is always in view the missile can be guided all the way.

The sophistication of these attack helicopters is amazing. They are not just airborne anti-tank guns, each one is much nearer to being a complete anti-tank unit in itself. In time the AH-64 will carry the Hellfire missile, which homes onto a laser spot and needs no wire guidance at all. The laser beam can be directed from the AH-64, or from some other source so that all that the helicopter needs to do is to see the target and fire its Hellfire, whereupon it can drop down behind cover and move off, leaving the missile to fly straight on to the laser spot. The ideal position for this sort of action is for the helicopter to be behind a large wood, or a long hill, where it can pop up and down as it pleases, just rising high enough to lift the missiles clear of the cover. There seems to be no answer to this sort of attack because the helicopter is not in view for long enough to be engaged. With the right kind of electronic equipment it can fire at night just as well as by day, and the only limitations on these operations would appear to be crew fatigue and ammunition supply, and these will almost certainly be critical.

So far there has been no chance to use this airborne firepower, but to be successful it is already obvious that attack helicopters must be used en masse and not one at a time although the temptation to split them up is going to be very strong. The idea will be to produce a devastating but short-term blast which withers the enemy. The helicopters then move off to somewhere else, since it is fatal to keep them operating from one place for too long, as once the enemy gets to know where they are he can start to take evasive action and bring up his counter-measures. Helicopters do not hold ground, they are self-propelled firepower, moving about the battlefield at three miles a minute, providing a massive airborne punch wherever and whenever it is needed, but never staying in one place longer than it takes to throw the punch.

Scout Helicopters

Backing up the attack helicopters are scout helicopters, in the ratio of about three scouts to five attack machines. The scouts go forward and find the targets, then they select the routes for the attack machines to come up. While they are coming they look for alternative positions, and for withdrawal routes. Scouts operate in much the same way as destroyers did for battleships, they are the eyes and ears of the fighting machines. But they are also the eyes and ears of the troop-carrying machines which move about equally as much as the attack variety. The air-mobile troops in the helicopters hold the ground, or move forward and take over the ground gained by the fire from the attack machines. In a fast-moving war against the numbers of divisions that the Soviets can put into the field the only way that the West is going to survive is by rapidly moving its smaller armies to any threatened place, and for this the only practical means is by helicopter. This really does mean that any nation which is going to honour its obligations to its allies or is going to defend its own boundaries must buy or build helicopters and keep them maintained. Whilst there is no substitute for massed firepower, equally there is no substitute for rapid mobility, and both are needed on the modern battlefield.

The future use of Airborne Units

The great debate on the value of airborne forces started as soon as World War II was over, and it has carried on ever since. General after general and air marshal after air marshal have solemnly pronounced upon the value of airborne troops and the cost that they demand from other forces. The argument is no different from that which has raged around any other special force, no matter when it was raised, whether it be marines, or even air forces themselves. Airborne troops have to be specialized, and all armies have been careful to take only the best possible men into the airborne units, with the result that they have become an élite corps. Élite units always come under attack from those who have given up their best men to them because these men could give good service in their home unit. It is an old dichotomy and it will never be resolved; if the best is wanted, and in airborne units it has to be the best, then one must pay for it and the payment is in one way, by creaming off the top layer of manpower.

The real drawback to this selective manning comes when the airborne unit has completed its mission and is fighting the ground battle. Because the men are good and because they are highly trained they tend to fight better than any other units. The ground commander is, therefore, tempted to keep them, and when that happens the casualty list grows. A prime example of this occurred on Corregidor when 503 PIR took 'Topside' with only light casualties, then stayed to winkle out the Japanese garrison and lost a further 850 men. The Germans were of course the worst of all in this respect for they formed their large parachute army in 1944, and never used it in action. The circumstances, however, were slightly different; the units were never intended to fight an airborne war at all, it was simply a method of getting good units into the ground battle, but it must have had an effect on the whole army, and one wonders if it was worth it.

The long training required to build up an airborne assault team makes it highly vulnerable to casualties, and there is an inclination to hold it back and only use the team for specific purposes. This too is counter-productive because it is difficult to decide when to commit the force, and the troops are kept out of the land battle, waiting for their opportunity. It builds up resentment from the conventional units who are taking the brunt of the fighting and who know that their good men, whom they badly need, are sitting by some airfield miles away from the battle. This happened all through the long summer of 1944 when the ground troops stormed across France and the airborne divisions re-formed and trained in England, standing by for successive operations that never came off. However, they were better off than the German parachute divisions, most of whom were destroyed in that ground battle. This could easily have happened to the Allied airborne units had they been left in the line after 'Overlord'.

The special men are not drawn only from the army. The aircrew of the transport aircraft have to be trained too, and without such training an operation can become a disaster, as Sicily showed only too clearly. Here again there is opposition, because unless every transport aircrew is trained in airborne techniques, and kept up to scratch, it means that for every separate operation the trained aircrew have to be collected and allotted to aircraft. Obviously it would be better and easier to train all of them, but this is not always so simple as it might seem, and it takes time.

One of the principles of military operations has always been to have one unified and responsible command structure, ideally one single commander for all. So far, with one exception, this has been the stumbling block of all airborne warfare, for the airborne method lies exactly along the dividing line between air and land operations. Only the Germans succeeded in getting it right when they put all airborne forces under Luftwaffe command, but the Luftwaffe was in any case an army air force and well oriented towards land operations. Even so, when the Wehrmacht saw how successful and important the airborne troops had become there was much jealousy and petty squabbling among the generals, although when the operations were quite independent of the army, such as in Crete, there was little trouble from the soldiers and the airborne units were left to get on with it.

The same difficulty exists among present-day Western nations. Air forces are now too large and too expensive to be part of the army, and all are quite independent and fiercely proud of it. For many years the Royal Air Force relegated troop-carrying to second place compared to other duties, and there was much the same attitude in other countries. But the troops have to be carried in air force aircraft, and the air plan is the responsibility of the airmen. Once the troops are on the ground the ground force commander takes over. It is not an ideal arrangement. In World War II it was to some extent overcome by having combined planning staffs, but even so there was constant quarrelling and the disastrous choice of drop zones at Arnhem shows that wise courses did not always prevail no matter how closely integrated everyone thought themselves to be. The only way to achieve successful airborne operations in any future war is going to be by nominating an overall commander who completely controls both air and land forces, and he must be a land commander, for that is where the battle is going to be fought. Despite all the differences, the parachute and the aeroplane are still in the end only the means of getting the troops to the battle; the fighting takes place on the ground.

With helicopters this desirable arrangement usually exists already, although most air forces fly the larger machines and leave the army to take the rest. Luckily those armies who have enough helicopters to carry troops find that this arrangement works reasonably well, and it means that the response to requests for flights is both quicker and more suitable since the pilots understand what the soldier wants.

The case for having some sort of long-range strategic intervention force seems strong enough, and at the moment and for the foreseeable future this means a parachute force. It need not be too strong, certainly the size of the force must be tailored to the transport fleet available to fly it, and the aircraft need to have a reasonable range so that there is no difficulty about refuelling on other than very long journeys. The aircraft also need to be pressurized and capable of flying the same sort of flight pattern as a civilian airliner, in case it is necessary to practise some sort of deception on the approach to the target. With such a force, and it need be no more than a brigade in strength, any medium-sized world power could feel capable of carrying out its obligations to NATO or the UN, and at a reasonable cost.

The tactical movement of troops is equally necessary and needs to be fulfilled by troop-carrying helicopters. There must be enough of these to enable the army's tactical reserve to be moved about the battlefield, and obviously the size of this force will vary with each country. The advantage of this tactical movement is to make the force several times more effective than it otherwise is, and because the amount of training needed for helicopter operations is so much less than for parachute assaults, losses can quickly and easily be made up from other formations. But it is not enough just to put the tactical reserve into the air in helicopters, they must also be backed with some airborne firepower, and a few squadrons of attack helicopters would be well worth the money. However, if the expense is too much, and it will be for some smaller countries, it is better to spend the available money on troop-carriers rather than try to have a little of everything.

It is time now to return to the question posed at the beginning of this chapter: Will the airborne method of warfare solve the military problems of future wars? The answer has to be that they cannot, but they can contribute a great deal to the solution. Although they are élite, expensive forces with much material and equipment involved in their being, they are an essential part of any modern defence force, and to ignore them for reasons of economy or tactical blindness is to invite defeat. There is no more fitting way to end this debate than with the often-quoted remark of Benjamin Franklin on seeing a balloon for the first time, in 1785: 'Where is the Prince', he said, 'who can afford so to cover his country with troops for its defence, as that 10,000 men, descending from the clouds, might not, in many places, do an infinite amount of mischief before a force could be brought to repel them?'.

Glossary

AA   Anti-aircraft, specifically anti-aircraft defences.

Canopy   The part of a parachute which consists of the supporting material which produces the retarding force. Originally made from silk, but from 1942 onwards in nylon.

Container   The early paratroops could not carry any equipment with them so this was packed into metal cylinders called containers and dropped separately from the same aircraft. There was a parachute on one end of the cylinder – often an old man-carrying parachute – and some sort of shock-absorber on the other. The arms and ammunition of the stick would be packed into three or four containers and dropped by the navigator of the aircraft at the time that the men were jumping. Often the container would have a coloured canopy to aid the men in finding it.

Despatcher   The man who stands at the door of the aircraft and controls the stick as it jumps. He is also responsible for checking that all the men are correctly equipped and strapped up before they jump. This task was originally carried out by the senior man in the stick. In the USA the despatcher is referred to as the jumpmaster.

Dropping height   All parachutes have a minimum height below which there is not enough time to allow the canopy to open and slow down the load. For most modern parachutes, a safe dropping height is 700–800ft (230–260m).

Dropping speed   All parachutes have a maximum speed above which it is dangerous to drop them as the canopy may be damaged or may fail to open. With some aircraft the band between stalling and dropping speed is very fine and it calls for nerve and skill on the part of the pilot to keep within it while over the DZ.

DZ (drop zone)   The area marked out for parachutists to land.

Flak   (*Flugzeugabwehrkanonen*) German AA fire.

Heavy drop   That part of a parachute assault which consists of the vehicles, ammunition supplies, guns and similar large objects. Usually carried and dropped by aircraft which carry nothing else, though in some cases the crews of the equipment will jump from the same aircraft. The heavy drop is a special study, and the loads are invariably attached to skidboards or platforms to allow them to slide out of the aircraft and to carry their parachutes.

Jumpmaster   See **Despatcher**.

LZ (landing zone) The ground on which gliders or helicopters are intended to land.

Parapack A large canvas-wrapped bundle of equipment carried on a bomb-dropping pylon under the aeroplane and dropped with the stick, in much the same way as a container. US origin.

PIAT Infantry anti-tank defence weapon. (British WWII)

Platform See **Heavy drop**.

Reserve A second parachute carried on the chest for use in emergency. Although carried by all US troops from the beginning of their formation in 1940, reserves were not carried by British forces until 1956, by which time every other country had adopted them.

Retro-rockets Rockets which fire so as to slow down movement rather than induce it. Used to reduce the landing run of certain German gliders during World War II and now used to cushion the landing shock of Soviet heavy drop platforms.

Rigging line The thin nylon line which runs from the edge of the canopy down to the gathering point above the shoulder. Generally a man-carrying parachute has 28 rigging lines in four batches of 7.

Rip cord The wire which opens the pack of the main parachute when pulled by the parachutist.

RV (rendezvous) Gathering point for troops on a DZ. A large stick dropped by a fast aircraft can be spread out as far as a mile along the DZ and it is necessary to have a pre-planned RV, which is generally in the middle of the DZ, to which all men make their way as fast as they can after landing. The RV is usually marked by some discreet signals, particularly at night.

Skidboard A large plywood board on which a heavy drop load slides over the rear door sill of the aircraft.

Slick US Army slang for a troop-carrying helicopter.

Static line A strong line attached to the main pack of a parachutist which opens his parachute as he falls away from the aeroplane. The man thus has to do nothing to actually operate his parachute beyond jumping through the door. Static lines are used on all military parachutes.

Stick A group of parachutists dropping in the same drop zone.

Strop An extension line to the static line to enable the parachute to be used in different aircraft. Some aircraft require the man to have fallen well clear before his canopy is pulled out, and in these cases it is easier to add a clip-on strop than to modify the entire parachute.

185

Bibliography

There are certain acknowledged works which are the main sources for any study of airborne warfare. I have used these extensively and have not been ashamed to draw on them, particularly for the sections on World War II, which has now been studied in depth by several authors. The reader who wishes to pursue this subject further is recommended to start with the books on the following list, which have been the core of this book.

Crookenden, Napier, *Dropzone Normandy*, Ian Allan, 1976

Department of the Army, Washington DC (Historical Division), *United States Army in World War II*

Gavin, Lt-General James, *War and Peace in the Space Age*, Harper, New York, 1963

Otway, Lt-Col T. B. H., *Airborne Forces*, The War Office, London, 1951

Ryan, Cornelius, *The Longest Day*, Gollancz, 1960

——*A Bridge Too Far*, Hamish Hamilton, 1974

Taylor Telford, *The March of Conquest*, Edward Hulton, 1959

Tugwell, Maurice, *Airborne to Battle*, William Kimber, 1971

Secondary sources are numerous and almost defy cataloguing. The following list is a generalization of what has been used in this book. Any reader who intends to read further than the basic list is recommended to use his judgement and critical faculties since there is much in print that is worthless.

Divisional Histories (both British and American) have been produced by many publishers and date from about 1948 to the present day. All are a mine of information about particular operations and occasions.

Anderson, W. E., *Banner Over Pusan*, Evans, 1960

Churchill, Winston S., *Second World War*, Cassell & Co.

Clark, Alan, *The Fall of Crete*, Anthony Blond, 1962

Eisenhower, Dwight D., *Crusade in Europe*, Heinemann, 1948

Fleming, Peter, *Invasion 1940*, White Lion, 1957

Hart, Basil H. Liddell, *The Other Side of the Hill*, Cassell & Co., 1948

MacDonald, Charles, *By Air to Battle*, MacDonald, 1970

Merglen, A., *Histoire et avenir des troupes aeroportées*, Arthaud, Paris, 1968

Mrazek, James, *The Fall of Eben Emael*, Robert Hale, 1972

——*Fighting Gliders of World War II*, Robert Hale, 1977

Newnham, M., *Prelude to Glory*, Sampson Low, 1952

Norton, C. G., *The Red Devils*, Leo Cooper, 1971

O'Ballance, Edgar, *The Indo-China War 1945–54*, Faber and Faber, 1964

O'Neill, Robert J., *The Indo-China Tragedy 1945–54*, Frederick Warne & Co, 1968

Pelling, Henry, *Britain and the Second World War*, Fontana, 1970

Pond, H., *Sicily*, William Kimber, 1962

Seth, R., *Lion with Blue Wings*, Gollancz, 1955

Slim, Field-Marshal W., *Defeat into Victory*, Cassell & Co., 1956

US Army, *Historical Study, Airborne Operations—A German Appraisal*, Department of Defense, Washington DC, 1951

Wilmot, Chester, *The Struggle for Europe*, Collins, 1952

Acknowledgements

I have had the privilege to serve with the British airborne forces for most of my service life, making a grand total of over twenty years in which I have worn a red beret. Throughout that time I have been conscious of the bond and comradeship which binds airborne soldiers together, regardless of their nationality, language or politics. The best years of my life have been spent among these men, years in which I have benefited from the experiences of others and been helped and guided by those who knew how to steer the enthusiasm and energy of the youngsters around them. I have gained from what they have given me, and I have never been entirely sure that I have passed on that knowledge when it became my turn to do so. Now that I am within a few weeks of my retirement from service life this book will, I hope, redress the balance slightly and hand on to others something of what I have absorbed and admired in my years of parachuting.

In the mechanical production of this book I have been helped by many people, and it would be invidious to try to name them all here. This is my opportunity to express my gratitude to all those who have assisted me by lending me books from their libraries, by answering my many questions, and by writing to me. I have been particularly helped by the staff of the US Army Audio-Visual Library in the Pentagon and by Mr Potts and his staff in the War Office Library in London. Mrs Ponting deciphered my appalling manuscripts and produced legible copy from them and my wife put up with endless evenings of loneliness and boredom while I sat in my study hammering at the typewriter.

John Weeks
April 1978

(*Bundesarchiv*)

Index

airborne assault, by glider, 69; last German, 109; less expensive than seaborne?, 76; only Germany and Russia serious in 1939, 12; launched 2,000 miles distant, 179; successful in Normandy, 92; 'airborne carpet', 18, 98

airborne command post, use of by French at Suez, 143

Airborne Corps, XVIII US, 62, 94

Air Command, German XI, composition, 23

Air Commando, No 1, 68, 70

Air Commando, No 2 British, 119

airborne forces: classical use, 20; effective use in Congo, 148; use of Dakotas, 116; First Army's haphazard use, 43; future of, 179 *et seq*, 182–3; used as ground troops, 46; for Home Defence, 116; Japanese resistance against, Leyte, 72; effective Japanese use of, 76; first used in Pacific, 64–5; Japanese only ones in Far East 1942, 64; Japanese parachutist's uniform, 137; purpose of, 8; readiness force, first use of, 152; as reinforcements, 156; role in Overlord, 86; with seaborne landing, 72; in Sicily, 46; street fighting, 102; use of in Vietnam, 152–3, 156

airborne forces, national: American: 56–63; Belgian: 177; *see also* Congo; British: 116–22, 170; Canadian: 89; French: 170; in Vietnam, 127–31; German: 32–41, 176; corps formation, 23; modern uniforms, 133; Indian: 122; Israeli: training and equipment, 148–9; Italian: Folgore Division uniform, 137; modern, 177; Japanese: 81–4; Soviet: superiority, 177; not used operationally since WWII, 168; *see also* NATO and Warsaw Pact; Turkish: 177

airborne fort, plan, 8

airborne operations: first Allied, 43, 65; Burma biggest in Far East, 68; French skill in Vietnam, 131; Japanese against Chinese, 65; 'Market Garden' biggest, 97; in Pacific, 64; Rhine crossing best executed, 112; Vietnam cradle of theory and practice, 125; Western Desert, 38

air support, 69, 74

Airborne Task Force, 176

airborne troops: advancing, 31; Australians with Americans, 66; German characteristics, 32; German, little used, 1944–45, 40; German, moved to Russia as ground troops, 31; German strength in 1944, 39; for Rhine crossing, 111; for sabotage, 132; for street fighting, 104; poor use of in Tunisia, 46; unsuitable for prolonged operations, 40

airborne warfare: Allied revised strategy, 55; briefings in air, 152; British War Office policy, 121; ends in Far East, 138; Stanleyville rescue classic example of use of, 148; Crete made British think, 31; Crete operation ends German interest in, 31; most dangerous type, 44; effectiveness in Crete, 30; end of in Pacific, 76; German activity diminished, 31; Germany first to exploit, 32; Hitler's views, 38; Pyongyang drop in Korea an advance, 132; in Pacific, 64; theory of, 109; good strategic use of in Jordan and Lebanon, 145; strength and weakness, 24; British techniques in Malaya, 132

aircraft: Albemarles, 49; Antonov AN-12, 168, 169; AN-125, 177; B-18, 56; Boeing 707, 179; Curtiss JN-4, 13; C-47, 42, 44, 46, 54, 56, 73, 74; Japanese C-47, 72; DC-3, 13, 60; Fieseler Storch, 50; Halifax, 49, 90; Handley Page, 8; Hastings and Beverleys in Lebanon and Jordan, 145; Hercules, C-130, 125; Jumbo Jet, 179; Junkers, 10, 24, 27, 28, 50, 109, 125; Lockheed C-130 Hercules, 145; Lufthansa aircraft as transports, 9; Messerschmitt, 16, 35, 50; Messerschmitt 'Gigant', 53; Stirlings, 86; Stukas, 54; TB-3, 9, 10; Transell, 173; Whitley bombers, 43, 116

aircraft, use of: American in Korea, 131–2; at Arnhem, 107; as carriers in Korea, 132; used by 1 Cav Div, 156; lack of suitable, 82; towing, 49; Soviet transport similar to US, 167; under overall commander, 96

airdrop exit, 35

Air-landing, not glider-borne for early British forces, 121

air-mobile division: 158–66; concept of, 158; formation, 159; origin in Vietnam, 125; role of 101 Airborne, 156; air-mobile forces, Israeli, 149; air-portable div, French, 170, 176; air-portable troops, German, 176

airstrips: makeshift in Crete, 28; needed by Allies on Noemfoor, 67; air transport, at Suez, 143

Albert Canal, obstacle for Belgian invasion, 20

Ålborg, Danish airfield captured, 15

Allied airborne divisions, in one army, 94

Allied Expeditionary Force, for Rhine crossing, 111

Ardennes, battle of, 109–11

Arnhem: 76, 81, 94–108; *see also* 'Market Garden'; Bridge, 81; casualties, 108–9; landings, 72; Polish brigade fights, 122

Arnold, Gen, supports Wingate, 68–9, 87

Ashford, Major, 45

Austria, occupied by Germany, 11

balloon jumping, 118

Barbarossa, Operation, regrouping for, 30

Bassenge, Gen-Maj Oswalt, 10, 11, 12; opposition to SA, 12

Bastogne, glider at, 110

Belgium, invasion of, 20

blitzkrieg, suitability of a/b troops, 9

Bone airfield, 43

Bradley, Gen Omar, 86

Brayley, Lt, 45

Brereton, Gen Lewis H, 94, 96

'bridge too far, A', 109

British Corps XXX, 98

Browning, Maj-Gen Frederick, 42, 68, 96, 98, 102, 107, 109, 121